Solving the Anorexia Puzzle:

A Scientific Approach

About the Authors

W. Frank Epling, Ph. D. is a professor of behavioral psychology in the Department of Psychology at the University of Alberta. He is also a clinical psychologist in Student Counselling Service at the University and has extensive experience in the field of abnormal behavior. After completing his Ph.D. degree at Washington State University, Dr. Epling travelled to England. During the 1970's, he was a consulting psychologist at Rainhill Hospital in Prescot, a lecturer at the University of Southampton, and a clinical psychologist Whitecroft Hospital on the Isle of Wight. Following his stay in Britain, Dr. Epling took an appointment as Chief Psychologist at Yorkton Union Hospital, Yorkton, Saskatchewan, Canada. In 1977, he joined the University of Alberta where he has had a successful research career. He has published numerous scientific articles and book chapters in the fields of behavioral psychology, nutrition, and anorexia.

W. David Pierce, Ph. D. is a professor of behavioral psychology in the Department of Sociology at the University of Alberta. He is currently Director of the Centre for Experimental Sociology, a research facility for the experimental analysis of human behavior. In 1975, Dr. Pierce received his Ph.D. degree from York University in Toronto, Canada and subsequently took a faculty appointment at the University of Alberta. He is a member of the American Psychological Association and the Association for Behavior Analysis. His research is focused on the interplay of behavior principles, biology, and culture. Dr. Pierce has conducted scientific research with animals and humans on the allocation of behavior in complex-choice settings — as well as research on the interrelations between eating and running, anorexia and nutrition. He has published more than 40 scientific articles and bok chapters, and is currently writing a book on *Contemporary Behavior Analysis* — to be published with Dr. Epling as coauthor.

Solving the Anorexia Puzzle

A Scientific Approach

W. Frank Epling, Ph. D.
W. David Pierce, Ph. D.
The University of Alberta

Foreword by P. J. V. Beumont, Ph. D.
University of Sydney

Hogrefe & Huber Publishers
Toronto • Lewiston, NY • Bern • Göttingen • Stuttgart

Library of Congress Cataloging-in-Publication Data

Epling, W. Frank.
     Solving the Anorexia Puzzle: A Scientific Approach / by W. Frank
Epling, W. David Pierce.
          p.   cm.
     Includes bibliographical references.
     ISBN 0-88937-034-6 : $29.50 (U.S.)
     1. Anorexia nervosa. 2. Exercise addiction. [1. Anorexia
Nervosa. 2. Eating Disorders.] I. Pierce, W. David. II. Title.
     [DNLM: WM 175 E64s]
RC552.A5E65 1991
616.85'262--dc20
DNLM/DLC
for Library of Congress   90-4426
                                          CIP

Canadian Cataloguing in Publication Data

Epling, W. Frank
     Solving the anorexia puzzle

     Includes bibliographical references.
     ISBN 0-88937-034-6
     1. Anorexia. 2. Anorexia nervosa. I. Pierce, W. David. II. Title.
     RC552.A5E7 1991   616.85'262   C90-093866-8

Copyright © 1991 by Hogrefe & Huber Publishers, Inc.
   14 Bruce Park Avenue
   Toronto, Ontario M4P 2S3

   P.O. Box 51
   Lewiston, N.Y. 14092

Printed in Canada

ISBN 0-920887-20-1   Hogrefe & Huber Publishers • Toronto • Lewiston, NY • Bern • Stuttgart
ISBN 3-456-81865-3   Hans Huber Publishers • Bern • Stuttgart • Toronto • Lewiston, NY

Table of Contents

Foreword

Fifty years ago, the motor vehicle had not completely dominated the streets of our cities, and some deliveries were still made by horse-drawn carts. The horses wore blinkers; little leather shields attached on either side of the bridle which ensured that they could look only straight ahead. These blinkers were meant to stop the horses shying from the traffic around them. The drivers of the carts did not wear blinkers. Instead they had an uncanny ability to see around corners and to choose a twisting route through the streets to avoid all potential traffic hazards. The distinction between those who wear blinkers and those who look around corners applies as well to writers of books on anorexia nervosa.

In her book *Fasting Girls*, Joan Brumberg [1988] argues at great length that anorexia nervosa is a very distinct culturally-determined condition. Although she does refer to biological and psychological factors, her reader is left with the impression that one must be white, female, middle-class and preferably American in order to qualify for the diagnosis. She dismisses the suggestions of some highly experienced clinicians that they can discern cases of anorexia among patients who were reported as puzzling in the earlier medical literature. She does not even consider the possibility that animals might develop an anorexia nervosa-like condition. Perhaps the idea would seem preposterous to her.

In fact, animal models provide a series of pertinent observations through which our understanding of anorexia nervosa is slightly advanced [Beumont, 1984]. Anorexia nervosa is an "illness" and not a "disease:" it is a human experience rather than a pathological change to the structure and function of one of the organs of the body. Because it is a very human condition, largely restricted to certain types of society and certain groups within those societies (adolescent girls and young women in affluent Western-type communities), it would indeed be too much to expect that any animal model could accurately reflect *all* aspects of the illness. However, the spontaneous hypophagias that occur in relation to events such a rutting, hibernation and incubation in animals in their natural habitat have interesting features in common with the human ailment. Similarly, some of the experimental findings on laboratory animals are extremely helpful in explaining the pathogenesis of the disturbance.

If some authors wear blinkers, Epling and Pierce do their level best to look around corners. In this book, they have drawn together the results of laboratory experiments on animals and clinical observations on patients to present a strong case for the existence of an activity anorexia, a syndrome of hyperactivity and food avoidance that links the animal and human phenomena.

One of the most comprehensive studies to investigate hyperactivity in anorexia nervosa patients was carried out by Kron *et al*, [1978]. In a series of 33 patients, they found that hyperactivity was a feature at presentation in 25, and further noted that 21 reported unusual physical activity prior to the onset of dieting and weight loss. Ten of 13 patients available for long-term follow-up continued to report high levels of activity. They concluded that the high levels of activity seen in these patients was "…an early and enduring feature of anorexia nervosa and not merely secondary to either a conscious attempt to lose weight or weight loss *per se*."

From my clinical experience, I have no doubt that activity anorexia is an important sub-category of anorexia nervosa , like the more commonly recognized bulimia nervosa. Some years ago my colleagues and I described a series of 15 patients who fulfilled the diagnostic criteria of anorexia nervosa but in whom excessive exercising was the prominent feature of the clinical presentation [Touyz *et al*, 1987]. A comparison of some clinical data concerning these patients with control "non-exerciser" and anorexic subjects is shown in Table 1.

All our patients had started with a "pursuit of fitness" rather than a "pursuit of thinness." In all, this had progressed from regular exercise to compulsive over-eating which they were no longer able to control. This development is well-illustrated in the following 2 case vignettes.

Case 1: Patient A was a 15 year old school girl who lived with her parents and three siblings on a farm near a small country town. The parental marriage was unhappy and her father was openly critical of his wife and children for their laziness. The patient's premorbid involvement with exercise consisted of occasional school athletic events and ballet classes once a week. Her early development was unexceptional.

A year prior to admission she won the school cross-country race, although she had not trained for it. Her father was delighted, and confided in her that he had been a keen competitive middle-distance runner in his youth. Together they planned a training school schedule directed at the state junior championship. She joined an athletic club and also trained under his guidance on a track set up at the farm. She ran each day a minimum of 8 km. Her total food intake increased greatly and she felt anxious less she was eating too much.

TABLE 1

Comparison of "exercisers" and "non-exercisers"

	Exercisers (n = 15)		Non-exercisers (n = 17)	
	n	5	n	5
Family interest in physical activities	11	73	4	24
Onset of excessive exercise before dieting	9	60	1	6
Dieting before exercise	6	40	16	94
Initial motive for exercise:				
Weight loss	5	33	11	65
Fitness	10	66	6	35
Peak activity:				
Less than one hour a day	0	0	14	82
One to two hours a day	1	7	3	18
More than two hours a day	14	93	0	0
Debting:*				
Present	15	100	7	41
Absent	0	0	10	59
"Withdrawal" symptoms:				
Present	15	100	8	47
Absent	0	0	9	53
Body Ideal:				
Fit	12	80	2	18
Thin	3	20	15	88
Sports injuries sustained	10	67	1	6

* Debting: the deliberate balance of energy intake against energy output. i.e. attempting to take only as muany calories as ahve been used during prior exercise

Three months prior to admission she was spending at least 2.5 hours every day running. She read a book on diet and fitness and became determined to turn "fat into muscle," although she had no desire to lose weight as such. She avoided foods she considered fattening, such as puddings and fried foods. Her mother disapproved of her changed dietary habits, so she surreptitiously disposed of some foods and hoarded fruit in her room.

She now began to feel that she could not bear to be physically inactive. She neglected her studies to undertake all the chores on the farm, ran before school and at each recess, as well as in the afternoons. Although she felt exhausted all the time, she continued her strenuous training program. She sustained a stress fracture of a metatarsal, but despite a swollen and painful foot, competed in another long-distance running event for her region, which she won. By this time she had noticed a loss in weight, felt proud of this additional achievement, and took to weighing herself twice daily.

Eventually her performance deteriorated. Her reaction was to further increase the time spent training, running at least 80 km each week. Although she was refusing fatty or sweet food, she still ate substantial meals and lots of fruit, giving an estimated energy intake of about 2 000 calories a day. But she insisted on "earning" each meal by exercising beforehand, and then "burning off" any excess by further exercise afterwards.

She withdrew completely from her schoolfriends and siblings and was always irritable and tense. Her mother had long realized that she was ill, but her father at first colluded with her behavior. Eventually she was referred to our clinic for assessment. This involved a 4-hour car drive. She delayed their departure by undertaking an hour's run beforehand as she could not tolerate the thought of being inactive for so long, and when they stopped en-route for a drink, she insisted on running around the block several times.

On admission, her weight was 42 kg (85% of ideal). She had little difficulty in accepting a high calorie diet and restoration of normal body weight, but found it most distressing to stop her exercise program. She has now moved to a boarding school in the city, attends as an outpatient, maintains a normal diet, but still finds it uncomfortable to restrict exercising to a level considered appropriate by the school.

Case 2: Patient B was referred to our unit at the age of 37 years. The younger son of a wealthy but aloof British family, he had attended boarding school from an early age. His mother he described as domineering, his father has an alcohol problem. Patient B had three sisters. One had been treated for anorexia nervosa, as had her two sons. Patient B's own health during childhood and early adult life was good.

He migrated to Western Australia at the age of 22 to live with an Australian woman he had met in London. They married and had two children within 5 years. Their marriage was happy and their sex life active and mutually satisfying. He had varied success at work, was involved in a series of business ventures, and was financially rather insecure. Otherwise, he seemed to be coping well, living an active social life, and avidly absorbed in developing his long-standing ambition of being an amateur air pilot. His wife describes him at this stage as being "averagely lazy," seldom helping with household chores, and not too concerned with tidiness, promptness, etc. but social and fun-loving.

When he was 30, he volunteered for an assessment at a fitness laboratory in Perth and was told that he was in excellent condition, his weight being 65 kg (10 stone 4 lbs) — ideal body weight for his height of 170 cm (5'7") is 58-74 kg (9 stone 2 lbs — 11 stone 6 lbs). He was delighted at this assessment and thought he should become even fitter. He became committed to regular exercising, jogging, and swimming; he became concerned about his diet, avoiding fats and simple carbohydrates and eating healthy foods (complex carbohydrates).

An insidious change came over his personality. He began to structure his life around his exercising and fitness to such an extent that he was meticulous about time of meals, what exactly was eaten, and how each hour of his day was spent. His meticulousness spread to other aspects of his life - he took over household chores and wanted everything precisely in place.

At about this time (1977), the family moved to Sydney to be reunited with his wife's parents. He regretted the move almost immediately. He hated the business he had gone into with his brother-in-law (managing a squash court complex) but was quite obsessed in his attention to details. He became very conscious about his weight and deliberately changed his diet to one of low energy content. His concern manifested itself in calculating his intake in calories. His weight fell to 52 kg (a little over 8 stone) and he continued to exercise more than ever. His social activities decreased dramatically and he lost all interest in sex.

In 1981 his wife persuaded him to seek medical advice. He saw two psychiatrists and his calorie intake was reported to be about 1400 calories a day, energy deficient in view of his exercising, but adequate in its content of the essential food components. He increased his diet to 2500 calories a day and over a 4-month period gained weight to 60 kg (9 stone 6 lbs), became angry with his therapist, and discontinued attendance. He decided not to decrease his intake of energy, but to increase expenditure.

Commitment to exercising now became permanent; he worked out a rigid schedule involving long runs in the mornings and evenings, the use of every opportunity to exercise during the day (standing rather than sitting, walking to business appointments in the city rather than taking taxis). "I am never happy unless I am burning calories." His meticulousness about exercise was paralleled by his meticulousness about eating. He insisted on eating at fixed hours, would refuse dinner engagements as they would necessitate an alteration of his eating routine, and would refuse business engagements if they interrupted his time for lunch and morning tea. (Despite this, however, he did well in his new job as a sales representative and has been salesman of the year for the past 2 years).

He carried a pocket calculator with him as well as a calorie counter and calculated everything that he ate and all the energy he expended (i.e. one mile run at 50 kg = 80 calories) and ensured that he was always in a negative balance. Twice a week he weighed himself and then on two separate scales in the city. If he had lost weight, he felt good, and would allow himself a sweet cake in the coffee shop. Over the year his weight fell to 50 kg (8 stone).

He was totally preoccupied with thoughts of food and what he needed to do in the realm of exercise in order to justify eating. He became weaker and felt exhausted after his exercise regime. Eventually he consulted a physician who arranged a full medical workup and reported that his gonadotrophin and testosterone levels were low and he had a raised cholesterol level — this alarmed him and he was referred to us.

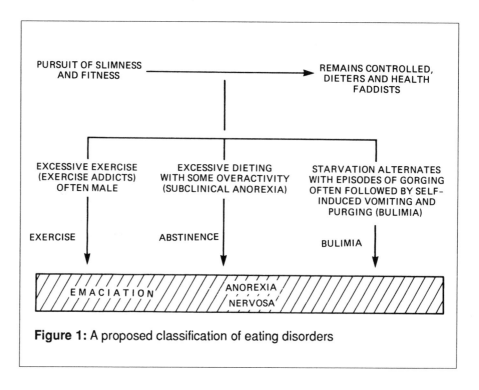

Figure 1: A proposed classification of eating disorders

He was treated as an outpatient on 3500 calories a day varied diet and a restricted exercise program but he found it difficult to comply and complained of tremendous anxiety when he wasn't exercising, of continued preoccupation with food, and of overwhelming indecision when having to choose what to cook.

Our concept of exercise anorexia is similar but not identical with activity anorexia (see Figure 1). We thought that the overactivity was a reflection of the current preoccupation with exercise and fitness in our community. However, Lasegue [1883], and Gull [1884], had commented that hyperactivity was a cardinal feature of the illness in the classical descriptions, and Epling and Pierce are right in insisting that the relationship between overactivity and food avoidance is a persistent characteristic of anorexia nervosa. I have found their observations of great value in better understanding the confusing clinical picture that my patients presented.

P. J. V. Beumont

REFERENCES

BEUMONT, P.J.V. (1984). A clinician looks at animal models of anorexia nervosa. In N.W Bond (Ed.), *Animal Models of Psychopathology*. Academic Press: Sydney.

KRON, L. KATZ, J.L., GORZYNSKI, G. AND WUNER, H. (1978). Hyperactivity in anorexia nervosa. A fundamental clinical feature. *Compr. Psychiatry*, 19, 433-440.

TOUYZ, S.W., BEUMONT, P.J.V. AND HOOK, S. Exercise anorexia: A new dimension of anorexia nervosa? In P.J.V. Beumont, G.D. Burrows and R.C. Casper (Eds.). *Handbook of Eating Disorders, Part I; Anorexia and Bulimia Nervosa*. Elsevier: Amsterdam.

Preface

This book is an account of our research and theory concerning activity anorexia. We argue that any human being can, under certain circumstances, become anorexic. The conditions that produce anorexia are a complex interplay of environment and biology. Social and cultural practices lead many people to diet and exercise. Under some conditions, dieting and exercise produce a biological response that leads to an activity anorexia. This anorexia involves a vicious cycle of increasing physical exertion and decreasing appetite.

In Part One of this book, we describe current medical and psychological views of anorexia nervosa. The reader is presented with the diversity of opinion regarding this syndrome. After the basic overview, we have detailed the growing incidence of anorexia in our society. Surprisingly, the evidence suggests that both males and females, and older as well as younger people, are among diagnosed anorectics. Statistics show that up to 20 percent of anorectics may eventually die from the disorder. Section one of the book ends with a consideration of conventional treatment techniques. We evaluate long-term psychiatric care, family therapy, behavior modification and the role of drugs in the treatment of anorexia nervosa.

Part Two of the book presents a new understanding of anorexia in humans and other animals. This understanding is based on a so-called "secondary symptom" of anorexia nervosa — the presence of excessive physical activity is common among these patients. Professionals usually view excessive activity as another way that an anorexic individual can lose weight "by burning off calories." We argue that substantial evidence indicates that excessive physical activity is not a secondary symptom, but is central to an understanding of anorexia. We support this claim with findings from human and animal research.

Separate research areas indicate that, contrary to common sense, increasing amounts of physical exercise may reduce a person's appetite. Also, lower food intake can induce physical activity. These two effects may combine to produce an "activity-based anorexia" that occurs in animals and accounts for a significant number of cases of anorexia nervosa. Although the underlying process is based on evolved physiological mechanisms, current cultural practices are shown to setup the necessary conditions for activity anorexia.

The final section of the book details the implications of our theory for the assessment, treatment and prevention of activity anorexia. We attempt to specify the assessment criteria for activity anorexia and differentiate this disorder from anorexia nervosa. The classification is functional rather than psychiatric. A psychiatric classification is usually based on a set of symptoms attributed to an underlying personality disturbance. In contrast, a functional diagnosis is based on the objective causes of self-starvation. These causes refer to the biological and environmental conditions that regulate food intake and body weight. A functional classification of anorexia has practical implications. In the final chapter, we suggest treatment and prevention strategies based on a scientific understanding of anorexia.

W.F. Epling
W.D. Pierce

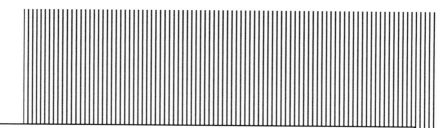

The major topics are:

● **PHYSICAL ACTIVITY AND ANOREXIA NERVOSA**
● **ACTIVITY ANOREXIA IN ANIMALS**
● **THE BIOLOGICAL BASIS OF ACTIVITY ANOREXIA**
● **THE SOCIAL CONTEXT OF ACTIVITY ANOREXIA**
● **SUMMARY AND OVERVIEW**

Summary

· Activity anorexia is not a mental disorder.

· Many cases of anorexia nervosa are actually instances of activity anorexia.

· Activity anorexia was discovered in animals and a similar process occurs in humans.

· There is an evolutionary basis to activity anorexia and specific physiological mechanisms control the cycle.

· Culture and social conditioning initiate the activity anorexia cycle in humans.

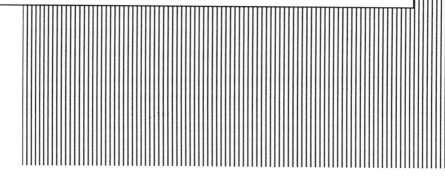

Introduction:
A Scientific Approach to
Anorexia

Activity anorexia is not a mental or psychological disorder. There are a significant number of people in our society suffering from activity anorexia who are incorrectly labelled neurotic. These people are diagnosed as having anorexia nervosa. Additionally, there are individuals in athletics and physical fitness who appear to self-starve as a result of the combined effects of dieting and exercising. This book emphasizes a scientific view of human self-starvation. We suggest that most cases of anorexia nervosa are, in fact, instances of activity anorexia [1]. These cases are recognized by the excessive exercise and hyperactivity of the patients.

The basic premise is that people go on diets that lead to excessive physical activity. The dieting athlete may increase training, the sedentary person may begin jogging, the person with anorexia nervosa may be hyperactive. Paradoxically, excessive exercise or hyperactivity begins to interfere with eating and the loss of weight results in further physical activity. Thus, declining food intake produces activity and activity suppresses food intake. The process is apparently a vicious cycle that is not consciously controlled by the anorectic. Physiological mechanisms involving brain opiates seem to explain the activity-anorexia cycle.

Activity anorexia is controversial because most people believe that persons who willfully starve themselves must be mentally ill. A young woman goes on a severe diet and continues to the point of starvation. How can this person be anything but mentally disturbed? The answer from most doctors is that indeed she is. In fact, anorexia nervosa is currently classified as a neurotic disorder by psychiatrists and psychologists. Mental illness is suggested by the many symptoms that accompany willful starvation. These symptoms include fear of being fat, obsessive food rituals, distorted body image, and disturbed perceptions of self. There is no doubt that such symptoms are associated with anorexia nervosa. However, the presence of excessive activity at the onset and during the course of illness suggests activity anorexia rather than anorexia nervosa.

The numerous and varied symptoms may arise from the common experiences of anorectics rather than be the cause of willful starvation. Most people believe that perceptions, attitudes, feelings, and personality explain what they do. Modern psychiatry has reinforced the view that cognitive and mental events cause human behavior. This is convincing to people because such mental activity often accompanies bizarre behavior. However, a well known dictum of the scientific method is that correlation does not entail causation. Although these mental events occur and are associated with disturbed eating, this evidence is not sufficient to claim that they are causes. The evidence presented in this book suggests that food restriction and excessive activity are the underlying determinants of most human anorexia.

Current cognitive theories of anorexia nervosa have emphasized beauty standards and cultural values of thinness [2]. From this perspective, an individual develops an image of the ideal person that is based on cultural standards. Television, magazines, and other sources have frequently conveyed stereotypes of the perfect body type. A person who has internalized these standards may incorrectly infer that excessive thinness is desirable. Although social-cognitive theories of anorexia nervosa offer an explanation of the tendency to diet and exercise in Western culture, these accounts do not recognize fundamental interrelations among food intake, physical activity, and body weight. From our perspective, this omission is critical because clinical reports indicate that hyperactivity or increased exercise is a prominent and enduring feature of anorexia nervosa [3, 4, 5]. Our estimate is that more than half of diagnosed anorectics show excessive activity. Thus, a significant number of human anorexias may be activity induced.

1   PHYSICAL ACTIVITY AND ANOREXIA NERVOSA

Most reports of excessive physical activity have viewed this behavior as an interesting, but seemingly unimportant, symptom of the anorexia syndrome. For example, Dr. Feighner and his colleagues have described diagnostic criteria that include periods of overactivity as one of six possible secondary symptoms [6]. In the traditional view of anorexia nervosa, activity is secondary because it is simply a way that the anorectic reduces calories. That is, activity is a manifestation of the desire to lose weight.

Although the traditional interpretation seems reasonable, there is growing evidence that it is wrong. Excessive physical activity appears to be central to many cases of human self-starvation. The evidence for the primary importance of activity comes from a variety of sources. Controlled experiments with animals have shown that physical activity can make an animal give up eating when food is relatively abundant [7]. Less controlled research with humans has also suggested the link between activity and starvation [1].

There is growing evidence that physical activity is central to the understanding of human anorexia. For example, one study attempted to measure the symptoms of anorexia nervosa by requiring judges to rate the behavior of anorectics [8]. Anorectics differed from other psychiatric patients on resistance to eating, methods of disposing of food, and overactivity. Dr. Anthony Crisp, a prominent Professor of Psychiatry and expert on anorexia nervosa, mentioned activity symptoms of 30 patients. He stated that "the patients were often restless, slept badly, and typically suffered early morning waking and or waking in the middle of the night." He went on to point out that phenomena such as overactivity, restlessness, insomnia, and ritualistic behavior develop during the course of self-starvation and recede when the individual has again stabilized eating [9].

In another clinical report, Dr. Kron and his associates tried to define the core pathology of hospitalized patients with anorexia nervosa. The summary of their findings makes it clear that excessive physical activity is critical to the onset and progressive development of anorexia:

> We reviewed the charts of 33 patients hospitalized with this illness during the past 10 years... In 25 of the 33 charts, the presence of hyperactivity during the present illness was recorded; only one patient was specifically noted to show unremarkable physical activity... Among the 13 patients interviewed directly, ten described themselves as continuing to be highly active physically... Physical activity appeared to be more excessive, disorganized, and aimless during the acute phase of anorexia nervosa... These preliminary findings suggest that "hyperactivity" is an early and enduring clinical feature of anorexia nervosa and not merely secondary to either a conscious attempt to lose weight or weight loss per se [5, p. 439].

The central importance of physical activity for anorexia is further documented by recent evidence dealing with the sequence of symptoms during the illness. Professor Beumont and his colleagues asked 25 anorectics to identify their symptoms and the order of occurrence [10]. Of the 28 reported symptoms, only "manipulating food servings" and "increased sport activity" were present in all patients. Generally, the ordering of the symptoms indicated that changes in dieting and food intake were followed by increased physical activity. Interestingly, this course of onset parallels the development of anorexia in laboratory animals.

2   ACTIVITY ANOREXIA IN ANIMALS

Activity anorexia was discovered by controlled experiments with laboratory animals [1]. The basic experimental situation is based on work concerning self-starvation in animals. In our laboratory the process of activity anorexia begins when rats are fed a single-daily meal and allowed to run on an activity wheel. It is important to note that the size of the meal is more than adequate for survival. Also, animals are not forced to exercise on the wheel. They can choose to remain in an attached cage or just lie in the wheel. In fact, the animals start running and this activity increases daily. The change from many meals per day to one produces the increasing physical activity.

Figure I.1   A laboratory rat in a running wheel. The apparatus is used for the experimental study of activity anorexia. When animals are fed once a day, they run in their wheels and stop eating.

Wheel running rapidly increases to excessive levels. A typical adolescent rat (60 days old) may run up to 20 kilometers per day at the peak. Ordinarily, these animals would run less than 1 kilometer a day. This excessive activity is surprising because the animal is expending many more calories than it is consuming. For this reason, the activity is life threatening.

A more startling effect is that food intake at the meal declines as running becomes excessive. At the end of one week, the animal may not eat at all. The animal is giving up eating in spite of increasing energy expenditure through wheel running. If this process is allowed to continue, the animals die of starvation. The seemingly willful starvation of these animals appears similar to cases of human anorexia.

The animal model describes a basic biobehavioral process that may extend to humans. The model does not, and can not, depict the complex social conditions that predispose some individuals to contact the basic process. There is, however, reasonable evidence that sociocultural factors set the conditions that encourage people to diet and exercise.

The person who is subjected to strong social pressure to diet does not willfully restrict food intake. In both laboratory animals and humans, food restriction is imposed. That is, the experimenter controls the diet in the laboratory and the "diet and exercise culture" regulates the eating practices of people.

3   THE BIOLOGICAL BASIS OF ACTIVITY ANOREXIA

Although activity anorexia seems to involve a deliberate choice to not eat, it is in fact a normal physiological response of organisms to food deprivation. An evolutionary account of activity anorexia points to the survival value of such behavior [7]. During times of food scarcity, organisms can either stay in one place and conserve energy (e.g. hibernate) or become mobile and travel to another location (e.g. migration). If travel leads to abundant food and remaining in the same place leads to starvation, then those animals that travelled would reproduce and the tendency to become active during periods of food scarcity would increase in the next generation. Many species, including humans, increase activity in times of food shortage. Although persons with anorexia appear to have an abundant supply of food, sociocultural conditions prevent access to this supply and anorectics experience the equivalent of a famine. Contact with the socially-imposed food shortage then initiates the activity-anorexia cycle.

The fact that increasing energy expenditure through walking, running, or exercise is accompanied by decreasing food intake violates common sense. From an energy balance or homeostatic perspective, food intake should increase with energy expenditure. This is in fact the case if an animal is given time to adjust to a new level of activity and food is plentiful. If a person adapts to a new exercise regime, calorie intake will adjust to meet the new demands. Also, when dieting is gradual and moderate, the activity cycle does not occur.

When food is severely limited, however, mobility and travel should not stop until organisms detect an adequate supply. Under these conditions, the animal or person may not eat if the environment signals only small and infrequent quantities of food. This is because the time and energy wasted by obtaining small amounts of food is better spent on travel. Increasing contact with food would indicate a replenished supply and travel or mobility should reduce or stop at this time. In humans, dieting to lose weight can produce and maintain conditions of food depletion even though food is readily available. Anorectics therefore may not experience increased contact with food, activity continues to spiral upward, and food consumption remains low or declines.

The evolutionary history of people has resulted in physiological mechanisms that regulate and respond to food supply. Neurologically, a brain structure called the hypothalamus has been found to play a role in the regulation of eating and physical activity [11]. Another promising line of research suggests that brain opiates called endorphins regulate eating, activity and menstrual cycle [7]. The effect of endorphins on menstrual cycle is interesting because many women athletes and anorectics have problems with menstruation [12, 13].

4 THE SOCIAL CONTEXT OF ACTIVITY ANOREXIA

The scientific analysis of activity anorexia suggests that choosing to diet or exercise is determined by biological and environmental conditions. The most important aspect of the human environment is social. The social environment consists of the practices of other people and is a major determinant of human behavior. What a person eats or drinks, how or when the person exercises, what inner feelings are reported, how persons describe themselves, and what kind of personal relationships are formed — all depend in part on the reactions and responses of other people.

Social reinforcement of particular behavior can increase the tendency to diet or exercise. An individual may learn these responses in order to escape or avoid criticism for being overweight or to gain approval for being slim and fit. The type and intensity of dieting and exercise is initially regulated by the responses of others. However, once social reinforcement has encouraged food restriction, especially in the context of increasing exercise, the activity anorexia cycle may be contacted. When the process is initiated, the person may be trapped by the activity-food-reduction cycle.

Although the failure to eat may be due to biological factors, the experience and description of activity anorexia will depend on social conditioning. For example, persons suffering from activity anorexia may be convinced by mental health professionals that their behavior is an attempt to "manipulate other family members." Indeed, the apparent willful starvation may upset the family and there may be numerous conflicts that arise. Persons who undergo therapy may learn to label their emotional states and behavior in accord with the expectations of professionals or family members. For example, the anorectic may be told that the pursuit of thinness represents a denial of sexuality. Her psychiatrist may say that she must accept her passage through adolescence and the full-female shape of an adult. Eventually, she is convinced and begins to talk differently about herself.

It is well known that some individuals are more likely to develop anorexia than others. This variation is due to both biological and social differences. Biological factors involve differences in normal body weight, metabolism, sex of individual, age, stature, and so on. Social differences depend on variation in social experiences. People learn many things from others by direct experience and by observing other people [14]. Those who share similar social attributes (e.g. status, race, sex, and demographic location) often have similar learning experiences. However, some experiences and social models in a person's life are unique.

People watch different television programs, read different magazines, and have different friends even though they come from the same community. One individual may learn to eat in moderation, another may learn to eat to excess. In Western culture, the mass media conveys values of thinness and physical fitness that are linked to an increased incidence of anorexia. There is, however, considerable variability in the degree of acceptance of these values. It is likely that greater acceptance correlates with the tendency to diet and exercise thereby increasing a person's chances of triggering the activity-anorexia cycle.

Humans self-impose food restriction, typically called diets, for a variety of reasons. All diets would not be expected to generate excessive activity [1]. The type, severity, and pattern of diet are important factors contributing to physical activity. For example, many anorectics change their meal pattern from several meals to one per day. This change in the number of meals may be important in generating activity anorexia. Other patterns of food intake may not lead to excessive activity. Clearly then, given these restraints, not all people who are very active or who go on diets would be susceptible to activity anorexia.

5 SUMMARY AND OVERVIEW

Activity anorexia develops from an interplay of culture and biology. Cultural and social practices predispose some individuals to contact the activity-anorexia cycle. This cycle is the result of species evolution and is mediated by physiological mechanisms regulating eating and physical activity. Once initiated, this cycle of increasing activity and decreasing food intake is resistant to change.

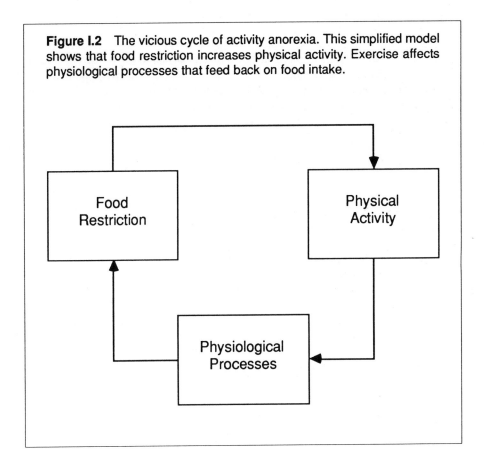

Figure I.2 The vicious cycle of activity anorexia. This simplified model shows that food restriction increases physical activity. Exercise affects physiological processes that feed back on food intake.

Human self-starvation is still viewed as a psychiatric disorder called anorexia nervosa. The first section of this book (Chapters 1 to 6) is a critical analysis of the history, diagnosis, and treatment of willful starvation as a mental illness. The analysis is based on the author's acceptance of the scientific method and the possibility of scientific accounts of human behavior. From our perspective, accounts of human behavior that rely on subjective mental processes are open to severe criticism. Unfortunately, much of the research and theory on anorexia nervosa is mentalistic and subjective. Although we have attempted to accurately describe traditional perspectives of anorexia nervosa, we were forced by our assumptions to challenge some of these views. Nonetheless, many of the current ideas and conceptions of this disorder remain useful and are integrated within our approach.

The second section of the book details the evidence for activity anorexia. We provide an analysis of the social and cultural factors that predispose people to diet and exercise. We also consider human and animal research on physical activity and food intake, and the relationship of this research to an animal model of activity anorexia. This is followed by a discussion of the evolutionary and physiological bases of this form of self-starvation.

In the final section of the book, we detail the assessment criteria for activity anorexia. A functional definition of anorexia is introduced that allows for a new classification of human self-starvation based on the determinants of weight loss and food reduction. The major advantage of a functional classification is that treatment may be tailored to the specific factors that maintain anorexia. This functional approach is used to design treatment and prevention strategies for individuals suffering from activity anorexia. Our suggestions for preventing and treating activity anorexia incorporate many of the established therapies but redirect these interventions toward the diet and exercise cycle. In addition, we offer several new treatment tactics.

REFERENCES

Although many of these references may be of interest, we have indicated (with an asterisk*) those that are written for the non-specialist reader.

1. Epling, W. F., Pierce, W. D. and Stefan, L. (1983). A theory of activity-based anorexia. *The International Journal of Eating Disorders*, 3, 27-46.
2. Garner, D. M. and Garfinkel, P. E. (1978). Sociocultural factors in anorexia nervosa. *Lancet*, Sept., 674.
3. Crisp, A. H., Hsu, L. K. G., Harding, B. and Hartshorne, J. (1980). Clinical features of anorexia nervosa: A study of a consecutive series of 102 female patients. *Journal of Psychosomatic Research*, 24, 179-191.
4. King, A. (1963). Primary and secondary anorexia nervosa syndromes. *British Journal of Psychiatry*, 109, 470-479.
5. Kron, L., Katz, J. L., Gorzynski, G. and Weiner, H. (1978). Hyperactivity in anorexia nervosa: A fundamental clinical feature. *Comprehensive Psychiatry*, 19, 433-440.
6. Feighner, J. P., Robins, E., Guze, S. B., Woodruff, R. A., Winokur, G., and Munoz, R. (1972). Diagnostic criteria for use in psychiatric research. *Archives of General Psychiatry*, 26, 57-63.

7. Epling, W. F. and Pierce, W. D. (1988). Activity-based anorexia: A biobehavioral perspective. *The International Journal of Eating Disorders, 7*, 475-485.

8. Slade, P. D. (1973). A short anorectic behavior scale. *British Journal of Psychiatry*, 122, 83-85.

9. Crisp, A H. (1965). Clinical and therapeutic aspects of anorexia nervosa: A study of 30 cases. *Journal of Psychosomatic Research*, 9, 67-78.

10. Beumont, P. J. V. , Booth, S. F. , Abraham, S. F. , Griffiths, D. A. and Turner, T. R. (1983). A temporal sequence of symptoms in patients with anorexia nervosa: A preliminary report. In P. L. Darby, P. E. Garfinkel, D. M. Garner and D. V. Coscina (Eds.), *Anorexia nervosa: Recent developments in research*, (pp. 15-28). New York: Alan R. Liss, Inc.

11. Cumming, D. C. (1989). Menstrual disturbances caused by exercise. In K. M. Pirke, W. Wuttke, and U. Schweiger (Eds.), *The menstrual cycle and its disorders: Influences of nutrition, exercise and neurotransmitters,* (pp. 150-160). New York: Springer-Verlag.

12. Pirke, K. M., Schweiger, U., Broocks, A., Spyra, B., Tuschl, R. J. and Laessle, R. G. (1989). Endocrine studies in female athletes with and without menstrual disturbances. In K. M. Pirke, W. Wuttke, and U. Schweiger (Eds.), *The menstrual cycle and its disorders: Influences of nutrition, exercise and neurotransmitters*, (pp. 171-178). New York: Springer-Verlag.

13. Stunkard, A. J. and Stellar, E. (1980). *Eating and its disorders* (Research publications: Association for Research and mental disease, Vol., 62) New York: Raven Press.

14. *Bandura, A. (1977). *Social Learning Theory*. Englewood Cliffs, NJ: Prentice Hall.

PART I

Anorexia Nervosa

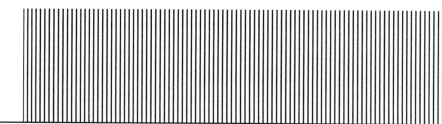

The main topics are:

- **THE MEDICAL MODEL OF ANOREXIA NERVOSA**
- **PSYCHOANALYSIS AND ANOREXIA NERVOSA**
- **MENTAL ILLNESS AS A MYTH**

Summary

- The history of anorexia nervosa is outlined.

- A discussion of physical and mental causes of abnormal behavior is presented.

- Psychoanalysis and the mental illness view of anorexia are examined.

- The authors suggest that mental illness explanations are not scientific. An account of anorexia must point to the biological, behavioral, and cultural conditions that regulate eating — physical activity is a primary factor.

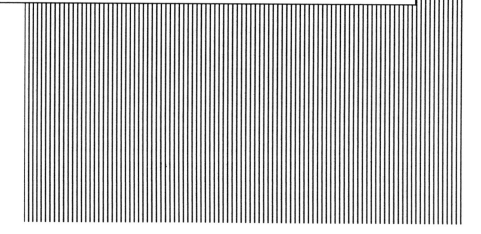

CHAPTER

Anorexia as a
Mental Illness

1

Anorexia nervosa refers to willful self-starvation and is generally regarded as a psychiatric disorder. Anorexia is a term derived from the Greek word "orexis" that refers to appetite or desire. The prefix "an" means "the absence of" and therefore, anorexia is the absence or loss of appetite. The word nervosa comes from the Latin root "nervus" and in this context has the meaning of imprisoned or captured. The person is a "prisoner" of a neurotic mental state.

Today, anorexia nervosa is a clinical label that is applied to a person who is "locked into" a mental illness that results in self-starvation. Although this disorder is receiving increased attention by practitioners, scientists, and the popular media, the first case history was documented nearly three centuries ago.

In 1689 the English physician, Richard Morton, described a condition of willful starvation in a young woman who died a few months after her visit to him. He attempted to distinguish this condition from the loss of appetite that accompanied the medical disease of tuberculosis. Morton called the illness "nervous consumption" and vividly described his 18-year-old patient as follows:

> In the month of July she fell into a total suppression of her monthly courses from a multitude of cares and passions of her mind, but without any symptom of the green-sickness following upon it. From which time her appetite began to abate, and her digestion to be bad; her flesh also began to be flaccid and loose, and her looks pale ... she was wont by her studying at night, and continual pouring upon books, to expose herself both day and night to the injuries of the air ... I do not remember that I did

ever in all my practice see one, that was conversant with the living so much wasted
with the greatest degree of a consumption (like a skeleton only clad with skin) yet
there was no fever, but on the contrary a coldness of the whole body ... only her
appetite was diminished, and her digestion uneasy, with fainting fits, which did
frequently return upon her [1].

Dr. Morton also described a case of anorexia nervosa in a young man. He stated that
"the son of the Reverend Minister Steel, about the sixteenth year of his age, fell gradually
into a total want of appetite, occasioned by his studying too hard, and the passions of his
mind, and upon that into a universal atrophy, pining away more and more for the space of
two years, without any cough, fever, or any other symptom of distemper" [2, p. 143].

The next documented report of anorexia appeared nearly two centuries later. In 1868
another English physician, Sir William Gull, published a detailed account of deliberate
self-starvation. He initially referred to the condition as "apepsia hysterica" but by 1873 he
considered the term "anorexia nervosa" more descriptive of the illness.

Gull suggested that the disease arose from a "morbid mental state" and a "disturbed
nerve force." He saw the person controlled by a deranged mind and this mental condition
gave rise to the various symptoms that he observed in his patients. A similar mental account
was provided by the French physician, Lasegue, who published an independent report in
1873 that called the disorder "hysterical anorexia." Lasegue stated that this kind of
starvation resulted from psychic disturbances and noted his patient's "complacent attitude" of contentment with her emaciated state [3].

The current psychiatric understanding of anorexia nervosa has built upon the early
accounts of Morton, Gull, and Lasegue. Today, however, professionals prefer to discuss
the mind in terms of disturbed thinking patterns and disorders of personality. Modern
psychiatry and clinical psychology have replaced "morbid mental state" with mental
illness concepts that maintain the opinion of anorexia as a neurotic disorder.

In our view, "neurotic" is a descriptive label for seemingly irrational behavior but is not
an explanation. A scientific account provides an explanation by pointing to the biological
and environmental determinants of self-starvation. However, Gull's description of the
symptoms of anorexia nervosa still remains useful to a scientific understanding of the
disorder. In this regard, he noted disrupted or absent menstrual cycles, extreme thinness,
constipation, slow pulse rate and breathing, and excessive activity in the absence of
physical illness. The presence of physical activity may be the most important observation
in terms of the causes of self-starvation.

1   THE MEDICAL MODEL OF ANOREXIA NERVOSA

A major contemporary view of anorexia nervosa has evolved from the physical disease
model. If a person coughs, has difficulty breathing, is feverish and has no energy, a possible
diagnosis is pneumonia. The symptoms or observable features are assumed to be caused
by the underlying physical disease. This assumption has proven useful because many

physical disorders, like pneumonia, have resulted from initially unobservable causes. In the case of pneumonia, the discovery of pneumonia bacteria has allowed for an understanding of the symptoms and led to the eventual treatment of the illness.

The physical disease model has, of course, often been used to account for the abnormal behavior of people. The assumption is that unusual and irrational actions are the result of disease or injury. This is a significant step toward a more scientific understanding of abnormal behavior.

Many physicians assume that unusual behavior is due to some physical disease. This view is often successful in identifying those behavior problems with organic causes. For example, Alzheimer's Disease is a degenerative brain disorder that occurs during middle age and produces unusual behavior patterns. The person with this illness may appear absent-minded, irritable, have difficulty in concentration, and frequently exhibit paranoid beliefs. Many other physical diseases produce unusual behavior. Today, finding a physical cause is important to medical progress, especially in the area of psychological and psychiatric problems.

The physical illness model has been extended to many other types of unusual behavior including anorexia. Even when physical causes are not identified, the physical disease model is used to understand irrational actions. In this case, physicians act as though there is an underlying organic disorder.

Physical and Mental Causes of Anorexia

Other physicians have argued that some abnormal behavior patterns are not due to organic problems, but rather to non-physical (i.e. mental) reasons for the illness. This shift to mental causes is understandable when physical factors cannot be readily identified. The inference that irrational actions are due to unobservable mental events seems to answer the question of why the person is behaving so strangely. That is, saying that the anorectic is ill due to mental disturbance provides an explanation and allows for medical treatment. Although mental explanations are acceptable in everyday life, a genuinely scientific account of self-starvation cannot rely on inferred and subjective processes. There is no doubt that persons who are anorexic have many unusual thoughts and feelings. However, as we will show later, these experiences are by-products rather than causes of self-starvation.

Many physicians and other health professionals recognize that physical causes provide a more adequate explanation of unusual behavior than do various appeals to ad hoc mental problems. The view of anorexia nervosa as a mental illness was challenged in 1914 by a new medical discovery. A pathologist, Dr. Simmonds, reported a lesion in the anterior lobe of the pituitary gland of an emaciated woman [4]. This organic damage seemed to explain why a person willfully refused to eat. Finding a physical disease in this situation made an appeal to mental states unnecessary. Based on this evidence, the medical profession began to classify many cases of anorexia as Simmonds' disease. However, a difficulty was that most cases of anorexia did not show this kind of pathology. Thus, there was a need to distinguish Simmonds' disease from anorexia nervosa.

Anorexia nervosa was used as the diagnosis when physical damage could not be established. The problem was that without physical damage or disease there was no explanation for self-starvation. In order to provide a medical understanding of anorexia nervosa, the mental-illness view was reconsidered. A 1938 account of anorexia nervosa by Drs. Farquharson and Hyland suggested that the illness resulted from "some prolonged emotional conflict, either avowed or concealed" [5].

Diagnosis of Anorexia Nervosa

Following the lead of Farquharson and Hyland, other investigators attempted to differentiate anorexia nervosa and Simmonds' disease. This effort finally culminated in the 1971 publication by Dr. Ushakov who presented the following criteria for distinguishing Simmonds' disease from anorexia nervosa.

1. Anorexia nervosa presents mostly in early adolescence;

2. More frequent in girls than in boys;

3. Lack of pronounced changes of secondary sex characteristics;

4. Lack of signs of premature senility;

5. Loss of hair and teeth extremely rare;

6. Psychogenic reasons for food rejection, with loss of appetite;

7. The patient is hypersensitive to any offer of help and is eager to be slim; persistently resists any treatment, which is regarded as an obstacle to slimming — these characteristics do not apply to patients with Simmonds' disease;

8. Absence of weakness, even with a significant degree of emaciation, is typical of the initial and later stages of development of hypophyseal deficiency;

9. In anorexia nervosa the patients remain active, very sensitive, and have morbid aspirations toward their goal; in contrast, patients with Simmonds' disease are passive, apathetic and disinterested [6, p. 286].

Anorexia nervosa is currently considered a psychiatric disorder characterized by a voluntary refusal to eat, extreme loss of weight, and in some cases, death. The diagnostic manual of the American Psychiatric Association details the official criteria for the diagnosis of anorexia nervosa [7]. Several of the primary symptoms must be present before a person is classified as anorexic. Primary symptoms include behavior directed toward losing weight, weight loss, peculiar patterns of handling food, intense fear of gaining weight, disturbance of body image, and in females, irregular or absent menstrual cycle (amenorrhea). Secondary features are not required for diagnosis but occur with some frequency. These include denial of illness and resistance to therapy, delayed psychosexual development in adolescents, and in adults, loss of sexual interest.

Table 1.1
The Diagnostic Criteria for Anorexia Nervosa

According to the Diagnostic and Statistical Manual of the American Psychiatric Association [7]

1. Refusal to maintain body weight over a minimal normal weight for age and height, e.g., weight loss leading to maintenance of body weight 15% below that expected; or failure to make expected weight gain during periods of growth, leading to body weight 15% below that expected.

2. Intense fear of gaining weight or becoming fat, even though underweight.

3. Disturbance in the way in which one's body weight, size, or shape is experienced, e.g., the person claims to "feel fat" even when emaciated, believes that one area of the body is "too fat" even when obviously underweight.

4. In females, absence of at least three consecutive menstrual cycles when otherwise expected to occur (primary or secondary amenorrhea). (A woman is considered to have amenorrhea if her periods occur only following hormone, e.g., estrogen, administration.)

The Harvard physician, Dr. Hilde Bruch, has suggested another set of criteria for "primary anorexia nervosa." In this classification system there are four psychological characteristics that are essential. First, in agreement with the American Psychiatric Association manual, the patient shows a delusional disturbance of body image and body concept. Second, the person fails to recognize hunger and nutritional needs. Third, there are deep feelings of inadequacy and inferiority; the anorectic suffers from a paralyzing sense of ineffectiveness. Fourth, obsessive hyperactivity is usually present such that the true anorectic denies feelings of fatigue [1,8]. In our view, the presence of hyperactivity is a central feature of anorexia. Dr. Beumont in Australia and Drs. Crisp and Stonehill in England reported excessive physical activity in virtually all of their patients [9, 10].

There are other classification schemes that attempt to identify the person with anorexia nervosa. Drs. Paul Garfinkel and David Garner have suggested several diagnostic criteria. They emphasize self-inflicted loss of weight associated with avoidance of food, self-induced vomiting, abuse of laxatives, excessive exercise, or some combination of these. They also note a secondary endocrine disorder which appears as amenorrhea in females and a reduction of sexual interest in males [11]. This diagnostic system is compatible with the one suggested by Dr. John Feighner and his colleagues. In addition to the above criteria, Feighner adds that the onset of illness must occur before age twenty-five, and there must be at least a 25 percent reduction of normal body weight [12].

Regardless of the diagnostic criteria, anorexia nervosa is still viewed as a mental illness. This view of anorexia and other abnormal behavior became firmly established at the turn of the 20th century, when the Viennese physician, Sigmund Freud, was developing his theory of psychoanalysis. This theory was based on his clinical observations and analysis of upper-class Viennese women who came to him with problems of "hysteria."

2   PSYCHOANALYSIS AND ANOREXIA NERVOSA

Following the rise of Freudian psychoanalysis, anorexia nervosa has been seen as an illness largely due to mental disturbance [13]. The theory of psychoanalysis is based on Freud's conclusion that neurosis occurs when unacceptable and unconscious impulses threaten to break into the conscious mind. The source of these impulses is the "id" or the primordial reservoir of instinct. When these unconscious urges are recognized by the ego (i.e. the source of self-awareness) the person is driven to self-gratification. However, the superego or conscience (i.e. the source of morals and values) works to oppose the impulses of the id and, in the ensuing fight, the ego has recourse to a variety of defense mechanisms.

The most important ego defense is repression, in which the ego forces the threatening urges back into the unconscious. This defense requires considerable psychic effort, weakens the ego, and creates neurotic anxiety. Often the unconscious urges are of a sexual origin and are expressed in ways that camouflage their true meaning. In this mental illness view, the anorectic is expressing neurotic anxiety related to sexual impulses. The psychoanalytical understanding of anorexia nervosa is seen in this passage from Drs. Rosen, Fox, and Gregory's text on abnormal psychology.

> ...*Whether occurring in a neurotic or a schizoid individual, anorexia nervosa is often related to sexual events in the patient's life history - the onset of puberty, guilt felt in connection with sexual activity or fantasy, and so forth. The motivation of the disorder is often a fear of sexual maturity; self-starvation may be an attempt to remain undeveloped, flat chested and unfeminine. ... Young anorexia patients will often openly express their pleasure in being a child and their desire to remain a favored daughter rather than a grown woman. It is common for symptoms to begin following a weight-reducing diet. ... Another motivation, deeply unconscious, is an association of food with impregnation, so that fear of eating represents a fear of becoming pregnant. Such primitive or infantile associations typically arise in girls with a very repressive upbringing. Having little or no sexual information but seeing their mother's abdomen growing, they assume that the baby is in the stomach and comes from eating some foods. In fact, such beliefs are common in many children but are corrected by added information with maturity. In some persons such childhood ideas are never expressed and corrected and the false belief continues well into adolescence, albeit at an unconscious level* [14, pp. 177-178].

The anorectic's refusal to eat and resulting severe loss of weight are considered to be expressions of an underlying personality disorder related to sexuality. A similar view has been expressed in a 1985 book on the treatment of anorexia, in which Drs. Wilson, Hogan and Mintz suggest that anorexia commonly arises from the young girl's terror of becoming fat. This terror, the authors assert, arises from anticipation of the hazards and responsibilities of adult sexuality [15].

Contemporary psychoanalysts such as Dr. Beattie relate anorexia more to the mother-daughter relationship than to sexuality. In her 1988 article, Dr. Beattie states that "the girl's ambivalent struggle for ... autonomy from the mother persists long past the Oedipal phase and revives intensely at puberty, with its pressures towards physical and psychosocial maturation" [16, p. 455]. From this perspective, disordered eating results from hostile-dependent conflicts and struggles for independence from the mother. In general, psychoanalysts relate anorexia to personality problems that arise from psychosocial and sexual stages of development.

Anorexia as Neurosis

We have seen that, on the whole, psychoanalysts see the anorexic personality as the root cause of the illness. A young woman may starve herself because she has developed a personality type which predisposes her to a neurotic concern with weight. In this regard, Dr. A H. Crisp has stated that "at one end of the spectrum the anorectic is seen to be very much in control of her destiny; however, at the other end, and this is the view that I adopt, the anorectic is seen to be at bay. She only appears to be in control of her destiny. In fact, she is devoid of choice and is driven by fear" [17]. In Dr. Crisp's view the anorectic has an excessive fear of being fat. The refusal to eat is therefore an expression of this phobia.

Other psychiatrists believe that the phobic reaction to food is an unconscious strategy that the person uses to obtain secondary goals. The anorectic is said to use her behavior to gain control over family members or to deny her blossoming sexuality. Dr. V. Rakoff has remarked that:

> ...it (extreme thinness) signals to the self in the mirror and to the world at large some aspiration. The signals are various: 'I am beautiful;' 'I am sexually desirable;' 'I am one of you;' 'I am virtuous;' 'I am not like you;' 'I am not sexually mature — I am only a little girl' ... it (anorexia nervosa) is an exercise of intense self-control, such as doing 150 pushups, or swimming a mile a day, or wearing a hair shirt. Yet it is intensely demonstrative and is not secret and intimate. It is a signal to the field which in addition to any other messages also conveys, 'see how I can control myself (and you).' In short, it is contextual and manifests a considerable degree of 'field dependency,' a conformity to some ideal perceived by the patient as necessary for self-acceptance and acceptance in 'the field' [18].

In Dr. Rakoff's view, physical activity (i.e. pushups and swimming) is equated with "wearing a hair shirt." We think this is an unnecessary generalization, which Dr. Rakoff makes only because of his broad interpretation of the concept of intense self-control. Other psychiatrists equate this physical exercise with an extreme need to burn off calories rather than merely a need for control. In fact, we have found that physical activity itself arises from food restriction rather than these psychological needs.

Psychoanalysis continues to be an influence in the area of mental health and is still used to understand and treat anorexia nervosa. Dr. David Rampling published a 1978 paper on psychoanalytical theory and practice as it pertains to anorexia nervosa, in which he states:

> *The development of anorexia nervosa represents a regression in psychosexual develop-*
> *ment as a maladaptive solution to the maturational demands of adolescence, which the*
> *patient construes as maleficent and frightening. The libidinous feelings attending sexual*
> *maturation, along with their potential for consummation in an extrafamilial and*
> *heterosexual relationship, are the core issues around which fears evolve. ... Adjectives*
> *such as obstinate, manipulative, deceitful, and stubborn are frequently applied to*
> *anorexic patients, all of which describe manifest behavior, but convey nothing of the*
> *despair and helplessness motivating these desperate individuals* [19, p. 297].

The specific, underlying psychic forces (i.e. sexual desires, maternal conflicts, etc.) may change from person to person, but from a psychoanalytical perspective the dynamics remain similar. This conceptual framework is one example of the application of the medical model to anorexia nervosa. It concludes that the cause of self-starvation is a personality disorder and the anorectic is mentally ill. Other psychodynamic theories differ in the psychic mechanisms that give rise to the disorder but all view the individual as mentally disturbed.

3 MENTAL ILLNESS AS A MYTH

Mental illness explanations of behavior have some serious conceptual and logical difficulties [20]. The psychiatrist and critic of the medical model of mental illness, Dr. Thomas Szasz, has stated that mental illness is a myth. He concludes that "our adversaries are not demons, witches, fate, or mental illness. We have no enemy whom we can fight, exorcise, or dispel by 'cure'. What we do have are problems in living — whether these be biologic, economic, political, or sociopsychological" [21].

Although Szasz is referring to mental illness in general, it is important to note that the understanding of anorexia nervosa as a type of mental illness is also a myth. There are a number of reasons for such a conclusion. These involve: a) the incorrect application of the physical disease model; b) problems with the basic assumptions that lead to the concept of mental illness; and c) circular reasoning that yields false explanation.

As we mentioned earlier, the medical model of mental illness gains its support from the physical account of disease processes. Specifically, there are physical diseases of the body that affect what people do. Some of these illnesses produce alterations of the nervous system which may result in bizarre or unusual behavior. Such abnormal behavior is not due to a disorder of the mind; rather it results from physical changes of the neurological system. When neurological impairment cannot be established, it is tempting to appeal to a non-physical or mental cause(s). A mental disturbance, however, has no physical referent except the bizarre behavior. When health professionals use mental causes to account for self-starvation, they are actually providing a non-medical explanation since no physical-disease agent exists. Explanations of abnormal behavior that rely on non-physical causes are, therefore, incorrect applications of the medical model.

Mental illness theories do not meet the scientific criteria of independent observation and replication of results. In everyday life, people seldom question common sense mental interpretations of behavior in terms of observation and replication. However, these criteria are more central to adequate scientific accounts.

Another problem that is raised by mental illness explanations is the use of inherently untestable assumptions. Of course, scientists have often hypothesized unobservable events and causes. For example, the atom was an unobservable physical entity when first described. The difference between the atom and a mental entity like the "ego" is that atoms have physical referents (i.e. mass and location) but the ego's referent is the behavior it is said to explain. In other words, it is not possible to specify or measure aspects of the "ego" independent of human action. Concepts such as ego could be made more scientifically palatable if they referred to a set of testable conditions that commonly influenced human behavior. At the present time, however, few mental concepts have been defined in this way.

Nonetheless, an appeal to mental causes has attained popular acceptance in modern times. It sounds reasonable to say, "her behavior expresses an unconscious conflict with sexuality that is resolved by a refusal to eat." The difficulty with an interpretation of this sort is that people may not eat for a variety of reasons. Perhaps friends have strongly encouraged a thin appearance; family members may have teased the person for being too fat; Simmonds' disease may be unrecognized, and so on.

Circular reasoning is another common error when the medical model is applied to mental illness. When a young woman is extremely thin, refuses to eat, perhaps claims to be larger than objective evidence suggests, and generates a high score on an eating disorders test, she is likely to be diagnosed as suffering from anorexia nervosa. The diagnosis is a label for the unusual behavior. A logical problem occurs when the label is used to explain why the person behaves in this manner. Since the label stands for the behavior, it cannot be the explanation.

There are psychiatrists and psychologists who employ mental explanations but who believe that the mental causes of abnormal behavior will eventually be linked to physiological and chemical processes. To these specialists, mental disorders are in fact due to physical causes in the brain. This perspective holds that mental diseases are no different than other bodily dysfunctions except they occur in the neurological system. However, when mental reference is replaced by physiological description, the mental interpretation of an illness then becomes unnecessary.

Another troublesome aspect of reducing mental processes to neuroanatomy is that mental illness may often be due to social problems. It is unreasonable to expect that the most advanced understanding of the brain can help those who have social and economic difficulties. The point is that specific physical changes in the nervous system (or elsewhere) cannot be linked to particular social or economic actions. Additionally it is clear that belief statements, such as "I am overweight and need to lose a few more pounds" are socially regulated and there is no point in looking for their location in the brain or nervous system. Finally, brain processes do not account for the disrupted social relationships that may occur during anorexia (i.e. family conflict).

We suggest that sociological factors (e.g. values and norms of society and groups) and social learning (e.g. social reinforcement, modeling and imitation) account for many personal problems, unusual beliefs, and conflicts in social relationships. People learn to regulate their food intake and reduce body weight because of socially prescribed standards. Following this, physiological processes of decreased appetite and increased physical activity maintain the person's refusal to eat. Therefore, both social learning and physiology are required to provide a reasonable account of anorexia.

Whatever the criticism of the mental disease model of anorexia nervosa, it continues to be a major influence in the field. Although logical and conceptual difficulties exist, researchers holding this perspective continue to provide detailed observations of the disorder. These observations have been valuable for building a scientific theory of how individuals can starve themselves to the point of death. Modern doctors and researchers are increasingly more diverse in theoretical orientation. Even though mentalistic factors continue to predominate, there is increasing awareness of and concern with the influence of sociocultural factors and the way the individual interacts with others.

REFERENCES

Although many of these references may be of interest, we have indicated (with an asterisk*) those that are written for the non-specialist reader.

1. *Bruch, H. (1973). *Eating disorders*. New York: Basic Books.
2. *Dally, P., Gomez, J. and Isaacs, A. J. (1979). *Anorexia nervosa*. London: William Heinemann Medical Books, Ltd.
3. *Dally, P. (1967). *Anorexia nervosa*. New York: International Universities Press.
4. Simmonds, M. (1914). Ueber embolische prozesse in der hypophysis. *Archives of Pathology and Anatomy*, 217, 226-239.
5. Farquharson, R. F. and Hyland, H. H. (1938). Anorexia nervosa: A metabolic disorder of psychologic origin. *Journal of the American Medical Association*, 111, 1085-1092.
6. Ushakov, G. K. (1971). Anorexia nervosa. In J. G. Howells (Ed.), *Modern perspectives in adolescent psychiatry*. Edinburgh: Oliver and Boyd.
7. American Psychiatric Association. (1987). *Diagnostic and statistical manual of mental disorders (DSM-IIIR)*. Third edition, Revised, Washington, DC: American Psychiatric Association.
8. Bruch, H. (1965). The psychiatric differential diagnosis of anorexia nervosa. In J. E. Mayer and H. Feldman (Eds.), *Anorexia nervosa: Symposium am 24/25 April 1965 in Göttingen*. Stuttgart, Germany: Georg Thieme Verlag.
9. Beumont, P.J.V., Booth, A.L., Abraham, S.F., Griffiths, D.A. and Turner, T.R. (1983). A temporal sequence of symptoms in patients with anorexia nervosa. In P. L. Darby, P. E. Garfinkel, D. M. Garner, and D. V. Coscina (Eds.), *Anorexia nervosa: Recent developments in research*, (pp. 129-136). New York: Alan R. Liss.
10. Crisp, A.H. and Stonehill, E. (1976). *Sleep, nutrition and mood*, (pp. 22-23). London:

John Wiley.

11. Garfinkel, P. E. and Garner, D M. (1982). *Anorexia nervosa: A multidimensional perspective*. New York: Brunner/Mazel.

12. Feighner, J. P., Robins, E., Guze, S. B., Woodruff, R. A., Winokur, G. and Munoz, R. (1972). Diagnostic criteria for use in psychiatric research. *Archives of General Psychiatry*, 26, 57-63.

13. *Freud, S. (1933). *New introductory lectures in psychoanalysis*. New York: Norton.

14. *Rosen, E., Fox, R. E. and Gregory, I. (1972). *Abnormal psychology*. Toronto: W. B. Saunders Co.

15. Wilson, C. P., Hogan, C. C. and Mintz, I. L. (1985). *Fear of being fat: The treatment of anorexia nervosa and bulimia*. New York: Jason Aronson.

16. Beattie, H. J. (1988). Eating disorders and the mother-daughter relationship. *International Journal of Eating Disorders*, 7, 453-460.

17. Crisp, A. H. (1983). Some aspects of the psychopathology of anorexia nervosa. In P. L. Darby, P. E. Garfinkel, D. M. Garner & D. V. Coscina (Eds.), *Anorexia nervosa: Recent developments in research*. New York: Alan R. Liss, Inc.

18. Rakoff, V. (1983). Multiple determinants of family dynamics in anorexia nervosa. In P. L. Darby, P. E. Garfinkel, D. M. Garner & D. V. Coscina (Eds.), *Anorexia nervosa: Recent developments in research*. New York: Alan R. Liss, Inc.

19. Rampling, D. (1978). Anorexia nervosa: Reflections on theory and practice. *Psychiatry*, 41, 296-301.

20. *Szasz, T. S. (1961). *The myth of mental illness: Foundations of a theory of personal conduct*. New York: Dell Publishing Co.

21. Szasz, S. T. (1973). The myth of mental illness. In T. Millon (Ed.) *Theories of psychopathology and personality*. Toronto: W. B. Saunders Co.

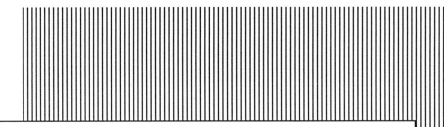

The main topics are:

- SOCIAL-COGNITIVE MODEL
- THE BEHAVIORAL MODEL
- SOCIAL LABELING AND ANOREXIA NERVOSA

Summary

- The social-cognitive view emphasizes thoughts, actions, and social reactions.

- Observational learning and the socialization of the values of thinness and fitness are discussed.

- Behavioral views of anorexia focus on operant conditioning of eating and the regulation of body weight.

- Anorexia nervosa can be viewed as learning to play the sick role. Social labeling occurs when the person is diagnosed as neurotic.

- People with activity anorexia are locked into a biobehavioral process. There is no point in labeling them as neurotic — in fact, this may create serious negative consequences for the patient.

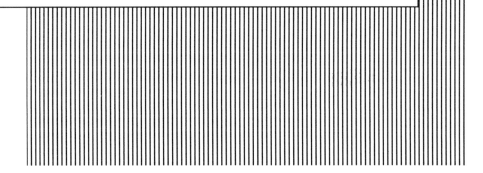

CHAPTER

Non-Medical Perspectives of Anorexia

2

Psychological theories offer new ways of understanding unusual and irrational behavior. Two major approaches to psychological science are cognitive and behavioral [1, 2]. Cognitive psychologists are concerned with how people understand themselves, others, and their environment. In contrast, behavioral psychologists are not interested in how people interpret the world. They prefer to directly study the behavior of people without making inferences about what people think. In this chapter, we present analyses of anorexia based on cognitive and behavioral theories.

Cognitive theories emphasize disordered thinking [3]. Instead of looking for disorders of personality (see Chapter 1), cognitive psychologists attend to the person's current beliefs, attitudes and expectations. These thought processes, or cognitions, are indirectly observed by analyzing the verbal and non-verbal actions of people. Cognitive psychologists argue that social factors have a strong influence on thinking. Social factors involve the person's interaction with family, friends, and other people. The integration of social and cognitive perspectives has lead to the social-cognitive model of anorexia nervosa.

1 THE SOCIAL-COGNITIVE MODEL

Three separate factors are important to the social-cognitive approach: a) the overt behavior or conduct of the individual, b) personal characteristics involving styles of perceiving and thinking about the world, and c) the person's environment which consists of social situations and interactions with other people [4]. These three factors influence one another in an interlocking system. For example, cognitive factors may involve various expectations, beliefs and attitudes of the person. A belief in the attractiveness of a slim figure may combine with beliefs about self (i.e. I am overweight) to initiate dieting and food regulation (overt behavior). Once dieting has started, the loss of weight may cause others to express approval or admiration by remarks such as "you are looking so trim; I wish that I had your will power." The reactions of others may confirm the belief that being thin is good and may increase the tendency to diet.

An important part of this perspective concerns the social experiences of the person. Past and present interactions with others affect the way the person sees and interprets the world (i.e. cognitive processes), and thus influences the way a person thinks about himself and

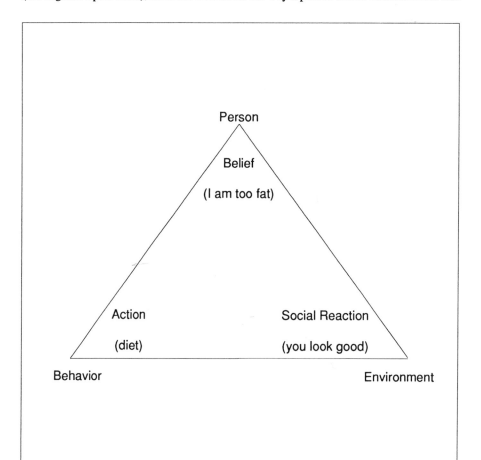

Figure 2.1 The social cognitive model of human behavior. In this model the person's beliefs influence behavior that affects social reactions. These reactions, in turn, alter the person's beliefs.

his environment. To illustrate, a child raised in a household where the mother expects children to "clean the plate" may have very different beliefs about food than children whose mothers are less adamant. Current social interactions may also produce a change in attitude and belief. However, in this case, an attitude change may be less likely because people generally choose to interact with others who share their opinions while rejecting those who challenge their beliefs [5]. From a social-cognitive perspective, such biased information-processing makes it hard to change the anorectic's way of thinking about food and body weight.

The social experiences of a person are sometimes shared with others and these experiences are often unique. Based on this fact, each person has an individual cognitive style that is carried into particular situations [1]. How the person interprets the situation is seen as an important determinant of individual behavior. If the family meal is defined as threatening because of an acquired belief in thinness, the anorectic may respond with hostility to members of the family.

Social-cognitive researchers point out that a person's understanding of stressful events can lead to eating problems. People who respond to stress by increasing or decreasing food intake have interpreted the situation in a way that makes sense to them. For example, an anorexic person may think: "I can't handle this event; I need the affection and sympathy of others; perhaps I can get attention by starving."

The importance of situational factors that trigger anorexia nervosa has been described by several researchers [6]. Breakup of the family, death of a parent, going to college, pregnancy in a parent or sibling, sibling promiscuity and other events have been implicated as stressful circumstances that precede anorexia. Of course, all persons faced with family crises do not become anorexic. In the social-cognitive view, experiences of the anorectic have predisposed the individual to react to the crisis by giving up food. Some investigators suggest that the major predispositions are feelings of worthlessness and low perceived control over one's life [7]. The importance of perceived control is illustrated in a case history provided by Professor Vivian Rakoff:

In the case of Miss C., the anorectic symptoms represent a profound rejection of her overwhelming family. The father, a well-known artist, presented an eccentric, disheveled appearance. He was obese and dirty in a way rarely seen among middle-class people; his skin was grey with ingrained filth; his jacket from one suit and his trousers from another were spattered and caked with stains and encrustations. His teeth were broken and yellow, and his hands and fingernails were blotched with nicotine stains. The mother was also obese. She was, however, clean, and for attendance at interviews she dressed herself in her best and tried to arrange her hair. But everything about her seemed to escape her attempts at control; her hair eluded the many combs and pins and hung in untidy tendrils down her neck; rolls of fat bulged her too-tight dress. Above her very shabby shoes which seemed too small for her, her fat feet puffed upward in cushions. It soon became apparent that the appearance of the parents was an exact reflection of the chaos of the household in general. The conversation in the family was calm and reasonable; there was distress and bewilderment and genuine concern for the patient. She, however, sat throughout the interview looking down at her hands. She would not speak to or look at her parents, and indeed rejected conjoint therapy. Her explicit verbal statements and her anorexia nervosa conveyed the same message: 'I will not be like them. I want to lead an orderly, clean, controlled, ordinary life. I don't want to be in a house where meals aren't cooked, where the kitchen is like a stable, every surface cluttered with dirty dishes and fragments of food.

Figure 2.2 Fashion designs of course often work with an idealization of beauty involving extreme slenderness.

In Miss C's family, there was little overlapping of identities. Perhaps the mother was overinvolved with the father's career, but this is purely conjecture. The overt picture is one of hyper-autonomy: an overfilled house, the children left essentially to rear themselves. The mother, having been defeated by the demands made on her, retreated into benign passivity. Miss C's yearning for order and control would most readily be expressed in the one area where she could exert her will: her appetite and her body. For her this became the focal expression of her aspiration for a life as totally unlike that of her parents as she could manage [8, pp. 35-36].

In the social-cognitive view, the low perceived control of Miss C. is related to her eating problem. One's perceptions of control are part of the more general belief in being able to cope effectively with tasks and situations. According to Dr. Albert Bandura, people form efficacy expectations about their capabilities of handling situational requirements [9]. One person may believe that it is possible to cope with social pressures to be trim and slim while another believes that the pressure is too much to deal with. Maladaptive eating may arise from this low perceived efficacy.

Social-cognitive psychologists also emphasize the importance of learning by observation, and one aspect of observational learning is that people acquire new ways of acting by imitating what others do [4]. The model (or the individual who is imitated) often provides information about how to behave in particular situations. The learner is said to cognitively represent the actions of the model. Cognitive representation involves mental coding, rehearsal, memory, and reproduction of modeled action. In this way, the person effectively learns from what others say and do.

Family members, peers, heroes, and popular figures serve as particularly significant models. Another kind of model is called symbolic: the model represents some culturally-fixed social value or standard. Many popular television programs and books present stereotyped characters who convey these social ideals.

In terms of anorexia nervosa, magazines, books, and television present an ideal standard of beauty for women. During the last century, social models have suggested to women that "being thin is good." Dr. Hilde Bruch has commented that "magazines and movies carry the same message, but most persistent is television, drumming it in, day in day out, that one can be loved and respected only when slender" [10, p. viii]. Symbolic modeling affects both parents and children. A daughter may see television models that represent the ideal figure and then attempt to emulate these individuals. Parents are also affected by such models and teach this standard of beauty to their children. The critical role of symbolic models for anorexia nervosa has been addressed by Dr. David Garner and his associates:

If a thin shape has been considered desirable in Western society during the last century, in the last decade there has been an almost fetish-like quality to the preoccupation with thinness for women. The examination of virtually any women's fashion magazine today illustrates the point more elegantly than written description. It was our impression several years ago that not only were women being confronted more aggressively by the media with the 'thin body image,' but also these 'ideals for feminine beauty' were notably thinner than they had been in the past [11, p. 69-70].

People therefore learn many things by observation and imitation. Some models influence many people (e.g. television models) while others are unique to the person (e.g. family and friends). One child may observe parents eat in moderation, another may see them eat to excess. The value of dieting and exercise is communicated by some parents but not others. Peers and mass media not only convey the value of thinness but also provide information about how to lose weight. A survey of women's magazines demonstrates that dieting is a popular topic. The person is told to be thin and is provided with a variety of reducing diets. Most observational learning is sex-typed and social models that portray the value of being thin are typically young women. Both men and women are affected by this message. Men come to find thin women more attractive; women try to make themselves match the social standard and men's expectations. Of course, not all young women are equally affected since the models and experiences of each person are different.

The social-cognitive perspective emphasizes the way people interact and subsequently interpret themselves and their circumstances. What a person does is said to be explained by the underlying cognitions. Beliefs about control and expectations of personal competence are suggested as important factors related to anorexia. In addition, cognitive representation of the action of social models, allows people to acquire social standards and values. The value of being thin is communicated to young women and this is held to be another factor leading to anorexia. Generally, social-cognitive theorists argue that in order to understand the behavior of people, it is necessary to know how, and what, they think.

The social-cognitive model is important for a scientific analysis of activity anorexia because the model points to specific conditions that lead a person to combine dieting and exercise. That is, the conditions that lead a person to be overly concerned about thinness and fitness probably bring on an increased tendency to diet and exercise. When the individual combines excessive exercise with severe dieting, a vicious cycle of activity anorexia may be the result.

2 THE BEHAVIORAL MODEL

Behavioral psychologists provide an alternative to the social-cognitive interpretation of maladaptive behavior [12]. Behaviorists argue that there is no need to guess about people's perceptions, beliefs, and attitudes. They suggest that an objective science cannot be based on subjective assumptions about cognitive processes. The difficulty is that thinking is only accessible to the person doing it. Although a person's report of internal thoughts may be accurate, the report cannot be independently verified — and independent verification is the hallmark of science. Behaviorists state that thoughts and feelings are produced by experience and are directly related to what the person does. Since this is the case, it is possible to avoid subjective reports by analyzing the relationship between environmental events and behavioral responses.

The behavioral approach comes from a branch of psychology that emphasizes the study of behavior for its own sake [13]. Behaviorists suggest that the causes of behavior must be stated in terms of observable environmental events. Likewise, they state that a scientific

---

Table 2.1
The Behavioral Model of Human Behavior

Specific Events or Stimuli Set the Occasion for Behavior. The Response Produces Consequences that May Increase this Behavior (i.e., Reinforce) in the Future.

Sd	R	Sr
Dinner on table	Refuse to eat	Attention from parents
Occasion	Response	Consequence
Discriminative Stimulus	Operant	Reinforcer

---

analysis of human behavior is possible. A person drives a car, goes to a movie, talks on the telephone, eats to excess, cries, and works. All of these are objective activities that can be scientifically investigated.

When it comes to anorexia nervosa, behavior analysis has focused on eating, body weight, physical activity, and so on. What anorectics say about themselves is not seen as a reflection of cognitive processes. Such statements are simply analyzed as another side of the behavior of the individual. The explanation of verbal and non-verbal behavior is based on identifying those stimulus events that precede or follow behavior.

The behavioral approach is based on the process of operant conditioning. A common observation is that successful behavior tends to be repeated and unsuccessful actions are not. An operant is any behavior that operates upon the environment to produce effects. The effects produced by such behavior are called consequences. Some consequences are reinforcing and thus strengthen (or increase) the behavior that produces them. Other consequences serve to weaken (or decrease) behavior.

The process called positive reinforcement occurs when a response is followed by an event that strengthens it. To illustrate, a person who buys lottery tickets (operant) may have his or her action reinforced by winning money (reinforcement). Winning increases the behavior of buying tickets, but, in fact, the total amount of money spent in any such activity may far exceed the winnings. Positive reinforcement works to maintain the betting habit even though the person loses in the long run. The gambler's behavior is self-defeating but very persistent.

Positive reinforcement may involve social, rather than monetary, consequences. In this case, a person's behavior is followed by approval, attention, admiration, and so on. Adult attention is an especially powerful reinforcer for children. Interestingly, studies show that even negative attention (i.e. attention that adults feel is unpleasant to the child) can strengthen behavior [14]. Parents who nag their child to eat may inadvertently reinforce the child's refusal to eat. Like the gambler, the anorectic's behavior is often viewed as self-defeating. Behaviorists suggest that the gambler is not trying to lose and the anorexic child is not trying to starve — both are examples of the effects of positive reinforcement.

People behave differently depending on the situation. A person who is talking loudly may become silent upon entering a library. In technical terms, the individual's differential response is called discrimination [12]. Discrimination occurs when behavior is reinforced (or punished) in one situation but not in another. Many signs and signals (e.g. police sirens, sale signs, smiles and frowns, etc.) set the occasion for specific responses. When an event signals or cues the person to do something, the event is called a discriminative stimulus.

The person who receives a "nudge under the table" may change the conversation or "shut up." The social cue is a discriminative stimulus which sets the occasion for a change in the conversation. The discriminative stimulus changes behavior because this event (i.e. the nudge) has reliably signalled unpleasant consequences for continuing the topic of conversation. In a different example, parents may differentially reinforce eating on time. Food is made available during the established meal periods and then removed. The child who arrives late for dinner is not fed. Differential reinforcement makes "time of day" a discriminative stimulus for eating [15].

Behavioral psychologists suggest that most human behavior is regulated by discriminative stimuli. These events "tell" the person when, where, and how to behave. Discriminative stimuli regulate behavior because they indicate the consequences (i.e. reinforcement or punishment) of behaving in a certain way. At dinner time, the anorexic child may refuse to eat more often when parents are present than when nursing staff are watching. This suggests that the "presence of parents" is a discriminative stimulus that sets the occasion for refusing to eat (the operant). Parents may reinforce this behavior while nursing staff effectively ignore it.

In their book on abnormal behavior, Drs. Ullmann and Krasner have pointed to the importance of operant conditioning for an analysis of anorexia nervosa. They state that "perhaps the most useful way of conceptualizing anorexia is to view non-eating behavior as an operant maintained by environmental consequences (operant conditioning). The behavior of refusing to eat, irrespective of how it developed, is maintained by the reactions of individuals to it" [16, p. 295].

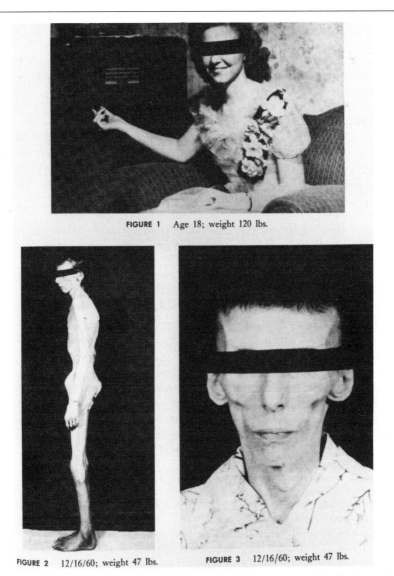

FIGURE 1 Age 18; weight 120 lbs.

FIGURE 2 12/16/60; weight 47 lbs.

FIGURE 3 12/16/60; weight 47 lbs.

Figure 2.3 Photographs of the anorexic patient treated by Dr. Bachrach and his associates at the University of Virginia Hospital. The photographs show the patient before she became anorexic and two days after she was admitted to the hospital. Behavior modification increased her weight to approximately 85 pounds. Photographs are reprinted with permission from Bachrach, A. J., Erwin, W. J. & Mohr, J. P. [1965]. The control of eating behavior in an anorexic by operant conditioning techniques. In L. P. Ullmann & L. Krasner (Eds.), *Case studies in behavior modification*. (pp. 153-163) New York: Holt, Rinehart, and Winston.

As we have noted, important reinforcements of anorexic behavior are provided by friends, family and peers. Refusing to eat, and other associated behavior, can sometimes be traced to how others have reacted to dieting. The compassionate or negative attention of concerned family members and friends may actually work to maintain or increase the problem behavior. The extreme dieting of the anorectic is very difficult to ignore and so people inadvertently pay serious attention to it.

A useful procedure is to remove the person from those who reinforce problem behavior and re-establish appropriate eating. Interestingly, in 1868 Gull recommended that "if anorexia nervosa has been present for more than a year, or if the patient is emaciated, it is nearly always necessary to separate her from her family and bring her into hospital" [17, p. 103]. Although this recommendation was not based on an understanding of reinforcement, it may work in accord with operant-conditioning principles.

Behavior modification procedures attempt to restructure the person's environment. This restructuring involves the arrangement of occasions and consequences for eating and associated behavior. Dr. Arthur Bachrach and his colleagues reported one of the first applications of behavior modification for treatment of anorexia nervosa [18]. The patient was a seemingly hopeless case when the researchers were asked to intervene. At the start of the modification program, the woman weighed 47 pounds and was very close to death.

The first thing done was to observe and analyze the patient's immediate environment. She was in an attractive hospital room with pictures on the wall, flowers, and a view of the grounds through her window. She had access to visitors, a radio, books, records, television, and magazines. People would visit her, read to her, and put on the TV for her. It was obvious that she enjoyed these activities and enjoyed her visitors. The experimenters considered that these stimuli could be positively reinforcing. She was removed from her pleasant hospital room and transferred to a private room in the psychiatric ward which was furnished only with a bed, a night stand, a chair and a sink.

The investigators obtained the cooperation of the patient's family and the hospital administration, particularly the nurses. Their initial program involved the total cessation of any visits from outsiders, medical staff, or training faculty. The nurses kept contact with the patient to the barest minimum and entered her room only to change her linen and to bring her water and meals. The patient was told that each (researcher) ...would eat one meal a day with her. When the patient lifted her fork to move toward spearing a piece of food, the experimenter would talk to her about something in which she might have an interest. The required response was then successively raised to lifting the food toward her mouth, chewing, and so forth. Initially, any part of the meal that was consumed would be the basis for an additional reinforcement e.g. radio, TV set, or phonograph.... More and more of the meal had to be consumed in order to be reinforced, until she was eventually required to eat everything on the plate.... (At discharge) the experimenters enlisted the aid of the patient's family. They were instructed to avoid reinforcement of complaints, not to make an issue of eating, to reinforce weight maintenance verbally, to give her no special diet, to refrain from weighing her at home..., to discuss only pleasant topics at mealtimes, never to allow her to eat alone, to follow a rigid schedule for meals with an alarm clock at each meal ... and to encourage her to dine out with others under enjoyable conditions. [16, pp. 295-296].

This patient was near death and all other forms of treatment had failed to stop the anorexic behavior. Given the initial hopelessness of this case, it is indeed remarkable that behavioral techniques could save her life. Although behavior modification was successful in this sense, the procedures did not entirely remedy the problem.

During her stay in the hospital, the patient only regained fourteen pounds so that at discharge she weighed sixty-one pounds. After two and one-half years her weight stabilized between eighty and ninety pounds. Her normal weight was around 120 pounds so that the treatment had stabilized her weight at 70 percent of normal. There may have been biological changes due to starvation that were not solved with behavioral technology. Perhaps her body had adapted to starvation by lowering and defending a new physiological weight level or "set point" [19, 20].

Some psychiatrists have suggested that behavior modification for anorexia is no better than hospitalization. In their comments on hospitalization for anorexic patients, Drs. Dally and Gomez report that "the aim of inpatient treatment is to restore the patients' weight to normal, or to a figure reasonably near normal. This can be achieved in virtually every case; in over half by 'persuasion' alone, without the help of drugs" [17, p. 129-130]. We, however, are not convinced that mere persuasion is the correct description of hospital treatment. Dr. Halmi has outlined the implicit reinforcement and punishment practices of doctors and nursing staff on a hospital ward [21]. The unintentional arrangement of positive and negative consequences for eating and weight gain seem to explain the success of hospital treatment more than persuasion. However, the inadvertent arrangement of behavioral consequences by hospital staff is sometimes more powerful than planned intervention.

The behavioral model has provided important techniques for the treatment of anorexia nervosa. However, it has been less influential as a theory of how self-starvation develops. Behavioral researchers have focused on objective events that can be altered to improve the problem. In fact, behavior therapists contend that it is not necessary to know what produces self-starvation in order to change it. Anorexia nervosa may come about for a variety of reasons; however, once established, those conditions that maintain it can be changed.

An implicit assumption in the behavioral model is that the factors that produce the disorder are similar to the ones that change it (i.e. conditioning principles). Based on this reasoning, behavioral investigators have given little attention to the causes of anorexia (i.e. the etiology of the disorder). However, an understanding of the causes of anorexia may be critical for a definitive solution to this problem.

Although behaviorists have been more concerned with treatment than etiology, there is no fundamental reason for such an emphasis. Our animal research is based on behavior analysis and it is directed at the basic processes that result in anorexia. We argue that self-starvation in animals and humans is the result of behavioral (Chapters 7 & 8) and biological (Chapter 9) factors.

At the behavioral level, it is important to note that eating and exercise are interconnected [22]. Generally, physical activity lowers the reinforcing effectiveness of food. The result is that food-related behavior attenuates dramatically and dangerously (e.g. preparing and eating food). At the other end, food deprivation and weight loss increase the reinforcing effectiveness of physical activity (e.g. running). The net result is that behavior related to exercise, sports and fitness is strengthened. The compulsive runner may represent one instance of this motivational process. In extreme cases, the interaction of eating and exercise produces anorexia.

3   SOCIAL LABELING AND ANOREXIA NERVOSA

The behavioral model has been combined with sociological concepts of labeling and stigma to provide an alternative account of this abnormal behavior [16]. The person is not viewed as sick or suffering from a mental illness. Instead, the anorectic is a person who has learned a pattern of behavior or role that satisfies the expectations of others [23]. People who expect certain behavior will reinforce appropriate action and punish misconduct. Just as people learn the occupational roles of policeman, lawyer and physician, some people become socially conditioned to play the sick role.

An important part of role playing is meeting other people's expectations in order to receive a social label. For example, in order to be a lawyer an individual must go to university, pass courses in law, and ultimately pass the bar examination. A person who has satisfied these requirements is called a lawyer. Once the law degree is acquired, the person may practice law (i.e. the role). Each person plays a variety of formal and informal roles. The lawyer may also be a parent, friend, school-board member, and so on.

A person who has a serious disease also assumes a social role [24]. The ill person is called a patient, and medical doctors are responsible for assigning the person to this sick role. Role assignment begins when the doctor has made a diagnosis. The patient's role is to cooperate with medical personnel and try to get better. The doctor also plays a role. The medical role is to help the patient recover from illness. Help involves providing medical therapy and advice. The doctor-patient relationship is the interlocking of these two roles.

When people exhibit unusual behavior, they may be sent to a psychiatrist. In this case also, the person may be required to play the sick role even though there is no physical disease [25]. Ultimately, the patient can come to be labeled or perceived as mentally ill.

A person is labeled mentally ill for several reasons. First, the person may do something that is unpleasant or disturbing enough for someone to want to change it. When an adolescent consistently refuses to eat, parents, teachers, and the family doctor show a reasonable concern for the child's health. Second, the person does something that does not appear to make sense. For instance, the anorectic may refuse to eat when others do, prepare a meal and not eat it, say "I'm too fat" when others can clearly see she is not, and occasionally binge eat. Third, the relative power of the evaluator is important. A judgment of mental illness is most likely when the person is in a weak position. People are less likely to be described as mentally ill when they have high prestige and power — for example, Howard Hughes behaved in a bizarre and unusual manner but was never officially labeled as mentally ill. Fourth, when people do something that is socially inappropriate (i.e. violate group norms) they may be seen as abnormal or deviant. The anorectic is called sick because self-starvation breaks socially accepted standards. Finally, the label anorexia nervosa may be assigned in order to satisfy a demand for an explanation. The person is now said to "suffer from the illness" and this provides parents, relatives and others with an apparent reason for self-starvation. Family members can now tell concerned friends why their child is having a problem — "she has Anorexia Nervosa."

The same unusual behavior (i.e. delusions, hallucinations, etc.) may be labeled differently depending on the culture. In some societies, the person is "possessed" and abnormal behavior is caused by evil spirits; Western culture sees the person as sick and explains any unusual behavior in a cause-and-effect manner as the result of mental illness. Cultures also differ in terms of the people who can officially sanction and label individuals who show abnormal behavior. Cultural variation in official labeling of abnormal behavior is emphasized by Drs. Ullman and Krasner in the following passage.

> *The current concept of the etiology of abnormality in any particular society has a major impact on who the official labelers will be in that society. If the concept involves the explanation of abnormal behavior as a result of possession by evil spirits, the labelers and healers are likely to be priests. If the concept of etiology is that of a physical defect interfering with normal perception and action,the labelers and healers are likely to be physicians* [16, p. 35].

Although the official label of "mentally ill" is provided by psychiatrists and psychologists, the process of labeling begins with peers, parents or other members of the community. Those with a close relationship to the adolescent who is refusing to eat, may seek advice and counsel. In their search, they may eventually contact a professional who provides the diagnosis of anorexia nervosa.

Once the person is labeled as having anorexia nervosa, treatment can begin. One consequence of the labeling process is that, having neatly defined the abnormality, something can be done about it. For example, the person may begin drug therapy or be admitted to a hospital. Another consequence is that the person diagnosed anorexic is absolved of responsibility for action. A sick individual is suffering from a disease and is not responsible for refusing to eat. Even though these consequences are positive, there are long-term effects that are negative. A person who is given a psychiatric diagnosis is, in our society, stigmatized and may be treated with caution or avoided by others [26]. This, of course, may create a 'snowball' effect with harmful influences on the person's self-image and subsequent behavior.

We argue that many people who are diagnosed with anorexia nervosa are, in fact, exhibiting activity anorexia. When the eating problem arises from the interplay of behavior, environment, and biology, the person is not sick (in the sense of disease) and is not mentally ill. Labeling the person as neurotic encourages the patient to learn behavior that is appropriate to the diagnostic label. To illustrate, the anorexic individual refuses food; such refusal may occur when the self-imposed food restriction combines with excessive physical activity. Before diagnosis, the person may state that "I don't want to eat because I'm not hungry." Following diagnosis and treatment, the same person may report that "my anorexia resulted from an intense fear of being fat." The person is now acting in accord with the neurotic role.

In our view, there is no point in labeling people with activity anorexia as neurotic. Activity anorexia occurs before and independently of the social-labeling process. That is, under appropriate conditions any person may self-starve. The social labeling of a person as neurotic may produce negative consequences which, in the long term, will reinforce the abnormal behavior, and will also mislead professionals and can prevent effective treatment.

REFERENCES

Although many of these references may be of interest, we have indicated (with an asterisk *) those that are written for the non-specialist reader.

1. Markus, H. and Zajonc, R. B. (1985). The cognitive perspective in social psychology. In G. Lindzey and E. Aronson (Eds.), *Handbook of social psychology*, Vol. 1, 3rd edition, (pp. 137-230). New York: Random House.
2. *Mazur, J. E. (1986). *Learning and behavior.* Englewood Cliffs, NJ: Prentice Hall.
3. Garner, D. M. and Bemis, K. M. (1985). Cognitive therapy for anorexia nervosa. In D. M. Garner and P. E. Garfinkel (Eds.), *Handbook of psychotherapy for anorexia nervosa and bulimia*, (pp. 107-146). New York: The Guilford Press.
4. *Bandura, A. (1986). *Social foundations of thought and action: A social cognitive theory.* Englewood Cliffs, NJ: Prentice Hall.
5. Kiesler, C. A., Collins, B. E. and Miller, N. (1969). *Attitude change,* (pp. 155-188). New York: John Wiley.
6. Garfinkel, P. E. and Garner, D. M. (1983). The multidetermined nature of anorexia nervosa. In P. L. Darby, P. E. Garfinkle, D. M. Garner and D. V. Coscina (Eds.), *Anorexia nervosa: Recent developments in research,* (pp. 3-14). New York: Alan R. Liss, Inc.
7. Garfinkel, P. E., and Garner, D. M. (1982). *Anorexia nervosa: A multidimensional perspective.* New York: Brunner/Mazel.
8. Rakoff, V. (1983). Multiple determinants of family dynamics in anorexia nervosa. In P. L. Darby, P. E. Garfinkel, D. M. Garner, and D. V. Coscina (Eds.), *Anorexia nervosa: Recent developments in research.* New York: Alan R. Liss, Inc.
9. Bandura, A. (1977). Self-efficacy: Toward a unifying theory of behavioral change. *Psychological Review*, 84, 191-215.
10. *Bruch, H. (1978). *The golden cage: The enigma of anorexia nervosa.* Cambridge, Mass: Harvard University Press.
11. Garner, D. M., Garfinkel, P. E. and Olmsted, M. P. (1983). An overview of sociocultural factors in the development of anorexia nervosa. In P. L. Darby, P. E. Garfinkel, D. M. Garner, and D. V. Coscina (Eds.), *Anorexia nervosa: Recent developments in research*, (pp.65-82) New York: Alan R. Liss, Inc.

12. *Skinner, B. F. (1953). *Science and human behavior*. New York: MacMillan.

13. *Zuriff, G. E. (1985). *Behaviorism: A conceptual reconstruction*. New York: Columbia University Press.

14. Harris, F. R., Wolf, M. M. and Baer, D. M. (1964). Effects of adult social reinforcement on child behavior. *Young Children*, 20, 8-17.

15. Schacter, S. and Gross, L. P. (1968). Manipulated time and eating behavior. *Journal of Personality and Social Psychology*, 10, 98-106.

16. *Ullmann, L. P. and Krasner, L. (1975). *A psychological approach to abnormal behavior*. Englewood Cliffs, NJ: Prentice-Hall.

17. *Dally, P., Gomez, J. and Isaacs, A. J. (1979). *Anorexia nervosa*. London, England: William Heinemann Medical Books, Ltd.

18. Bachrach, A. J., Erwin, W. J. and Mohr, J. P. (1965). The control of eating behavior in an anorexic by operant conditioning techniques. In L. P. Ullmann and L. Krasner (Eds.), *Case studies in behavior modification*, (pp. 153-163) New York: Holt, Rinehart, and Winston.

19. Keesey, R. E. (1980). A set point analysis of the regulation of body weight. In A. J. Stunkard (Ed.), *Obesity*, (pp. 144-165). Philadelphia, PA: W. B. Saunders.

20. Mrosovsky, N. and Powley, T. L. (1977). Set points for body weight and fat. *Behavioral Biology*, 20, 205-223.

21. Halmi, K. A. (1985). Behavioral management for anorexia nervosa. In D. M. Garner and P. E. Garfinkel (Eds.), *Handbook of psychotherapy for anorexia nervosa and bulimia* (pp. 147-159). New York: The Guilford Press.

22. Pierce, W. D., Epling, W. F. and Boer, D. P. (1986). Deprivation and satiation: The interrelations between food and wheel running. *Journal of the Experimental Analysis of Behavior*, 46, 199-210.

23. Sarbin, T. R. (1954). Role theory. In G. Lindzey (Ed.), *Handbook of social psychology* (pp. 223-258), Cambridge: Addison-Wesley.

24. Parsons, T. (1958). Definitions of health and illness in the light of American values and social structure. In E. G. Jaco (Ed.), *Patients, physicians and illness*, (pp. 165-187). Glencoe, Ill: The Free Press.

25. Szasz, T. S. (1960). The myth of mental illness. *American Psychologist*, 15, 113-118.

26. *Szasz, T. S.(1961). *The myth of mental illness: foundations of a theory of personal conduct*. New York: Dell Publishing Co.

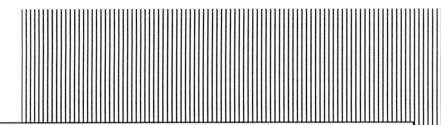

The main topics are:

- **INCIDENCE OF ANOREXIA NERVOSA**
- **RISK FACTORS AND ANOREXIA NERVOSA**
- **RECOVERY AND DEATH**

Summary

- The incidence of anorexia nervosa varies with geographical location, sex, and socioeconomic status.

- Adolescent females from the middle- and upper classes are more at risk for anorexia nervosa.

- Risk factors increase the chance of having anorexia nervosa.

- Disturbed eating attitudes and menstrual problems are note-worthy in the context of excessive exercise.

- The chances of death from anorexia nervosa range from 3 to 25 percent. The longer the follow-up after hospitalization, the higher the death rate.

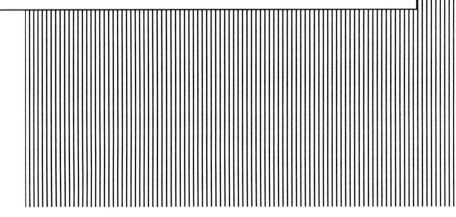

CHAPTER

Incidence, Risk and Recovery

3

The number of cases of anorexia in a population or subgroup is called the incidence. In this chapter, the incidence of anorexia nervosa is shown to vary by sex, age, social class, and other characteristics. Risk factors are prominent features which have been identified as being likely to precede the onset of diagnosed anorexia. Obesity and repeated dieting are examples of such risk factors. This chapter also details the evidence of long-term recovery from anorexia nervosa. Rates of recovery indicate the chances that an individual will recover or die from the disorder.

Anorexia nervosa is a disorder characterized by a voluntary refusal to eat, extreme loss of weight, and in some cases death. It is most common in young women but also occurs in men, children and adults. A typical anorectic is described as an adolescent girl from a middle or upper-middle class family. She is seen by many as a high achiever with good to excellent high-school grades. She is involved in many sports and extra-curricular activities.

1 INCIDENCE OF ANOREXIA NERVOSA

Geographical Location

Dr. Kalucy and his colleagues have reported that in London, England, as many as one in every hundred girls in high school may be an anorectic [1]. They have also suggested that the number of cases is increasing and that the risk of death is going up for hospitalized patients.

Several studies have documented the occurrence of anorexia nervosa in the general population. Dr. Theander, a medical researcher, identified cases of anorexia nervosa on the basis of clinical records from the departments of psychiatry, internal medicine, pediatrics, and gynecology at two Swedish university hospitals. He examined the records for women who were admitted to hospital for the first time. During the period 1931 to 1960, ninety-four women were admitted with anorexic symptoms. Given the number of people that these hospitals served, this figure suggested an incidence rate of 24 hospitalized cases of anorexia per million population [2]. The Swedish study has provided the lowest estimate of incidence. The reason for this may be that the estimate is based only on hospitalized cases of one sex.

In a more general study that included both sexes, and inpatients as well as outpatients, a greater number of anorectics were found. Three geographical areas, North-East Scotland (during 1966-1969), Monroe County in New York State (1960-1969), and Camberwell, England (1965-1971) were investigated. The researchers reported that there were 49 cases per million in Monroe County, 66 per million in Camberwell, and a high of 160 per million in North-East Scotland [3]. A more recent study of Monroe County, during the years 1960 to 1976, found that the number of women with the disorder was 116 per million, a figure more than twice the number found in the earlier study (49 per million) [4]. This finding is not unusual since other studies have reported a steadily increasing number of women with diagnosed anorexia nervosa.

The actual number of cases of the disorder are difficult to estimate. Since most studies rely on medical diagnosis to identify people with anorexia, there may be many unreported cases. Individuals with eating problems and low body weight do not always seek, or find, medical help. Some people cannot afford the cost of treatment; others are unable to find medical help in their community. In addition, the stigma of psychiatric diagnosis may prevent people from reporting an eating problem. Finally, physicians may assign a non-psychiatric diagnosis to cases of apparent self-starvation. No matter what the real number of cases, virtually all researchers agree that the incidence of anorexia nervosa is increasing.

Sex, Age, and Socioeconomic Status

Men as well as women are diagnosed as suffering from anorexia nervosa, but there has been some hesitation by physicians to diagnose anorexia nervosa in men [5]. Doctors tend to see few cases of anorexia and thus may be less familiar with male self-starvation. The influence of Freudian psychoanalysis may in fact have contributed to sex-typing of anorexia. Only women have "fears of oral impregnation." Also, professionals have sometimes failed to recognize anorexia in males because diagnostic criteria may require absence of menstruation. Finally, refusal to eat has been treated as a secondary symptom in men arising from other psychiatric disorders (e.g. depression) [6].

In the early nineteen seventies, Dr. Beumont and his associates reviewed seven studies of male anorexia, and found that there were 250 reported cases of male anorexia between 1930 and 1969 [7]. Dr. Beumont and his colleagues indicated that most of these cases did not satisfy the diagnostic criteria of anorexia nervosa. Only 25 cases of male anorexia qualified as "probably anorexia nervosa." This represents an incidence of approximately 10 percent of the total cases.

Thirty-four additional cases of male anorexia nervosa were reported by psychologist Derek Scott, in a 1986 review [5]. Thus, between 1930 and 1986 (56 years) there were only 59 reported cases of male anorexia that met the diagnostic criteria for anorexia nervosa. Most cases of male anorexia were not classified as anorexia nervosa. Many case histories were incomplete in terms of the information needed to make a diagnosis. In other cases, researchers concluded that the men were suffering from disturbances other than anorexia nervosa.

These findings are not surprising because the diagnostic criteria are strongly biased towards women. To illustrate, when a male is diagnosed as having depression, the refusal to eat may be seen as a secondary symptom of the depression. The same depressed state in a woman who is refusing to eat is viewed as a secondary symptom of anorexia nervosa. Our analysis of the research on male anorexia indicates that only 5 to 10 percent of the total cases of anorexia nervosa are men. One interpretation of this disparity is that the classification of mental illness makes it less likely for men to receive the diagnostic label of anorexia nervosa.

A functional definition of anorexia is used in this book. This method of classification is less biased and improves diagnosis. In this case, anorexia is defined by: a) refusal to eat, and b) greater than 25 percent loss of normal weight according to standardized weight to height tables. Classification of types of anorexia is based on the determinants of self-starvation. For example, if social conditioning produces a phobic avoidance of food then this is a sub-type of anorexia (i.e. phobic anorexia). Dr. Wolpe reports that cats will starve when eating is punished with a blast of air [8]. This suggests the possibility of phobic anorexia but further research is necessary. We argue that another type of anorexia is activity anorexia. This kind of self-starvation results from food restriction in combination with excessive exercise. The evidence for activity anorexia is well established in animals and appears to explain many cases of human self-starvation (see Part II of this book).

One important aspect of this functional diagnosis is that it allows interpretation of sex differences. When a type of anorexia occurs more frequently in one sex, this suggests a real difference rather than one imposed by the diagnostic criteria. At the present time, there has been no attempt to functionally classify anorexias. There may be several anorexias grouped under the label of anorexia nervosa, or others that are sub-clinical. If the label "anorexia nervosa" is ignored, and all cases of self-starvation are counted, the male to female ratio may still favor women. There could be different sex ratios for various kinds of anorexia but evidence is not available.

The incidence of anorexia nervosa also varies with a person's age. Young people are most likely to develop the disorder, usually in the early to late teens. However, anorexia is also reported in children and older adults [9]. Sometimes the eating problem begins in the adolescent years and continues into adulthood. Most mental illness theories (see Chapter 1) link anorexia with personality problems expressed during puberty. This has led practitioners to almost uniformly label teenagers with eating problems as anorexic. Such a tendency may distort the prevalence in adolescence. This distortion alone does not, however, fully account for the overwhelming incidence in this age group.

In 1980, Dr. Crisp and his colleagues reported on 102 women who were diagnosed with anorexia nervosa [10]. They found that most of the women ranged from 14 to 27 years old, the average age being 21 years. The age range was inflated since it was not based on onset of anorexia nervosa, but rather based on when Dr. Crisp first treated the patient. In another report, Crisp indicated that age of onset was considerably younger than 21 and anorexia nervosa usually began during puberty [9]. Dr. Beumont reported the same age of onset in men [7]. Twenty-three of 25 diagnosed male anorectics in Beumont's study were younger than 20 years; one man was 38 years old and age was not reported for another. The prevalence of anorexia in young people is interesting in terms of our model of activity anorexia (see Chapter 7). Younger men and women tend to be more physically active than older persons and this may contribute to the higher incidence of anorexia in this group.

Socioeconomic status is also related to anorexia nervosa. Several studies have suggested that middle- and upper-income groups have a greater number of diagnosed cases of the disorder. The 1970 to 1976 study of Monroe County in New York State did not find any cases of anorexia nervosa in the lower-income groups. However, middle, upper-middle, and upper-income groups all showed some rate of occurrence.

Interestingly, the higher the socioeconomic status of women, the greater the number of cases of anorexia nervosa. The highest status group had 320 cases per million. Even though there is reason to believe that anorexia varies with social class, some of the incidence may reflect ability to afford medical treatment. Importantly, those people who obtain medical attention are the ones that appear in studies of rates of occurrence.

The highest incidence of anorexia nervosa occurs in adolescent females from the middle- and upper-income groups [11]. We suggest that the higher incidence is related to socioeconomic and biological factors. First, women from middle- and upper-income groups are more likely to adopt the socially accepted values of thinness and fitness. Advertisers and the mass media have communicated these values and focused their sales campaigns on these women. Second, young women with money join more sports and recreational facilities than women of other social classes. Because of their youth, these women are very active and low in body weight. This increases the chances for combining dieting and exercise. Third, parents with money are more likely to have private health plans and they can afford the cost of psychiatric counseling and treatment for their children. Those who are seen by professionals are, of course, the only ones counted in reports of incidence.

Studies of the incidence of anorexia nervosa provide useful information about groups who are most susceptible to the disorder. In addition to sub-group characteristics like age and sex, there are several predisposing factors that place a person at risk for anorexia nervosa. For example, the person who repeatedly diets and regains weight has a greater chance of becoming anorexic than a person who does not diet. The importance of these risk factors is detailed below.

2   RISK FACTORS AND ANOREXIA NERVOSA

Obesity, Bulimia and Dieting

Childhood obesity may often be associated with development of anorexia. Obese adolescents who are prone to anorexia tend to binge eat and vomit (i.e. bulimia). Children who are teased about being fat may try to lose weight. They may go on a diet and tell family and friends that they are trying to reduce. At first, the child may simply try to decrease food intake. Since weight loss is slow, dieting becomes more intense, meals may be missed, and hunger becomes more extreme. At this point, giving in to such hunger is embarrassing and the child may wait until others have left the room or the house before eating. When the adolescent finally succumbs to hunger, a feeding frenzy usually occurs. This binge eating results in the child feeling guilty and nauseous. Guilt arises from breaking the self-made promise not to eat. The sick feeling comes from eating large amounts of food after a period of fasting. Both guilt and nausea contribute to the final 'redemptive' act of vomiting the meal. Interestingly, a similar process occurs when men are exposed to severe starvation [12].

Many other risk factors may come about from the "binge then vomit" pattern. The most obvious and alarming is the pattern itself. Bulimia or binge eating places a person at risk for anorexia. Other risk factors are secretive eating, concern with losing control, and preoccupation with food. Embarrassment leads to secretive eating, while social training to keep promises results in the person being concerned about giving in or losing control. Preoccupation with food may be due to long periods of fasting that increase food-related behavior. Men subjected to starvation conditions also become preoccupied with food [12].

Family Characteristics

Family characteristics are also crucial predisposing factors for anorexia nervosa. Anorectics frequently come from families where a parent or sibling has a weight problem. Weight problems can be related to either obesity or thinness. Some anorectics have parents who are involved in a nutritional profession (i.e. dietitian) [1]. Families who emphasize fitness and sports also place children at some risk for anorexia. Some researchers suggest that "achievement-oriented" families have more anorexic children than families which place less emphasis on success [1, 13, 14]. Children from families with these characteristics may develop a set of attitudes and behavioral dispositions that contribute to the development of anorexia [15].

More anorectics come from weight-conscious families than from other types of families. This does not mean that all, or any, children within a weight-conscious family will be prone to anorexia. Even though one sister is anorexic, another may have normal eating attitudes. Researchers have shown that non-anorexic sisters of anorexia patients have eating attitudes that are similar to the normal population.

Figure 3.1   Photograph of a young ballet student. Ballet dancers have high eating attitude scores and these scores are associated with anorexia nervosa.

Eating Attitudes

Abnormal eating attitudes are most definitely associated with the onset and long-term outcome of anorexia. Drs. Garner and Garfinkel have developed an Eating Attitudes Test (EAT) that measures attitudes toward dieting, overeating, and control of food intake. Test items that measure attitudes toward dieting include statements like "I am aware of the calorie content of foods that I eat." Measures of overeating include statements such as "I have the impulse to vomit after meals." Attitudes about control are measured by statements like "I avoid eating when I am hungry." The person answers these and other questions on a five-point response scale that goes from "always" to "never" [15]. The higher the test score the more anorexic the eating attitudes. Most diagnosed anorectics score 30 points or more on the test. Because of this, a person who has a test score of 30 or more is considered at risk for anorexia nervosa.

Drs. Garner and Garfinkel have shown that female ballet students, and young women training as fashion models, have more anorexic eating attitudes than university or music students [16]. Thirty-eight percent of the dancers and 34% of the models had eating-attitude scores greater than thirty. Only 9% of the music and university students had anorexic eating attitudes. During the course of this study, 11 of 183 (6%) ballet students became anorexic while 2 of 56 (3.5%) modeling students were diagnosed as having anorexia nervosa. None of the university or music students became anorexic. Only three modeling students had scores greater than 50 — two of these met the criteria for anorexia nervosa. For dance students, the higher the test score exceeding 30, the more likely the student was to develop anorexia. Four out of 6 ballet students with test scores higher than 60 were anorexic. Overall, the findings suggest that abnormal eating attitudes predict the onset of self-starvation.

The Eating Attitudes Test has been given to college students in an attempt to identify subclinical cases of anorexia. Drs. Button and Whitehouse asked 446 female and 132 male students to complete the test [17]. They defined anorexic eating attitudes as a score of greater than 32 (rather than 30) in order to reduce false positive results. None of the male students scored in the anorexic range. However, 28 female students (6.3%) were in this range.

These students were subsequently interviewed about symptoms commonly associated with anorexia nervosa. A similar interview was given to a control group of 28 female students who scored lower on the test. Students with anorexic eating attitudes showed many of the symptoms of anorexia nervosa while control students did not. For example, 14% of the students with high-test scores had not menstruated for more than 6 months while none of the control students had amenorrhea. Students with high test scores reported self-induced vomiting (39%), attempts to conceal not eating (36%), and overactivity (39%). None of the control students reported vomiting or concealment of not eating, and only 4 percent said they were overactive. The study suggests that there are many unreported, subclinical cases of anorexia among college women. Abnormal eating attitudes apparently also place women at risk for a subclinical form of anorexia.

Menses, Exercise and Anorexia

Problems with the menstrual cycle are an objective indication that a woman is at some risk for anorexia. Of course, problems with menstruation can occur for reasons not associated with anorexia nervosa. Because of this, menstrual difficulties are indicative of anorexia only when accompanied by other risk factors. Problems of reduced menses may precede or follow severe weight loss. In adolescent females, delay of the menstrual cycle is correlated with subsequent onset of anorexia. The same is true for young women who have stopped menstruating or who have irregular cycles [1].

Excessive exercise is also predictive of anorexia. The woman who is very concerned with physical fitness, and who uses exercise as a way to control weight, is inclined toward anorexia [1, 18, 19]. Ballet dancers are very active young women who have an unusually high incidence of anorexia [16]. These dancers are involved in a profession that requires both fitness and thinness. Many ballerinas combine dieting with their intense training. From our point of view, the combination of dieting and intense exercise is the most significant predictor of anorexia.

Interestingly, Dr. Frisch and his colleagues have reported that for ballet dancers "who are highly active ... there was a high incidence of primary amenorrhea, secondary amenorrhea, irregular cycles and delayed menarche — an incidence correlated with excessive thinness." [20]. In a later chapter of this book (Chapter 9), we will show that the menstrual cycle, exercise and anorexia are physiologically interrelated.

3 RECOVERY AND DEATH

Psychiatric illnesses rarely result in death but the person who is diagnosed with anorexia nervosa may eventually die. Dr. Theander identified 94 women who had been hospitalized during the years 1931 to 1960 [21]. Based on an initial follow up in 1966, he reported that 9 of the patients had died of starvation and another 3 had committed suicide. Fifteen years later, he again investigated the remaining women. An additional 3 had died from anorexia and there was one more suicide. It is difficult to interpret the meaning of the four cases of suicide. Whether suicide resulted from depression associated with anorexia or came about for other reasons is not known. When suicides are omitted, approximately 13 percent of the diagnosed anorectics died from their disorder.

Death from anorexia has been reported in several studies. Dr. Bemis reviewed these studies and found that estimates of death ranged from 3 to 25 percent [22, p. 597]. Bemis indicated that "some of the discrepancy in death rates may be attributable to the differing lengths of follow-up studies, as many of the longer studies have reported unusually high death rates." The implication is that the longer an anorectic is followed after treatment, the greater the chance of relapse and death.

A recent study by George Patton indicates that a death rate of 3 percent may be more accurate. The study was a comprehensive assessment of 481 patients over 10 years.

Predictors of death were the patients' lowest reported weight and repeated hospitalization. Patients whose lowest body weight was less than 35 kg (77 pounds) had a very high risk of death. After six years, nearly 50 percent of the patients had fully recovered from their eating disorder [23].

There is tentative evidence that relapse and death may be more frequent for male anorectics. In his review of male anorexia, Derek Scott reports that "of those 49 cases where some indication of outcome is given, about 55% had a favorable outcome and about 45% had an unfavorable outcome (including death in certain cases)" [5, p. 803]. Several researchers have suggested that the prognosis (or long-term outcome) for men with anorexia is poor [13, 24]. Since there are few reported cases of male anorexia, death rates are more difficult to obtain and assess. However, Drs. Hasan and Tibbett found that 1 of 10 anorexic males eventually died from the disorder [25]. This figure is close to the death rate for females as reported by Theander (see above).

In terms of recovery from self-starvation, Drs. Bliss and Branch have found that roughly two-thirds recovered or improved [26]. The other one-third continued to show anorexia and some of these eventually died. Dr. Dally and his associates followed 140 anorectics after they had been hospitalized for severe weight loss [13, p. 133]. The researchers found that approximately two-thirds of the patients had attained stable and adequate body weights, ten years after treatment. Patients who became anorexic before age 19 had a slightly better recovery rate than older patients.

Most researchers have reported less than 66 percent recovery. In several studies, less than 50 percent of the anorexic patients had achieved a satisfactory recovery [14, 27, 28, 29]. The researchers emphasize the long-lasting psychological and physical problems of the patients. Approximately 25 to 50 percent of the anorectics regain their symptoms following treatment [30]. The reappearance of symptoms is often accompanied by readmission to the hospital. Some patients may spend most of their lives recovering from, and becoming, anorexic.

REFERENCES

Although many of these references may be of interest, we have indicated (with an asterisk*) those that are written for the non-specialist reader.

1. Kalucy, R C., Crisp, A. H., Lacy, J. H. and Harding, B. (1977). Prevalence and prognosis in anorexia nervosa. *Australian and New Zealand Journal of Psychiatry,* 11, 251-257.
2. Theander, S. (1970). Anorexia nervosa: A psychiatric investigation of 94 female patients. *Actica Psychiatrica Scandinavica Supplement, 214.*
3. Kendell, R. E., Hall, D., Hailey, A. and Babigian, H. M. (1973). The epidemiology of anorexia nervosa. *Psychological Medicine, 3,* 200-203.
4. Jones, D. L., Fox, M. M., Babigian, H. M. and Hutton, H. E. (1980). Epidemiology of anorexia nervosa in Monroe County, New York: 1960-1976. *Psychosomatic*

Medicine, 42 , 551-558.

5.   Scott, D. W. (1986). Anorexia nervosa in the male: A review of clinical, epidemiological and biological findings. *International Journal of Eating Disorders,* 5, 799-819.

6.   Selveni, P. (1965). Interpretation of mental anorexia. In J. E. Meyer and H. Feldman (Eds.), *Anorexia Nervosa: Symposium am 24/25 April 1965 in Göttingen.* Stuttgart: Theime.

7.   Beumont, P. J. V., Beardwood, C. J., and Russell, G. F. M. (1972). The occurrence of the syndrome of anorexia nervosa in male subjects. *Psychological Medicine,* 2, 216-231.

8.   Masserman, J. M. (1943). *Behavior and neurosis.* Chicago: University of Chicago Press.

9.   Crisp, A. H. (1983). Some aspects of the psychopathology of anorexia nervosa. In P. L. Darby, P. E. Garfinkel, D. M. Garner and D. V. Coscina (Eds.), *Anorexia nervosa: Recent developments in research,* (pp. 15-28). New York: Alan R. Liss, Inc.

10. Crisp, A. H., Hsu, L. K. G., Harding, B. and Hartshorn, J. (1980). Clinical features of anorexia nervosa: a study of a consecutive series of 102 female patients. *Journal of Psychosomatic Research ,* 24, 179-191.

11. Joseph, A., Wood, I. K. and Goldberg, S. C. (1982). Determining populations at risk for developing anorexia nervosa based on selection of college major. *Psychiatric Research,* 7, 53-58.

12. Keys, A., Brozek, J., Henschel, A., Mickelson, O. and Taylor, H. L. (1950). *The biology of human starvation.* Minneapolis, Minnesota: University of Minnesota Press..

13. *Dally, P., Gomez, J. and Isaacs, A. J. (1969). *Anorexia nervosa.* London, England: William Heinemann Medical Books Ltd.

14. *Bruch, H. (1973). *Eating disorders: obesity, anorexia nervosa and the person within.* New York: Basic Books.

15. Garner, D. M. and Garfinkel, P. E. (1979). The eating attitudes test: an index of the symptoms of anorexia nervosa. *Psychological Medicine,* 9, 1-7.

16. Garner, D. M. and Garfinkel, P. E. (1980). Socio-cultural factors in the development of anorexia nervosa. *Psychological Medicine,* 10, 647-656.

17. Button, E. J. and Whitehouse, A. (1981). Subclinical anorexia nervosa. *Psychological Medicine,* 11, 509-516.

18. Crisp, A. H. (1967). The possible significance of some behavioral correlates of weight and carbohydrate intake. *Journal of Psychosomatic Research,* 11, 117-131.

19. Huenneman, R., Shapiro, L. R. and Hampton, M. C. (1966). A longitudinal study of gross body composition and body conformation and their association with food and activity in a teenage population. *American Journal of Clinical Nutrition,* 18, 325-334.

20. Frisch, R. E., Wyshank, G. and Vincent, L. (1980). Delayed menarche and amenorrhea in ballet dancers. *New England Journal of Medicine,* 303, 17-19.

21. Theander, S. (1983) Long-term prognosis of anorexia nervosa: A preliminary report. In P. L. Darby, P. E. Garfinkel, D. M. Garner and D. V. Coscina (Eds.), *Anorexia nervosa: recent developments in research,* (pp. 441-442). New York: Alan R. Liss, Inc.

22. Bemis, K. M. (1978). Current approaches to the etiology and treatment of anorexia nervosa. *Psychological Bulletin,* 85, 593-617.

23. Patton, G. (1989). The course of anorexia nervosa. *British Medical Journal*, 299, 139-140.

24. Crisp, A. H. and Toms, D. A.(1972). Primary anorexia nervosa or weight phobia in the male: report on 13 cases. *British Medical Journal.* 264, 334-338.

25. Hasan, M. K. and Tibbetts, R. W. (1977). Primary anorexia nervosa (weight phobia) in males. *Post Graduate Medical Journal*, 53, 146-151.

26. Bliss, E. L. and Branch, C. H. H. (1960). *Anorexia nervosa: Its history, psychology, and biology.* New York: Paul Hoeber.

27. Kay, W. D. K. (1953). Anorexia nervosa: A study in prognosis. *Proceedings of the Royal Society of Medicine,* 46, 669-674.

28. Kay, W. D. K. and Schapira, K.(1965). The prognosis in anorexia nervosa. In J. E. Meyer and H. Feldman (Eds.), *Anorexia nervosa: Symposium am 24/25 April 1965 in Göttingen.* Stuttgart: Thieme.

29. Rowland, C. V. (1970). Anorexia nervosa: A survey of the literature and review of thirty cases. *International Psychiatry Clinics,* 7, 37-137.

30. Moldofsky, H. and Garfinkel, P. E. (1974). Problems of treatment of anorexia nervosa. *Canadian Psychiatric Association Journal*, 19, 169-175.

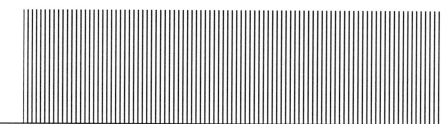

The main topics are:

- ● PSYCHOLOGICAL SYMPTOMS
- ● BEHAVIORAL SYMPTOMS
- ● PHYSIOLOGICAL SYMPTOMS

Summary

- Perception of body size has been central to anorexia nervosa. Current evidence suggests that most people "distort" their body size.

- Bulimia occurs in some cases of anorexia nervosa. Starvation and social learning seem to account for this symptom.

- Anorexia has been treated as a weight phobia. Evidence and logic argue against this view.

- Men who were forced to starve experienced most of the psychological symptoms of anorexia nervosa.

- Excessive exercise is the most important observed "symptom." Pronounced physical activity may account for many cases of human anorexia and form menstrual problems in anorexic women and athletes.

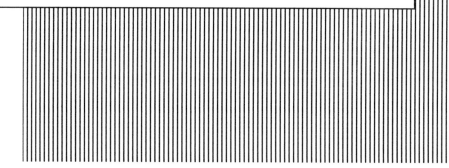

CHAPTER

Psychological and Physical Symptoms

4

The symptoms of anorexia nervosa are numerous, varied, and often contradictory. For example, the pursuit of thinness is said to be a result of "the desire to be sexually attractive" on the one hand, and "a denial of sexuality" on the other. Not only can some of the symptoms be contradictory but the occurrence of any particular symptom is uncertain. Thus, a "hostile-dependent attitude towards the mother" may be suggested for one patient but be absent in another. Variation in symptoms may be due to a diversity of views among therapists and researchers as well as to differences among patients. To illustrate, a psychoanalytical or Freudian therapist may see problems of ego, expressed as repression and denial of sexuality. In contrast, the cognitive-family therapist may report on the anorectic's belief that she can control others through extreme dieting.

There are many psychological symptoms that have been suggested over the years, and most of these are difficult to verify in an objective manner. For example, anorectics are said to be ineffective, distrustful of others, low in self-awareness, fearful of growing up, and driven by a desire for thinness. Other psychological symptoms are better researched — these include avoidance of food by vomiting, the fear of being fat, and unusual self-perceptions.

1 PSYCHOLOGICAL SYMPTOMS OF ANOREXIA NERVOSA

Distortion of Body Image

A commonly reported feature of anorexia nervosa is that the patients overestimate body size. That is, an extremely thin individual will tell friends, parents, and therapists that she is quite fat and needs to lose additional weight. According to some clinicians, this disturbance in perception of body-image is connected with a prolonged course of illness and a subsequently lower chance of recovery. Dr. Bruch has suggested that this symptom may precede the onset of anorexia and that it is always present in cases of primary anorexia nervosa [1]. However, it is also possible that body-image distortion is due to the same factors that produce anorexia. In this case, the disturbance would occur at the same time as excessive dieting or develop as weight loss became severe. Unfortunately, the research studies available to date are unable to accurately document the time of onset for this symptom.

Although therapists agree that anorectics have a distorted view of their bodies, the measurement of such an unusual perceptual disturbance is difficult. Based on the mental illness model (see Chapter 1), personality tests have been used to assess disturbed perception of body size. These tests involve free association to words as when the therapist says "fat" and the anorectic answers with the first word that comes to mind. Other tests require persons to describe what they see in ink blots (Rorschach test) or to provide sentence completions. In the latter method, the patient is asked to finish an incomplete statement (i.e. Often I feel that...) or to draw a self-portrait. The difficulty with these projective methods of assessment is that the interpretation of the results is frequently biased.

In the book *Modern Clinical Psychiatry*, Drs. Noyes and Kolb state that "the Rorschach is the projective test most likely to reveal nuclear conflicts, basic anxieties, and the level of emotional maturation. The validity and meaningfulness of projective test results are dependent on the skill, experience, and the personality of the psychologist" [2, p. 495]. The first part of this quotation indicates that the professional who employs these tests upholds the mental illness model. Nuclear conflicts and basic anxieties are only relevant to this perspective. Additionally, interpretations of the same test results frequently conflict. Different professionals interpret test responses from their own point of view and often arrive at different conclusions. For these reasons, projective tests may reveal more about the therapist's point of view than about the patient's personality.

There are more direct measures of body-image perception. One technique is to have people identify the body shape most like their own from a series of forms. Another involves asking individuals to draw a picture of themselves for which measures are taken, and compared with different parts of the body. A difficulty with this test is that the picture may reflect artistic ability rather than body image. In another procedure, patients stand in front of a large piece of blank paper with a pen in each hand. They are asked to indicate the edges of their hips, shoulders, abdomen and other parts of the body. Although these methods are more direct, they can be questioned with regard to validity and reliability. Validity refers to whether the test measures what it is intended to measure. That is, does placing marks on a sheet of paper truly reflect the individual's perception of body size? Reliability pertains to the accuracy of the measure. In other words, if an individual repeatedly placed two marks on a page for hip size, would the distance between the marks always be the same?

Perhaps the most objective measure of body image is based on presenting anorectics with distorted pictures of themselves. The patient is asked to pose for a revealing photograph that is then projected through a distorting lens designed to make the person appear fatter or thinner. The distortion is similar to the effect of mirrors used in carnival fun houses.

In a study by Dr. David Garner and his colleagues, this technique was used to compare female anorectics with thin, normal, and obese women. These people were presented with fat or thin images of themselves and asked to adjust the photograph until it looked like them. The majority of normal and thin people saw themselves as thinner than they actually were. About half of the anorectic and obese individuals also saw themselves as thinner than they really were. The other half of the people in these groups tended to see themselves as fatter. Body image overestimation only occurred in the anorectic and obese groups [3]. Because few women, in any group, correctly estimated actual body size, it seems inappropriate to call the anorectic's overestimation a distortion. In other words, the results of this study indicate that most people misperceive their body size.

With regard to the overestimation findings for anorectics we suggest a straightforward explanation. First, all judgments of body size are learned. Apparently, the value of thinness in our culture results in many women learning to describe themselves as thinner than they actually are. The same could be said for age since people commonly distort their true age. However, some women must verbally defend their thin appearance. This may occur when others tell them to stop dieting, or that they look too skinny. At least in the initial dieting phase, telling others that "I am still a bit fat" may provide a satisfactory answer to questions like, "don't you think you're getting a bit too thin?" Reduction in the frequency of questioning may socially reinforce reports of being too fat (see Chapter 2, *The Behavioral Model*).

Bulimia

One paradoxical symptom of anorexia nervosa is bulimia or ravenous overeating. Such overeating occurs in irregular bouts that are often called "binge eating." Bulimia has been reported for obese and normal weight individuals. Episodes of binge eating are frequently associated with anorexia and have been included as a clinical feature in Feighner's criteria of anorexia nervosa [4]. Also, some researchers have considered bulimia a variant of anorexia nervosa and have called it bulimia nervosa [5, 6]. Excessive eating is often followed by feelings of guilt and the bulimic may use a variety of techniques to eliminate the food. For example, a bulimic might secretly enter the bathroom to induce vomiting. Drs. Beumont and Abraham have described their patients who use vomiting to eliminate the food they have eaten.

> ...those (bulimics) who regularly induced vomiting stated that it either concluded a bulimic episode or occurred intermittently during its course. With each episode of vomiting, patients regurgitated between one and ten times until they felt that all food had been brought up. Eight patients used 'markers', commencing their overeating with substances such as red apple skin which they could recognize in the vomitus. A number also used a 'wash-out' technique, swallowing large amounts of water and regurgitating it until there was no residue of food. Vomitus was often hidden in disposable containers or plastic bags to avoid detection, and the absolute quantity of vomitus was described in terms such as 'saucepansfull' or even 'bucketsfull'. [7, p. 154].

Other bulimics may resort to the use of laxatives to rid their bodies of the unwanted meal. There are clinical studies that indicate bulimics may take from three to twenty times the recommended dose of laxatives immediately following the eating episode. Patients commonly report great pleasure in discovering the use of laxatives and how to induce vomiting since they now can control weight while eating as much as they want.

On the other hand, some bulimics resort to desperate tactics in an attempt to control binge eating and vomiting. In Beumont and Abraham's study of bulimia, they report that:

...all patients had attempted to resist the urge to bulimia. Resistance behaviors varied from simply avoiding situations seen as precipitating (e.g. going to parties) to freezing food at home or throwing it all out so as to avoid temptation. At the extreme end, some patients described locking themselves in the bathroom, cutting their finger tips so that they could not use them to induce vomiting ... and driving into the country where no food was available. One patient had even attempted to wire her jaws together, using a topical analgesic gel [7 p. 155].

Thus, the bulimic is torn between bouts of ravenous overeating and desperate attempts to resist it.

As with anorexia nervosa, bulimia is often viewed as an expression of the underlying personality or a result of disturbed eating attitudes. As a result, treatment focuses on changing the personality or relevant attitude(s). Because less attention is given to the behavior of gorging and vomiting than to psychic or cognitive factors, we refer to such treatment as indirect therapy. An alternative view stresses behavior change and the overeating and vomiting are seen as learned responses. In this case, treatment is focused on eliminating the behavior by conditioning techniques. Because treatment is specific to the problem behavior, we refer to this as direct therapy. Often professionals with an indirect orientation claim that direct therapy "treats the symptom and not the problem." On the other hand, professionals who use direct methods suggest that their treatment is most effective and quickly changes the problem behavior. These issues remain controversial within the professional community and are not resolved here. Some bulimics may respond best to indirect treatment and others may profit from direct therapy. A direct therapeutic intervention by one of the authors is described in the following passage.

Helen was an attractive 27-year-old mother of two children. She contacted Dr. Epling and requested a direct behavior modification treatment program to help control her vomiting. While she was slim, at 115 pounds and 5'8", she was not excessively underweight. She had occasionally forced vomiting since her late teens and had done this in order to, 'get rid of a large meal that could make me fat'. During the past three years she had been vomiting one or more times per day. Her concern was that the vomiting had increased over the past six months. She indicated that she felt out of control and could not stop binging and vomiting. Also, she said that she had been to see several other professionals but 'I was unhappy with them since they seemed to be focusing more on my interpersonal relationships and eating patterns.' The eating bouts were often at supper, where she frequently ate more than her husband, but these bouts also occurred at other times. She described eating her meal rapidly and always ate all of the prepared food including her husband's and children's leftovers. Following eating episodes, she felt uncomfortably full, anxious and guilty. Immediately after overeating she would go to the washroom and secretly induce vomiting 'in order to relieve the full feeling and my anxiety and guilt'. Interestingly, when eating out at restaurants or at friends' houses, she did not gorge or vomit.

A direct behavior modification program successfully treated Helen's bulimia and vomiting. Helen was required to monitor the frequency of bulimic episodes. She plotted

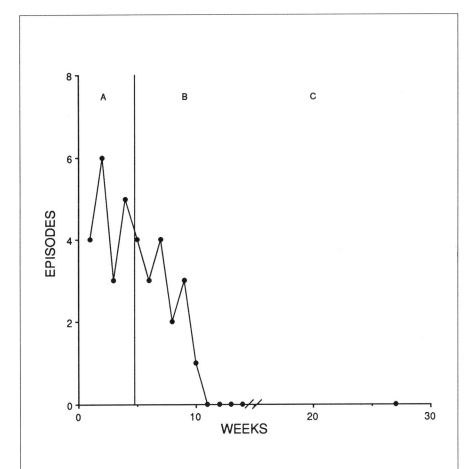

Figure 4.1   Helen's binge eating and vomiting episodes before, during and after treatment. During baseline (A), the number of episodes is approximately 5 per week. Treatment with behavior modification reduced the episodes to zero (B). After three months there were no reports of binge eating and vomiting (C).

the episodes on a graph that was taped to her refrigerator door. When she vomited, Helen was asked to snap a heavy rubber band that she wore on her wrist and immediately report the episode to her husband. He disapproved of her binge eating and vomiting and she had indicated that his opinion was important to her. Helen agreed to eat three regular meals each day and at each meal she was asked to eat slowly. Specifically, she was to chew each mouthful thoroughly and place her knife and fork on the plate between bites. Additionally, Helen was asked to leave a small amount of food on the plate and throw it away. The intervention was designed to reduce vomiting and increase appropriate eating habits.

The treatment was completed in three months and at a six-month follow-up she reported that binge eating and vomiting were no longer a problem. A major factor that contributed to the outcome, was Helen's cooperation. She was determined to stop binge eating and vomiting, and faithfully carried out the instructions.

Weight Phobia

A phobic reaction is an intense and disproportionate fear that is related to an issue, object or event. Typically, the person recognizes that the phobic situation does not present any real danger. Because of this, the fear is said to be irrational. The reaction to the feared object may include increased heart rate, faintness, nausea, tremor, and panic. Frequently, a feared event does carry some real danger and even non-phobic individuals may show some anxiety. For example, many people are afraid of snakes, spiders, dogs, dentists, medical injections, and the sight of blood. The difference between normal fear and phobic reaction is one of severity. Many people fear sharks; however, Dr. Epling recalls the case of a shark-phobic woman who would not leave her house in Birmingham, England. The reason for this strange behavior was that she was afraid she would see a picture of a shark, hear the word or see it in print. Any of these events would cause her to experience extreme panic.

In the case of anorexia nervosa, the person is often said to have a phobic reaction to weight gain. This is displayed as avoidance behavior, where the anorectic pursues a slim figure because it is a safeguard against the fearful state of obesity. In this case, the patient is not trying to attain some optimal thinness, rather the person is escaping from the "fear of fatness." Viewed as intense fear of fatness, anorexia nervosa is not a distinct psychiatric syndrome; it is a variant of phobic disorders. This point has been expanded by Dr. Crisp who states:

> *Essentially the (anorectic's) avoidance is of weight gain and of that distinct but terrifying prospect of normal adult weight from which the anorectic is separated by her regression. She construes her mature body weight as synonymous with 'fatness' simply because the pubertal process is the one that promotes the fatness she needs to avoid. In this sense she not only needs to avoid a mature body weight, but she needs to avoid any weight which will even rekindle the pubertal process.* [8].

Apparently, Crisp and others have regarded some cases of anorexia nervosa as a phobic reaction that is brought on by weight gain at puberty. Such a fear reaction is thought to be a result of a deeper "fear of sexuality" that is displaced to a more acceptable fear of fatness. In this view, normal body weight represents, or stands for, the sexually mature person. The anorectic is therefore intensely afraid of her sexuality which is a result of a repressive childhood. Dr. Bruch describes the case of Joyce in terms of weight phobia.

> *Joyce was ... quite explicit in describing her fear of becoming a teenager... She was also troubled about seeing her body change. From childhood on, she felt it was not 'nice' to look like a woman, that her tissues would bulge, that the female body was not beautiful. Her mother was in her forties when Joyce was born, and she had no memory of how her older sisters had looked as teenagers or how she had felt about them. In order to avoid the sagging flesh later on, she decided as an adolescent to avoid the curves and roundness of her own development. She wanted to have a body as good as it could possibly be, which meant to her to be thin. She brought her weight down to seventy pounds, taking inordinate pride in being so slim, with no curves, and in having achieved this herself* [10, pp. 64-65]. *

Although many experts have argued that anorexia is mainly a weight phobia, there are others that do not agree. In an article that closely examines the possibility of anorexia as weight phobia, Dr. Bemis has suggested problems with this characterization. In his paper he writes:

> *The distinction between simple avoidance of a feared stimulus (fatness) and ... a strong desire for the opposite of what is feared (thinness) may be illuminated by asking whether ... an elevator phobic engages in 'a relentless pursuit of an elevator free building.' Phobics do not pine for the opposite of what they avoid: there is no positive valence attached to the state of 'not being in an elevator.' While there may be relief to avoiding elevators, the individual who fears them is not apt to walk about all day euphoric with the thought 'How wonderful! I'm not in an elevator. Indeed, with each step I am getting further and further away from elevators'* [11].

However, unlike elevator phobics, anorectics do pursue and value thinness. Phobic individuals recognize and want to get rid of their fears. In contrast, anorectics do not recognize their fear of fatness and often resent the help they are offered.

It is difficult to see anorexia nervosa as a phobic reaction to fatness or weight gain. Also, it stretches common-sense credibility to argue that the real fear is of sexuality. How does fear of sexuality result in a fear of fatness rather than a fear of one's genitals? Additionally, why is this fear displaced to a phobic reaction to weight rather than to some other phobia? For example, if anorectics want to hide sexuality they could become introverted, develop poor grooming, cut off their hair, dress unattractively, eat to obesity and avoid members of the opposite sex. Although it is possible that some anorectics are weight phobic, it is unlikely that this explanation applies to most cases of self-starvation.

---

* Reprinted by permission of the publishers from *The Golden Cage: The Enigma of Anorexia Nervosa* by Hilde Bruch, Cambridge, Mass.: Harvard University Press, Copyright © 1978 by the President and Fellows of Harvard College.

Psychoanalytical experts are prone to see sexual conflicts and thus teach their patients to talk about sexuality and fear of fatness. There are reports that suggest that anorectics learn to interpret their excessive dieting as weight phobia. The terror of becoming fat is usually concealed or not admitted until therapy has gone on for some time [12, 13]. Rather than patients discovering their phobia, it is possible that some therapists reinforce verbal statements concerning fear of fatness. Another problem with the argument for weight phobia involves faulty logic. Fear of fatness is confirmed by observing the excessive loss of weight. Some people never watch television for a variety of reasons. It would be incorrect to conclude that the failure to watch television was due to "a fear of television shows." Although it is possible that a fear of television shows or fatness could lead to an avoidance of television or food, other reasons are at least as plausible (i.e. "I don't like television shows because they're boring"). Generally, there is no conclusive evidence that the anorectic is suffering from a weight phobia.

Explanation of Psychological Symptoms

We suggest that some of the psychological symptoms of anorexia are produced by social learning. Anorectics may deny illness, report being overweight, be preoccupied with preparing food, state that they fear being fat, and so on. These behavior patterns result from the social expectations of other people either before or during treatment. For example, socialization to the female role requires learning about the preparation of meals and the denial of food for oneself. This point is made by Susie Orbach in her book *Hunger Strike.*

> *...A woman comes to know that the food she prepares for others as an act of love and an expression of her caring, is somehow dangerous to the woman herself. Everyday women read in any newspaper or magazine of how they must restrain their desire for this very same food. Throughout history women have occupied this dual role of feeding others while needing to deny themselves. ... Women must hold back their desires for the cakes they bake for others and satisfy themselves with a brine-canned tuna salad with dietetic trimmings. Diet, deprive, deny is the message women receive, or — even more sinister — they must pretend that cottage cheese and melon is as pleasurable as a grilled cheese sandwich for lunch [14, p. 60].*

We would also add that the preoccupation with food could come about from starvation. When people are forced to starve (i.e. those in concentration camps of World War II), they are also obsessed with food. These people do not have food to prepare but they talk about their favorite meals, discuss recipes, and dream of food. Starvation and social conditioning could account for many of the other so-called symptoms of anorexia nervosa.

The strongest evidence that psychological symptoms result from starvation comes from a study by Dr. Ancel Keys and his colleagues at the University of Minnesota [9]. In this study, 36 young, healthy, and psychologically normal males volunteered to undergo starvation. The men were conscientious objectors to war and participated in the study as an alternative to military service. The men ate normally for the first 3 months of the study and various measures of personality, eating and behavior were gathered. Over the next 6 months, the food ration was cut in half and the men were reduced to approximately 75 percent of their original weight. Finally, the men were re-fed over the last 3 months of the experiment.

Starvation resulted in dramatic changes in behavior, personality and physical well-being. The behavioral and personality changes were, in many instances, consistent with psychological symptoms of anorexia nervosa. The men became preoccupied with food. Their conversation was dominated by food-related issues; their reading material was focused on cooking; some even began collecting cooking utensils. Eating habits began to change. The men spent the day planning how to eat the small daily food ration. On some occasions, the men would cut their food into tiny bites so that each morsel could be appreciated.

Some of the men became bulimic. They would lose control, gorge themselves, and then feel guilty about breaking the diet. In some instances, these bulimic episodes were followed by self-induced vomiting. There were other unusual changes in their emotional well-being. For example, some men reported long periods of depression, irritability, anxiety, and outbursts of anger. All of these effects have been reported as symptoms of anorexia nervosa.

The men were given a standardized personality test called the Minnesota Multiphasic Personality Inventory (MMPI). Test scores significantly changed with starvation. At normal weight the men scored in the normal range on the various personality dimensions. During starvation, many of the men had serious changes in personality. According to test scores, the men became neurotic and two volunteers showed signs of severe psychosis. The emotional and personality changes did not immediately recover when the men were returned to normal-eating conditions.

The emotional, behavioral and psychological changes of the men who were forced to starve are remarkably similar to the symptoms of anorexia nervosa. The most important feature of the starvation experiments is the time ordering of starvation and symptoms. Many professionals have suggested that the personality and emotional disposition of the anorectic causes the self-starvation. The Keys study makes it clear that the personality changes are the result of starvation rather than the cause. If anorexia is not the outcome of personality and emotional factors, then a scientific understanding must provide the determinants of self-starvation. We suggest that the combination of excessive exercise and dieting is a major determinant of human self-starvation.

2   BEHAVIORAL SYMPTOMS OF ANOREXIA NERVOSA

Although the psychological symptoms of anorexia nervosa are emphasized by professionals, there is also concern with the overt features of self-starvation. Anorectics engage in a variety of behavior that is related to weight loss, including unusual or peculiar methods of handling food, excessive physical activity, and disturbed sleeping patterns. Also, there are physiological consequences of starvation that include disruption of menstrual cycle, changes in sex hormones, growth of body hair and changes in skin color.

Eating, Hunger and Body Weight

Most authors agree that anorexia nervosa begins when the individual alters the pattern of food intake. Many anorectics are somewhat overweight prior to dieting. However, others are within a normal weight range. A majority of diagnosed anorectics report that they started dieting in order to lose weight. A few anorectics indicate that they don't eat much because they have no sense of hunger. Dr. Peter Dally and his colleagues believe that these few individuals are atypical in terms of the symptoms of anorexia nervosa [15, p. 12].

Usually, the anorectic begins by attempting to avoid fattening foods. These early attempts are often unsuccessful and may lead to more serious and abnormal dieting. The person may adopt and strictly follow a recognized diet plan. Although systematic evidence is not available, it may be that the type and severity of the chosen diet are important in the development of the disorder. Adherence to a diet plan may be furthered by having friends agree to follow the same plan. This is because the group can monitor and reinforce each other for sticking to the diet. Most people in such a group stop after reaching a weight target — but the anorectic does not.

The course of weight loss has been described by Dr. Crisp for two women who were treated for anorexia nervosa at 20 years of age [16]. Both women had a history of stable body weight that was within a normal range. Miss L. weighed about 130 pounds and Miss K. was 105 pounds. In each case, a period of overeating preceded dieting and weight loss. Miss L. moved away from home for the first time and started to gain weight four months later. After nine months away from home she weighed 15 pounds more than her previous weight. Miss K. suddenly gained 7 pounds during a holiday in Europe. This was the first time away from her parents and she met a waiter she was strongly attracted to who encouraged her to eat more than usual.

Both women began a strenuous dieting regimen at the peak of weight gain. Within seven and three months, respectively, they dropped below their previously stable weight. Even though they were back to their usual body weight neither would stop dieting. Miss L. lost about 50 pounds in fourteen months, and treatment was started when she weighed 98 pounds. The total weight loss of Miss K. was more serious since she was a smaller woman. Over a similar fourteen months of dieting she lost about 40 pounds and started treatment when she reached 70 pounds. Both patients were hospitalized and responded favorably to treatment, recovering most of their former weight after three months.

According to Dr. Crisp's findings, these anorexic women continued to have a desire for food while fasting. This observation is supported by Dr. Peter Dally and his coworkers who report that:

> *...hunger is not lost at first and the girl often has to battle hard against her pangs. Occasionally she lapses, but such is the sense of guilt and self- disgust afterwards that this gives her additional determination and willpower to succeed. However, as time passes and her food supply is increasingly reduced, hunger diminishes and may disappear altogether; this process can take up to a year or so* [15, p. 13].

In the two cases reported by Crisp, loss of appetite occurred between four and eight months after the start of dieting.

Interestingly, even though anorectics may not report hunger, they may at the same time become intensely preoccupied with food. The person may spend a lot of time shopping for groceries, making up food lists, reading cook books, preparing meals for others, and so on. Meals are often eaten very slowly with the person savoring each bite. In order to stretch meal time, food is cut into small bits and chewed slowly. Also, anorectics may insist on making their own dinners since the food must be prepared and displayed "just right." They often prefer to eat meals alone and are called secretive by others. This seemingly obsessive concern with food is described by Dr. Hilde Bruch:

> *Dora's parents had been reluctant to admit that their brilliant, admired daughter might be sick and in need of treatment. They finally came for help because her behavior interfered with the functioning of the family. She would get up early in the morning and prepare a huge breakfast and would not permit the younger children to leave for school until the very last morsel had been consumed. In another family the fifteen-year-old girl would begin baking cakes and cookies after she came home from school and would not permit her parents to go to bed until they had eaten every bite. What finally brought action was the mother's concern with her own weight, that she was getting fat under the pressure from her daughter* [10, p. 8]. *

As we stated earlier, preoccupation with food during starvation has been reported for experimental subjects who undergo forced starvation [9]. Some of the subjects and anorectics treated eating with great secrecy, prolonged their meal periods, and read or talked about food incessantly. The experimental subjects' diets are imposed on them and the reasons for food restriction are clear. The causes of starvation for anorectics are less conspicuous and their behavior seems incomprehensible. However, biological and social conditions also have a strong influence on the way people think, behave and view themselves and others. Because these determinants are not easily observed, the anorectic (but not the experimental subject) is said to willfully engage in self-starvation.

Activity, Sleep and Nutrition

Many professionals have reported excessive physical activity in anorectic patients. This hyperactivity is considered to be a side effect of the disorder. For example, Feighner lists periods of overactivity as one of six secondary symptoms [4]. Although it is recognized that extreme levels of activity are common in anorectics, the presence of this symptom is not required for diagnosis.

---

*   Reprinted by permission of the publishers from *The Golden Cage: The Enigma of Anorexia Nervosa* by Hilde Bruch, Cambridge, Mass.: Harvard University Press, Copyright © 1978 by the President and Fellows of Harvard College.

Table 4.1

Order and Frequency of Symptoms of Anorexia Nervosa [45]

Characteristic order	Symptom description	Frequency of occurrence
1.	Unsustained attempts to avoid fattening foods	0.80
2.	Adoption of recognized diet plan	0.96
3.	Strict adherence to diet	0.96
4.	Amenorrhea	0.88
5.	Calorie counting	0.80
6.	Preoccupied with weight	0.96
7.	Obsessive dieting	0.92
8.	Manipulating food servings	1.00
9.	Avoid some meals	0.68
10.	Increased sport activity	1.00
11.	Preoccupied with food	0.52
12.	Eating only irregularly	0.76
13.	Exercising alone	0.72
14.	Use of appetite suppressants	0.28
15.	Obsessed with exercising	0.72
16.	Replacing eating with other activities	0.56
17.	Purgative abuse	0.48
18.	Avoiding all set meals	0.88
19.	Denial of hunger	0.80
20.	Manipulating body fluids	0.32
21.	Gorging (bulimia)	0.76
22.	Self-conscious about emaciation	0.48
23.	Self-induced vomiting	0.64
24.	Deceiving family – eg, disposal of food	0.36
25.	Eating only with unobserved	0.56
26.	Episodes of total starvation	0.64
27.	Behaviors to prevent gorging	0.32
28.	Exhaustion	0.48

Attempts to food restrict precede exercise and sports activities. In this study, all patients reported "increased sport activity". Note that most psychological symptoms follow exercising and dieting. The table is reprinted with permission from Beumont, A. L., Booth, S. F., Abraham, D. A., Griffiths, D. A,. & Turner, T. R. [1983]. Temporal sequence of symptoms in patients with anorexia nervosa: a preliminary report. In P. L. Darby, P. E. Garfinkel, D. M. Garner & D. V. Coscina (Eds.), *Anorexia nervosa: Recent developments in research* (pp.129-136). New York: Alan R. Liss, Inc.

From the conventional viewpoint, pronounced physical activity represents another way to get rid of unwanted fat. However, we argue that in fact this activity is caused by declining body weight and changed eating patterns. In our view, activity is central to an understanding of most human anorexias.

In one study, Dr. Slade required judges to rate the behavior of anorectic patients on several dimensions [17]. He found that they differed from other psychiatric patients in food handling and overactivity. A study by Crisp and his associates found indications of excessive activity in 38 percent of their patients [18]. Other studies have reported intense athleticism in up to 75 percent of diagnosed cases of anorexia nervosa [19]. Crisp reported hyperactivity in all of 13 male anorectics [12]. Crisp and Stonehill, in the context of a broader discussion of sleep patterns of anorectics, reported excessive activity in all of the 60 patients they studied. They point out that overactivity, restlessness, insomnia, and ritualistic behavior develop during the course of anorexia and recede when the individual again stabilizes eating and body weight [20].

Dr. Beumont and his colleagues used a card sort technique to document symptoms and time of onset for 25 anorexic patients. This procedure involved giving patients a deck of twenty-eight cards with a behavioral symptom of anorexia nervosa on each card. Patients were asked to indicate whether or not they had the symptom and if so in what order it appeared. Importantly, all patients indicated "increased sports activity;" additionally seventy-two percent "exercised alone" and were "obsessed with exercising." Such vigorous activity appeared after an increasingly severe reduction of food intake [21].

In a recent clinical report, Dr. Kron and his co-workers attempted to define the core pathology of hospitalized patients with anorexia nervosa. The summary of their findings suggests that excessive physical activity is critical to the onset and process of at least some anorexias:

> ...We reviewed the charts of 33 patients hospitalized with (anorexia nervosa) during the past 10 years. In 25 of the 33 charts, the presence of hyperactivity during the present illness was recorded; only one patient was specifically noted to show unremarkable physical activity... Among the 13 patients interviewed directly, ten described themselves as continuing to be highly active physically... Physical activity appeared to be more excessive, disorganized and aimless during the acute phase of anorexia nervosa... These preliminary findings suggest that hyperactivity' is an early and enduring clinical feature of anorexia nervosa and is not merely secondary to either a conscious attempt to lose weight or weight loss per se [22, p. 439].

In addition to excessive activity, severe food deprivation is associated with disturbances of sleep [20]. Anorectics usually do not complain of problems with sleep and are likely to say that they are sleeping well. However, Dr. Crisp states that many anorectics experience early morning waking and many eat or exercise at this time. Sleep disturbance increases in proportion to the severity and length of starvation. Also, those people who are very active during the day are most likely to show restlessness during sleep [23]. Dr. Bruch describes a young woman who clearly illustrates the relationships among exercise, sleep and nutrition:

...Cora took up swimming, increasing the number of laps from day to day, finally spending five to six hours at it. In addition she would play tennis for several hours, run instead of walking whenever possible, and became an expert in fencing. She also worked many hours on her school assignments to achieve the highest grades. She kept busy for twenty-one hours, reducing her sleep time to three hours. When first seen she denied it, but much later she admitted that she also felt terribly hungry all the time. But she took so much pride in enduring it that she came to enjoy the sensation [10, pp. 5-6]. *

This frenzy of exercise is characteristic of the early stages of starvation. Increased mobility and arousal have been described for other starving populations. For example, a 1839 report on the destitute and starving poor in England documents an excited or nervous state for these victims [24]. Also, during World War One, German school teachers recounted increased activity in students who were malnourished [25]. Finally, increased restlessness and insomnia, particularly during the early morning hours, has been reported for starving people in post World-War-Two Germany [26].

In contrast, when starvation is sustained and extreme, people generally appear apathetic and lethargic. The survivors of Belsen concentration camp were close to death and when liberated they were very inactive [27]. This same immobility was described by a captured German medical officer who observed the slow starvation of men in prisoner-of-war camps. As starvation progressed, activity decreased and bed rest increased from eight to sixteen hours a day [28]. It appears, therefore, that the effects of starvation on activity and sleep depend on the degree of weight loss. During the early stages of starvation, physical activity and restlessness increase and eventually become excessive. At extreme levels of starvation activity drops and sleep increases. A similar effect occurs in laboratory animals and is described in Chapter Seven.

3   PHYSIOLOGICAL SYMPTOMS OF ANOREXIA NERVOSA

Amenorrhea and Exercise

Menstruation is closely associated with changes in body weight. Many health professionals consider amenorrhea or cessation of menstrual cycle to be a major diagnostic symptom of female anorexia nervosa. Experts have suggested reasons for this symptom that range from psychological to physical causes. For the most part, these explanations depend on the time of onset of amenorrhea. Some professionals have indicated that amenorrhea precedes the development of anorexia nervosa. In this case, they argue that loss of menses is due to the psychological state (i.e. stress or anxiety) of the person. This state eventually leads to other symptoms of self-starvation. In the two cases of anorexia

---

*   Reprinted by permission of the publishers from *The Golden Cage: The Enigma of Anorexia Nervosa* by Hilde Bruch, Cambridge, Mass.: Harvard University Press, Copyright © 1978 by the President and Fellows of Harvard College.

nervosa described by Dr. Crisp (i.e. Miss L. and Miss K.) amenorrhea occurred before extreme loss of weight. In both women, dieting reduced body weight to a point just below their normal weight. At this time, both women stopped menstruating and continued dieting. For these women at least, onset of amenorrhea preceded severe loss of weight.

Physiological changes due to dieting and loss of weight affect body chemistry. An alteration of hormonal balance produces irregularities in the menstrual cycle. If loss of menses is brought on by severe weight reduction, then onset of amenorrhea will develop after the appearance of anorexia nervosa. However, the majority of research evidence suggests that problems of menses precede the onset of the disorder [29].

Another physiological reason for menstrual problems is nutritional disturbance. Females on low-calorie diets may stop menstruating because of imbalanced nutrition (e.g. changes in carbohydrate levels). From this perspective, amenorrhea may occur prior to severe weight loss. This is supported by observations that some obese women will cease menstruation when shifted to a low-calorie diet [30]. In contrast to the psychological account of early onset of amenorrhea, the nutritional perspective views this symptom as a by-product of dietary practices and not fundamental to anorexia nervosa.

Previously, we described the pronounced physical activity of many anorectics. Researchers of anorexia nervosa report excessive physical activity in patients but they do not associate it with problems of menarche. Amenorrhea and hyperactivity are viewed as separate and unrelated features of anorexia nervosa. Our thesis is that excessive activity is central to many human anorexias. Amenorrhea is a primary feature of anorexia nervosa and it also occurs in women athletes. For this reason, it is important to document the relationship between physical activity and menstrual cycle.

Drs. Dally and Gomez reported that young adolescent anorectics had delayed menarche [15, p. 17]. Interestingly, this same problem was reported by Dr. Vincent for ballet dancers who often combine dieting with intense exercise [31]. Dr. Frisch and his colleagues conducted another study of 89 female ballet dancers. They found that nearly 70 percent of the dancers had menstrual difficulties. The researchers noted that for these women "who are highly active ...there was a high incidence of primary amenorrhea, secondary amenorrhea, irregular cycles and delayed menarche, an incidence correlated with excessive thinness" [32, p. 17]. The authors suggested that problems of menarche and low weight were due to the combined effects of heavy training and dieting.

Hard training and intense exercise may be the most important factors relating to amenorrhea. Studies show that onset of menstruation occurs later for girls who engage in strenuous athletic sports [33, 34]. The longer the duration of training, the greater the delay of menarche [35]. These studies strongly implicate level of exercise with delay of menstruation.

Other evidence indicates that intense physical activity disrupts regular menstrual cycle. Long distance runners often develop irregularity and cessation of menstrual flow. The frequency of such problems increases with weekly mileage [36]. Additional studies support the conclusion that runners are more likely than non-runners to develop problems of menarche [37, 38]. Finally, problems of menarche are observed when women are forced to exercise. Female recruits to a military academy who were required to participate in a vigorous training regime showed problems of reduced, delayed and irregular menstruation [39].

Thus, it appears that intense physical activity, whether chosen or forced, affects the menstrual cycle. It is likely that the high activity of anorectics is a fundamental factor, pertinent to an understanding of the associated problems of menarche [40, 41]. From our perspective, excessive activity is central to both amenorrhea and self-starvation.

Other Physiological Symptoms

There are many physical changes that result from severe malnutrition. These symptoms are similar regardless of how starvation is produced. For example, we have noted that starvation can be imposed by famine, war, poverty or culture (i.e. self-imposed). In each instance, the symptoms such as body-hair growth, coldness and rapid heart rate emerge during starvation and recede with weight gain [9].

Malnutrition can have numerous effects on the body when it occurs prior to or during puberty. As we have previously documented, starvation may delay the onset of menstruation. Current evidence suggests that when weight recovers the menstrual cycle begins and the woman is able to have children. This is documented for a women who started menarche at 25 years of age [42]. However, young women who develop anorexia during puberty may not attain full physical development. There is tentative evidence that the adolescent anorectic may never achieve maximum height. Also, breasts do not fully develop during the period of starvation and may be diminished in size even after recovery. Whether anorectics achieve complete physical development seems to depend on how long they starve themselves.

Dr. Gerald Russell has studied the physical development of young female anorectics. He notes that two of his patients were "treated effectively after a relatively short illness, and their breasts developed fully after a substantial and sustained weight gain. In two other patients, whose malnutrition had lasted somewhat longer, breast growth after weight gain was less complete" [42, p. 340]. Dr. Russell points out that, because of this problem of recovery, it is particularly important to identify and treat anorexia nervosa when it occurs before puberty.

There are several other physical problems which may develop during anorexia nervosa. The skin is often affected by malnutrition. The texture of the skin may become rough like sandpaper, dry, and inelastic. There may be lesions that appear on the feet and hands. The face becomes pallid and "some patients with chronic anorexia nervosa disguise this with make-up, so much so that they look like painted dolls" [15, p. 66]. The skin often changes color with tones of brown and yellow reported by many professionals. Some changes in coloration can even last when the person has recovered and persist for a year or more after weight gain.

In addition to changes in color, there may be substantial growth of body hair. This "lanugo" hair may cover large parts of the body including the trunk, limbs and face. Lanugo hair may be as long as three-quarters of an inch and it has a silk-like texture. Dr. Joseph Silverman, describes this hair as looking like a fur coat [43, p. 294].

Lanugo hair was reported during the Irish potato famine and presumably appeared because of starvation. Research has shown that this physical symptom is not as common for binge eating anorectics. This could be due to the fact that bulimics are less consistently malnourished [15]. Additionally, studies have reported that hair on the head is often thin and lifeless, and sometimes falls out. Finally, pubic hair is scanty in a small percentage of cases [44].

The anorectic may report "feeling cold" and their hands and feet may be cold to the touch. There are also changes in pulse and blood pressure. Slow heart rate or bradycardia is common among anorectics. Even after a bout of exercise heart rate may remain very low. During the final stages of starvation, when death is imminent, tachycardia or rapid heart rate may be observed. Usually, blood pressure declines in proportion to loss of body weight and the anorectic may feel faint and dizzy. There are also a few reports of epileptic seizures. These seizures appear to be induced by the drugs used to treat anorexia nervosa [15, p. 68].

Although there have been significant advances in modern medicine, anorectics continue to die of starvation. Anorectics die of extreme weight loss before, during, and after treatment. The reasons for death vary from suicide to medical complications resulting from severe emaciation.

In summary, there are numerous psychological, behavioral and physical symptoms of anorexia. We have argued that most, if not all, of these symptoms arise from starvation or as a result of social learning. This implies that the label anorexia nervosa is wrong. Since the neurotic symptoms are often produced by starvation, the person is not self-starving because they are neurotic. They are neurotic because they are starving. We are therefore left with the fact that some people refuse to eat and starve. The next step is to explain why they do this. We argue that an activity-anorexia cycle provides the explanation for many instances of human anorexia.

REFERENCES

Although many of these references may be of interest, we have indicated (with an asterisk*) those that are written for the non-specialist reader.

1. Bruch, H. (1965). The psychiatric differential diagnosis of anorexia nervosa. In J. E. Mayer & H. Feldman (Eds.), *Anorexia nervosa: Symposium am 24/25 April 1965 in Göttingen*. Stuttgart, Germany: Georg Thieme Verlag.
2. Noyes, A. P. and Kolb, L. C. (1963). *Modern clinical psychiatry*. Philadelphia, PA: W. R. Saunders.
3. Garner, D. M., Garfinkel, P. E., Stancer, H. C. and Moldofsky, H. (1976). Body image disturbances in anorexia nervosa and obesity. *Psychosomatic Medicine*, 38, 327-336.
4. Feighner, J. P., Robins, E., Guze, S. B., Woodruff, R. A., Winokur, G., and Munoz, R. (1972). Diagnostic criteria for use in psychiatric research. *Archives of General Psychiatry*, 26, 57-63.
5. *Garner, D.M. and Garfinkel, P.E. (1988). *Diagnostic issues in anorexia nervosa and bulimia nervosa*. New York: Bruner/Mazel.

6. *Johnson, C. and Connors, M.E. (1987). *The etiology and treatment of bulimia nervosa: A biopsychosocial perspective.* New York: Basic Books.

7. Beumont, P. J. V. and Abraham, S. F. (1983). Episodes of ravenous overeating or bulimia: their occurrence in patients with anorexia nervosa and with other forms of disordered eating. In P. L. Darby, P. E. Garfinkel, D. M. Garner and D. V. Coscina (Eds.), *Anorexia nervosa: Recent developments in research,* (pp. 15-28). New York: Alan R. Liss, Inc.

8. Crisp, A. H. (1983). Some aspects of the psychopathology of anorexia nervosa. In P. L. Darby, P. E. Garfinkel, D. M. Garner and D. V. Coscina (Eds.), *Anorexia nervosa: Recent developments in research,* (pp. 15-28). New York: Alan R. Liss, Inc.

9. Keys, A., Brozek, J., Henschel, A., Mickelson, O. and Taylor, H. L. (1950). *The biology of human starvation.* Minneapolis, MN: University of Minnesota Press.

10. *Bruch, H. (1978). *The golden cage.* Cambridge, MA: Harvard University Press.

11. Bemis, K. A . (1983). A comparison of functional relationships in anorexia nervosa and phobia. In P. L. Darby, P. E. Garfinkel, D. M. Garner and D. V. Coscina (Eds.), *Anorexia nervosa: Recent developments in research,* (pp. 403-416). New York: Alan R. Liss, Inc.

12. Crisp, A. H. and Toms, D. A. (1972). Primary anorexia nervosa or weight phobia in the male: report on 13 cases. *British Medical Journal,* 1, 334-338.

13. Rampling, D. (1978). Anorexia nervosa: Reflections on theory and practice. *Psychiatry,* 41, 296-301.

14. *Orbach, S. (1986). *Hunger Strike.* London: Faber and Faber.

15. *Dally, P., Gomez, J. and Isaacs, A. J. (1979). *Anorexia nervosa.* London, England: William Heinemann Medical Books Ltd.

16. Crisp, A. H. (1965). Clinical and therapeutic aspects of anorexia nervosa a study of thirty cases. *Journal of Psychosomatic Research,* 9, 67-68.

17. Slade, P. D. (1973). A short anorectic behavior scale. *British Journal of Psychiatry,* 122, 83-85.

18. Crisp, A. H., Hsu, L. K. G., Harding, B. and Hartshorn, J. (1980). Clinical features of anorexia nervosa: a study of a consecutive series of 102 female patients. *Journal of Psychosomatic Research,* 24, 179-191.

19. King, A. (1963). Primary and secondary anorexia nervosa syndromes. *British Journal of Psychiatry,* 109, 470-479.

20. Crisp, A. H. and Stonehill, E. (1976). *Sleep, nutrition and mood.* London, England: John Wiley and Sons.

21. Beumont, A. L., Booth, S. F., Abraham, D. A., Griffiths, D. A. and Turner, T. R.(1983). Temporal sequence of symptoms in patients with anorexia nervosa: a preliminary report. In P. L. Darby, P. E. Garfinkel, D. M. Garner and D. V. Coscina (Eds.), *Anorexia nervosa: Recent developments in research,* (pp. 129-136). New York: Alan R. Liss, Inc.

22. Kron, L., Katz, J. L., Gorzynski, G. and Weiner, H. (1978). Hyperactivity in anorexia nervosa: A fundamental clinical feature. *Comprehensive Psychiatry,* 19, 433-440.

23. Crisp, A. H. (1967). The possible significance of some behavioral correlates of weight and carbohydrate intake. *Journal of Psychosomatic Research,* 11, 117-131.

24. Howard, R. B. (1839). *An inquiry into the morbid effect of deficiency of food chiefly with reference to their occurrence amongst the destitute poor.* London, England: Simpkin, Marshall & Co.

25. Blanton, S. (1919). Mental and nervous changes in children of the Volkschulen of Trier, Germany, caused by malnutrition. *Mental Hygiene,* 3, 343-386.

26. Russell Davis, D. (1951). *Studies in malnutrition. M. R. C. special report series no. 275.* H. M. stationary office, London, England.

27. Lipscomb, F. M. (1945). Medical aspects of Belsen concentration camp. *Lancet*, 2, 313-315.

28. Leyton, G. B. (1946). Effect of slow starvation. *Lancet*, 2, 73-79.

29. Halmi, K. A. and Falk, J. R. (1983). Behavioral and dietary discriminators of menstrual function in anorexia nervosa. In P. L. Darby, P. E. Garfinkel, D. M. Garner and D. V. Coscina (Eds.), *Anorexia nervosa: Recent developments in research*, (pp. 323-330) New York: Alan R. Liss, Inc.

30. Russell, G. F. M. and Beardwood, C. H. (1970). Amenorrhea in the eating disorders: anorexia nervosa and obesity. *Psychotherapy and Psychosomatic Medicine*, 18, 358-364.

31. *Vincent, L. M. (1981). *Competing with the self: The pursuit of the ideal body form.* New York, NY: Berkley Books.

32. Frisch, R. E., Wyshank, G. and Vincent, L. (1980). Delayed menarche and amenorrhea in ballet dancers. *New England Journal of Medicine*, 303, 17-19.

33. Malina, R. M., Harper, A. B. and Avent, H. H. (1973). Age at menarche in athletes and non-athletes. *Medical Science and Sports Exercise*, 5, 11-13.

34. Malina, R. M., Spirduso, W. W. and Tate, C. (1978). Age at menarche and selected menstrual characteristics in athletes at differing competitive levels and in different sports. *Medical Science and Sports Exercise*, 10, 218-222.

35. Frisch, R. E., Wetz-Goldbergen, A. V. and McArthur, J. W. (1981). Delayed menarche, irregular cycles and amenorrhea of college athletes in relation to the onset of training. *Journal of the American Medical Association*, 246, 1559-1563.

36. Feicht, C. B., Johnson, T. S. and Martin, B. J. (1978). Secondary amenorrhea in athletes. *Lancet*, 2, 1145-1146.

37. Schwartz, B., Cumming, D. C. and Riordan, E. (1981). Exercise associated amenorrhea: a distinct entity? *American Journal of Obstetrics and Gynecology*, 141, 662-670.

38. Dale, E., Gerlach, D. H. and Wilhite, A. L. (1979). Menstrual dysfunction in distance runners. *Obstetrics and Gynecology*, 54, 47-53.

39. Anderson, J. L. (1979). Women's sports and fitness programs at the U.S. Military Academy. *Physiology Sports and Medicine*, 7, 72-78.

40. Cumming, D.C. (1989). Menstrual disturbances caused by exercise. In K.M.Pirke, W. Wuttke and U.Schweiger (Eds.), *The menstrual cycle and its disorders: Influences of nutrition, exercise and neurotransmitters*, (pp. 150-160). New York: Springer-Verlag.

41. Warren, M.P. (1989). Reproductive function in the ballet dancer. In K.M.Pirke, W.Wuttke and U.Schweiger (Eds.), *The menstrual cycle and its disorders: Influences of nutrition, exercise and neurotransmitters*, (pp.161-170). New York: Springer-Verlag.

42. Russell, G. F. M. (1983). Delayed puberty due to anorexia nervosa of early onset. In P. L. Darby, P. E. Garfinkel, D. M. Garner and D. V. Coscina (Eds.), *Anorexia nervosa: Recent developments in research*, (pp. 331-342). New York: Alan R. Liss, Inc.

43. Silverman, J. A. (1983). Medical consequences of starvation; the malnutrition of anorexia nervosa: caveat medicus. In P. L. Darby, P. E. Garfinkel, D. M. Garner and D. V. Coscina (Eds.), *Anorexia nervosa: Recent developments in research*, (pp. 293-300). New York: Alan R. Liss, Inc.

44. Emanuel, R. W. (1954). *Some physical aspects of anorexia nervosa.* Thesis, Oxford University.

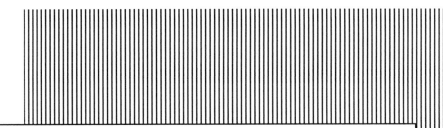

The main topics are:

- **CRITERIA FOR EVALUATING TREATMENT**
- **PSYCHOANALYSIS**
- **INSIGHT PSYCHOTHERAPY**
- **FAMILY THERAPY**
- **COGNITIVE PSYCHOTHERAPY**

Summary

- Indirect treatments focus on the personality, thinking style, or interpersonal conflicts of the anorectic — not on eating and body weight.

- About two-thirds (66%) of the patients with anorexia nervosa get better regardless of treatment. Effective therapies must exceed this figure.

- Psychoanalysis has focused on the unconscious sexual desires of anorectics. There is little evidence that it is an effective treatment.

- Insight psychotherapies provide alternative interpretation of personality and anorexia. The evidence on the effectiveness of these therapies is weak or lacking.

- Family therapy focuses on disturbed social relations and anorexia. The treatment appears effective — may be tailored to modify activity anorexia.

- Cognitive therapy emphasizes errors in logic and reasoning of the anorectic. Insufficient research — may be hepful for changing beliefs about diet and exercise.

CHAPTER

Indirect Treatment of
Anorexia Nervosa

5

Anorexia means loss of appetite. The clinical label "anorexia nervosa" suggests that anorexia is a neurotic illness. Treatments for loss of appetite that emphasize personality or thinking processes, may be called *indirect therapies*. These approaches attempt to cure the disturbed mental state that is the presumed cause of the appetite problem. In contrast, *direct therapies* concentrate on the appetite (and weight) problem and assume that personal adjustment will follow from weight recovery (see Chapter 6). This chapter outlines a number of indirect therapies for the treatment of anorexia. Psychoanalysis, insight and cognitive psychotherapy, and family therapy are indirect treatments that are discussed and evaluated in terms of their effectiveness.

The clinical orientation of the therapist influences the kind of treatment that a patient receives. Cognitive therapists are concerned with the patient's erroneous thinking and disturbed eating attitudes. Such cognitive processes are emphasized during the treatment of anorexia. From a cognitive point of view, long-term improvement requires changes in irrational beliefs and attitudes.

Distinctions in treatment orientation are somewhat artificial as many therapists adopt a "multidimensional" approach to anorexia nervosa. This means that practitioners combine diverse treatment techniques in an overall strategy to change and maintain weight, eating habits, and the general psychological well-being of the person. For example, a therapist may combine psychoanalysis, family counselling, and hospitalization (for severe cases) into an integrated treatment package.

Although therapists typically use a variety of techniques, our description and evaluation of treatment separates the approaches. Psychoanalysis and family therapy may be combined in treatment but it is necessary to outline and assess them independently.

1 CRITERIA FOR EVALUATING TREATMENT

Various therapies for the modification of anorexia are outlined and evaluated in this chapter. Interested persons may use the evaluations as a guide for selecting a suitable treatment. Many therapies require commitment by the patient in order to be effective. If a person does not feel comfortable with a particular approach, *no matter what the evaluation*, it is advisable to try an alternative treatment.

In our opinion, the most important question in the evaluation of treatment is whether the patient recovers from self-induced starvation. Such an evaluation of treatment must assess the adequacy of weight gain, the resumption of normal eating habits, and an accompanying change in eating attitudes. Additionally, the effectiveness of therapy must be assessed against recovery in the absence of treatment.

Behavioral scientists estimate that the majority of people with neurotic disorders improve without treatment (spontaneous recovery). For example, Dr. Hans Eysenck, a psychologist in England, suggests that 66 percent of people with neurosis improve without professional help [1, 2]. Many other studies of behavioral problems, ranging from delinquency to schizophrenia, find this same rate of spontaneous recovery.

In a review paper, Drs. Agras and Kraemer report that "... nearly two-thirds of a previously hospitalized anorexic population will be at normal weight, and the majority of these individuals will have resumed regular menstruation" [3]. This report is not unusual. An overview of the area by Drs. Bliss and Branch found that sixty-six percent of anorectic patients overcame self-starvation *regardless* of the type of treatment [4, emphasis ours]. Taken together, these studies suggest that 66 percent of people with anorexia improve independent of treatment. For this reason, a successful therapy must exceed this rate of spontaneous recovery. However, most clinical studies do not report rates of recovery. When these rates are not reported, our evaluation is based on the logic of the treatment and professional opinion.

2 PSYCHOANALYSIS

Psychoanalysis is an indirect therapy based on the writings of Sigmund Freud. The basic technique involves asking the person to relax and talk about "anything that comes to mind." While this free association is occurring, the therapist attempts to structure the communication of the client. Generally, the task is to have the patient talk about events in the past that presumably have created personality problems. Experiences such as trauma or seduction in early life are particularly relevant. Especially significant for the treatment of anorexia are events that center around sexual fantasies and desires. Discussion of the parent-child relationships helps to identify where particular sexual, oral and anal drives have been frustrated or repressed. The parent-child episodes may or may not have factual bases but the important point is that they are psychically real. Even if the events are fabrications of imagination, the fact that these fantasies occurred is itself important. This is because events that are viewed as real may have the same effects as actual life experiences.

A major objective of treatment is to have the patient release the reservoir of emotions. This venting of emotional "build up" is interpreted by the therapist as *catharsis*. A catharsis is a process of removing undesirable emotions that presumably are the causes of neurosis. For many clients, it is difficult to find the early life trauma that produced the neurosis. In these cases, psychoanalysts conclude that catharsis is not sufficient and other more rational techniques are required. The analyst then turns to interpreting the person's actions in terms of the conflicting forces of the psyche. The goal of interpretation is to provide the client with insight into the problem. However, the process of gaining insight is often difficult for the client. This resistance to accept interpretation is termed *blocking*, as when the client refuses to talk about relevant past events. Only by achieving a positive therapeutic and trusting relationship can this resistance be overcome.

As the therapeutic relationship evolves, the patient may express feelings toward the analyst. The therapist is often accused of sexual advances, hostile attitudes or indifference. The analyst may take these expressions as an extension of feelings toward significant persons in the client's actual life. Such inappropriate *transference* is used by the therapist as an occasion for interpretation that can help the patient to greater self-understanding. Based on the new insights, the client is then able to overcome resistance. When the client feels favorable, but unrealistic, emotions (e.g. love) toward the analyst it is termed *positive transference*. The expression of hostility and resentment towards the therapist is called *negative transference*. Generally, psychoanalytic therapy involves separate but interrelated techniques that attempt to achieve an emotional re-education of the person. These techniques are catharsis, insight, and transference interpretation.

When psychoanalysis is used to treat anorexia nervosa, the therapist attempts to establish insight about unconscious drives and motivations. For example, a 35-year-old woman with severe anorexia nervosa was treated with psychoanalysis. The case was claimed to be a success following 300 hours of analysis. Analysis centered on interpreting the refusal to eat as an expression of the woman's avoidance of oral castration of her father [5]. Modern psychoanalysis emphasizes the psychosocial development of the anorectic more than the resolution of sexual impulses. However, it is important to note that psychoanalysis usually involves rather lengthy treatment, regardless of the orientation of the analyst. This may be due to the time that is required to establish the therapeutic relationship that is essential for transference and re-education.

Evaluation of Psychoanalysis

Psychoanalysis is not currently a popular treatment for anorexia nervosa. One of the problems with this treatment is that patients may not gain weight or insight. A 1940 study of two female anorectics reported that fantasies of oral impregnation were the underlying reasons for self-starvation. In this account, the mouth was interpreted as the receptive organ that could be "impregnated" by food and the gastrointestinal tract was the womb. Therapy required that the patients become aware of these hidden motives. Unfortunately, the patients never did attain insight and failed to gain weight [6].

The failure of psychoanalytic treatment of anorexia nervosa was recently addressed by Dr. Kenneth Rockwell, who concluded that:

> *Psychoanalysis has had the longest time to establish its position in the treatment of anorexia nervosa. So far it has failed to do so. One might assume after so long a time that some quantitative data would have accumulated on the treatment efficacy of psychoanalysis. One would think characteristics of a subgroup of patients who had been treated with some success would have been delineated, too. At the present time there are no criteria for determining a subgroup of anorectic patients who might have a reasonable chance of benefiting from psychoanalysis...* [7, p. 16].

Professional opinion has shifted away from strict psychoanalysis because of weak evidence. Today, few psychoanalysts concentrate on unconscious sexual desires in the treatment of anorexia nervosa.

3   INSIGHT PSYCHOTHERAPY

There are a number of indirect treatment approaches that are not based on strict Freudian analysis. Freudian interpretations center on repressed sexual urges. Many therapists do not agree with this analysis and provide alternative interpretations of mental problems.

In most cases, therapy involves having patients talk about their relationships, feelings and problems with living. Group psychotherapy may involve discussion with other patients or family members. We use the term *insight psychotherapy* to describe any technique that emphasizes insight through discussion and communication. Most therapists use a variety of techniques based on different views of counseling. It is beyond the scope of this book to detail each variation of insight psychotherapy. However, it is useful to outline some of the major approaches.

Contemporary Psychoanalysis

Modern psychoanalysis has turned to the early mother-child relationship. Therapists see anorexia as a problem of the oral stage of human development. Some psychoanalysts believe that a domineering mother imposes a rigid caretaking schedule on the infant. In other words, the infant is fed, clothed, and comforted when it is convenient for the mother.

This kind of mother does not respond well to the child's needs and, in later life, the child is unaware of hunger and bodily sensations.

These therapists believe that individuals with such a rigid upbringing have no sense of personal control. Low self-control is said to underlie the feeling of ineffectiveness that characterizes the anorexic personality. Self-starvation is seen as an attempt to control bodily needs and thereby establish personal effectiveness. Therapy is designed to help these people resolve their feelings of ineffectiveness, understand their needs, and express unconscious feelings toward their mothers.

Treatment of anorexia based on fulfillment of oral needs is less interpretive than treatments focused on sexual desires. The oral interpretation assumes that eating problems are an expression of blocked oral gratification. A domineering mother is the source of this blockage. However, there is no evidence that rigid maternal care produces an anorexic child. More importantly, there is no evidence that understanding and resolving "feelings of ineffectiveness" can cure the eating problem.

Client-Centered Psychotherapy

Client-centered psychotherapy is an insight-treatment approach developed by Dr. Carl Rogers. In a recent survey of clinical and counseling psychologists, Dr. Rogers was considered to be the most influential person in psychotherapy [8]. The intent of his treatment technique is to help clients self-actualize by attaining their full human potential, and by opening them up to all their experiences. This approach is called *client-centered* because Rogers does not feel that the therapist should lead the person toward self-actualization. According to this perspective, the best person to guide self-inquiry is the client and not the therapist.

This form of therapy is based on *unconditional positive regard* by the therapist. Client-centered therapists believe that they must genuinely accept and value the person. Positive regard is given no matter what the client says or does (i.e. unconditional). Anorexia and other neurotic disorders are thought to arise from the conditional positive regard of others. These therapists believe that most human problems arise from attempts to please others and gain affection or love. Because of this, client-centered therapists feel it is essential to remove these social expectations. However, there is no direct attempt to lead the anorectic to a particular interpretation, rather the individual must engage in self-evaluation and in doing so arrive at an understanding of the eating problem.

Evaluation of Insight Therapies

Contemporary psychoanalysis and client-centered approaches to psychotherapy are contrasting examples of insight therapies. As stated earlier, most psychologists and psychiatrists are not committed to any single perspective. Rather, they utilize those techniques that seem most effective in terms of their clinical experience.

Although hard evidence is difficult to acquire on the effectiveness of insight psycho-therapy, a recent study indicates low success with this approach. The study was reported by Drs. Hall and Crisp at St. Georges Hospital in England. These researchers compared the outcomes of anorectics given 12 one-hour sessions of insight therapy with other anorectics given twelve hours of dietary advice [9]. Psychotherapy resulted in higher sexual and social adjustment scores than dietary advice. However, in terms of weight gain the results were reversed. In this case, dietary advice produced a reliable increase in weight but psycho-therapy did not.

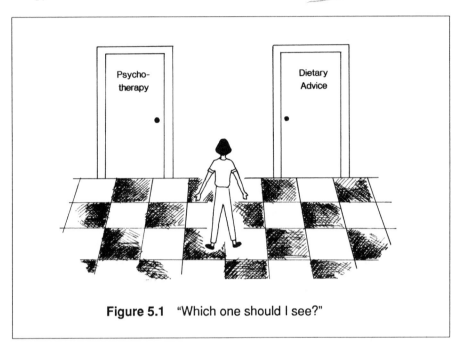

Figure 5.1   "Which one should I see?"

When patients weights were expressed as percentage differences from normal weight (i.e. normal in the sense of what a person's weight should be given height, age and bone structure), only dietary advice reliably increased weight toward normal. All patients were assessed on body weight one year after therapy. The dietary-advice patients sustained or gained weight; however, three of the eight psychotherapy patients had a major weight loss while five improved. Thus, five in 8, or 63 percent, of the psychotherapy patients had improved while all (100%) of the patients given dietary-advice gained or sustained weight. Although it could be argued that twelve psychotherapy sessions were not enough, the treatment did not produce a weight gain outcome better than 66 percent. We therefore conclude it was not successful. The researchers were interested in the effectiveness of psychotherapy; however, the results suggest that more attention should be paid to dietary advice.

Currently, few health professionals use insight therapy as an exclusive treatment for anorexia nervosa. Most agree that the first concern must be the resumption of eating and attainment of adequate body weight. However, many therapists do not feel that weight gain should be the primary focus of treatment. Dr. Rampling has argued that "... therapeutic zeal directed solely at restoring ideal weight invariably results in unhelpful confrontation and confirms the patient in her belief that she is not in control of her own destiny" [10]. A similar perspective is echoed by Dr. Bruch who recounts the treatment of "Willa" for bulimia, vomiting and anorexia nervosa. A program was set up to force feed Willa if she did not gain weight. Because Willa did not like force feeding, she began to eat foods that would produce rapid weight gain (i.e. ice cream and cake). In less than two months she went from 68 to 96 pounds and was discharged from the hospital as greatly improved. After returning to her family, she became depressed and suicidal. Dr. Bruch has suggested that this outcome was a result of the hospital treatment. When interviewed one year after discharge, Willa was desperately unhappy and weighed seventy-two pounds. Based on the history of Willa, Dr. Bruch concludes that:

> This story illustrates that there is more to the treatment of anorexia nervosa than inducing weight gain. The correction of the weight problem must be part of an integrated treatment approach. The patient needs to be instructed, and also the family, that in spite of outer appearances this is not an illness of weight and appetite — the essential problem relates to inner doubts and lack of self-confidence. However, in order to get help with these underlying problems, the body needs to be in a better condition. The patient is usually terror-stricken at the idea of having to gain weight, and it is important to give her a meaningful explanation why better nutrition is an essential precondition for coming to an understanding of her psychological problems [11, p. 93, emphasis ours].

There is disagreement regarding the importance of weight gain and recovery from severe anorexia nervosa. Dr. Peter Dally and his associates have indicated that the mental unrest of anorectics only reverses when the person recovers weight. They report that "noticeable psychological changes" occur after the patient recovers 80 percent or more of normal weight [12, p. 106]. In a previous chapter, we noted the development of psychological changes in individuals who were forced to starve. These personality changes typically subside as the person regains normal weight [13]. This suggests that weight gain may be primary, rather than secondary, to recovery from anorexia nervosa. It seems unjustified to claim that restoration of body weight is peripheral to any kind of starvation, including self-starvation. Additionally, it should be pointed out that weight gain may be achieved with techniques that range from coercive tube-feeding to positive incentive systems associated with behavior modification. Willa's experience may have been related to the coercive treatment. Positive weight-gain programs may be more effective in avoiding the negative psychological by-products.

Whatever one's perspective on weight gain, it is important to note that some objective criteria (if not weight gain) should be used to evaluate the treatment effectiveness of insight psychotherapy. If the goal is to have "control over ones destiny" then the psychotherapist ought to provide a reliable and valid measure of this capacity. More importantly, it seems reasonable to show that changes in "destiny control" are systematically related to long term

---

improvement in appetite and weight. It would be clinically unacceptable to improve perceived control and not affect the tendency to starve.

Some experts claim that insight psychotherapy is moderately effective in treating a range of psychological problems. Recent evaluation studies have shown that this may be the case [14, 15]. However, the definition of psychotherapy is much broader than ours. Approximately, 43 percent of the studies cited in the later article were in fact studies of behavior therapy and this may have contributed to their conclusion [14]. This is likely since other large scale evaluations, employing a definition of insight psychotherapy similar to ours, have not found it effective. Dr. Hans Eysenck, in a series of influential articles, found that persons undergoing psychotherapy did not improve more than untreated patients placed on a waiting list [16, 17, 18]. The finding was based on an evaluation of 24 studies covering over 7000 cases.

According to Eysenck, after two years, approximately 66 percent of the untreated patients got better. Patients receiving psychotherapy did not exceed this figure. Therefore, he concluded that psychotherapy was not effective. Although there have been many challenges to this conclusion, Dr. Edward Irwin at the University of Miami has convincingly argued that none of the challenges seriously alter Eysenck's original findings [19].

Based on our definition of insight psychotherapy, we would hesitate recommending this technique as the primary treatment of anorexia nervosa. Although there is no evidence that it is harmful, there is little evidence that it is effective.

4   FAMILY THERAPY

Many professionals who use the insight approach have recognized that this treatment may be more effective when combined with family therapy. We have listed family therapy as "indirect" since the primary goal is to improve family relationships rather than to regulate weight gain. From the family systems perspective, anorexia nervosa is brought about by disturbed interpersonal relations. From this perspective, the child's self-starvation arises in response to disordered family interactions (i.e. overprotectiveness and poor conflict resolution) and such interactions perpetuate the anorexia. The child's eating problem in turn maintains the disturbed family system.

Treatment with Family Therapy

Treatment is centered on identifying disruptive interaction patterns and improving communication. This is a recent approach developed in the United States by Dr. Salvador Minuchin and his colleagues and in Italy by Dr. Selvini-Palazzoli and her associates [20, 21, 22, 23]. The therapist often takes an active role and intervenes to correct conflicts among family members. The entire family is encouraged to attend therapy sessions. During these sessions, the therapist promotes open argument and discussion. Often a family member will prematurely concede an argument. In this case, the therapist challenges the winner to review the disagreement and to make certain that a fair agreement has been reached. This usually leads to further conflict resolution and improved communication.

The "family lunch session" is a structured opportunity for the therapist to make on-the-
spot changes in hostile interactions. Weight-gain programs, dieting and excessive involvement in sports are among the issues raised at these sessions. As may be expected, the
anorectic refuses to eat the meal and a power-struggle begins. These dynamic interchanges
are seen in the case of Deborah as reported by Dr. Minuchin and his associates.

*FATHER.   This is good food, and you eat it. Deborah, don't pull that shit on me.
Now eat it! If I thought it would kill you, I wouldn't let you eat it. Don't you tell me
about cottage cheese and protein. You're no goddamn doctor. Now eat it! Or you'll
find milk all over your hair and on your body and on your ... (Still sobbing, Deborah
takes the hot dog and crushes it.) Now I told you I'm going to give you a couple of
minutes, and then I'm going to feed you myself. Because eventually you're going to
get fed with a tube down your stomach anyway. Look at your body, and look at your
arms. Now come on, start to eat it. Start to eat! And don't be like a two-year old baby
and make a big fuss out of eating a stupid hot dog. A lot of kids wish the hell they had
a hot dog for lunch.*

DEBORAH: Well, give it to them!

*FATHER: I'm not going to give it to them. I'm giving it to you! And I'm not wasting
any food, either. Now Deborah, don't put me in a position where I'm going to get
violent. You eat the food, or you're not going to see me in this goddamn hospital
again. I don't care if they carry you out of here on a stretcher. Now, you eat it. Come
on, eat the goddamn hot dog! Deborah, if you don't eat this hot dog, you're going
to be sorry.*

DEBORAH: I don't want it! (She crumbles the mush in her hands.)

FATHER: You eat it! Don't you destroy it, or I'll get ten more. Now you eat it!

DEBORAH: I don't want it! Look at it! It's ugly!

*FATHER: Eat that hot dog! I'm not leaving this place, I swear to God, until you
eat it. Eat it! And drink this milk. And eat the peas. I don't mean leave it. Eat that hot
dog! God damn you! You son of a bitch! You eat the goddamn hot dog! I told you to
eat it! [He takes the crushed hot dog and shoves it into Deborah's mouth. She resists,
and is smeared with food. The therapist intervenes telling Mr. Kaplin to stop. Mr.
Kaplin sits down, visibly exhausted and ashamed of his failure [20, pp. 7-8]. **

Family lunch sessions are used to identify interactions that occur during eating. The aim
is to teach the anorectic to eat in the presence of the parents. Treatment is also designed to
reduce unnecessary involvement by parents. Therapists engage the concerned parents in
discussion so that the child can eat without being harassed. Both parents are taught to
maintain consistent and appropriate responses to the anorectic's behavior.

---

*   Reprinted by permission of the publishers from *The Golden Cage: The Enigma of Anorexia Nervosa* by
Hilde Bruch, Cambridge, Mass.: Harvard University Press, Copyright © 1978 by the President and
Fellows of Harvard College.

Figure 5.2   A family lunch session. Family therapists often arrange lunch sessions for the treatment of anorexia nervosa.

Although therapists are concerned with family interactions, they use a variety of strategies that are expressly designed to increase weight and improve the eating habits of patients. Contracts of agreement may be negotiated between parents and child. The intent of these contracts is to state in concrete terms what is expected of each family member. For example, the child may be required to eat a reasonable portion of the meal. In consultation with the therapist, the parents and child agree on how much is a reasonable amount to eat. Parents agree not to nag the child if this amount of food is consumed.

Evaluation of Family Therapy

Family therapy is becoming a treatment of choice for many professionals who treat anorexia nervosa. This acceptance may be based on the compatibility of family therapy with different approaches to anorexia nervosa. Therapists who practice insight psychotherapy or Freudian analysis recognize the importance of family dynamics. The interpretative orientation of these specialists can blend with the systems view of family therapy.

The growing acceptance of family therapy is also based on the findings of recent studies. A study by Dr. Rosman and his colleagues reported that 45 out of 53 patients, or 85 percent, were improved by family therapy [24]. The study was based on a survey of former patients who were contacted between 3 months and 4 years after therapy for anorexia nervosa. A subsequent assessment of the effectiveness of family therapy was conducted by Dr. Minuchin and his associates [20]. In this study, 16 therapists, who differed in training and experience, treated 50 anorectic patients. The patients were assessed after one and one-half to 7 years. According to the researchers, 43 of 50 patients, or 86 percent, treated with family therapy recovered from anorexia nervosa.

Our criteria of successful treatment requires greater than a 66 percent recovery rate. Both assessment studies substantially exceed this figure and this suggests that family therapy is an effective treatment for anorexia nervosa. There is, however, reason for caution. These outcome studies did not include an appropriate control group. Because of this, it is possible that factors other than family therapy contributed to the high recovery rate. To illustrate, families who agreed to this therapy may have been more committed to the recovery of their child. This selection bias could be the reason for success rather than the therapy itself. Nonetheless, the evidence is encouraging and suggests that this form of treatment should be considered as a primary intervention strategy.

The family therapy approach is consistent with the account of activity anorexia presented in this book. From our perspective, the diet and exercise culture is transmitted through family interactions. The family that encourages physical fitness and dieting is likely to push the adolescent toward the activity-anorexia cycle. Once this cycle is initiated it is self-maintaining and does not require social support. As discussed in Chapter 8, motivational conditions within the activity-dieting cycle produce the extreme food reduction (i.e. anorexia).

Hospitalization, forced bed rest, and direct behavior management can stop the activity-anorexia cycle. However, when the anorectic recovers, family members may inadvertently again prompt and reinforce excessive dieting and exercise. This is why family therapy is necessary for long-term recovery from anorexia. Family therapy may alter some of the social conditions that contribute to relapse.

5 COGNITIVE PSYCHOTHERAPY

Cognitive theorists argue that disturbed thinking underlies maladaptive feelings and behavior. According to cognitive therapists, anorexia is the result of distorted beliefs and attitudes (i.e. cognitions) about body weight. There is no need to explore the unconscious motivations of the anorectic that are, presumably, based on childhood experience. No matter how the person acquired the distorted cognitions, the task is to change them. The major goal of treatment is to alter these distorted ways of thinking.

Rational-Emotive Psychotherapy

A cognitive therapy based on the work of Dr. Albert Ellis is called rational-emotive therapy [25]. According to this model, people engage in a social comparison process. In other words, persons compare themselves to others and evaluate their abilities, competencies and physical attributes. Social comparison sometimes prevents them from accepting personal deficits or faults. As a result, the person feels self-contempt or defensive superiority. Rather than focusing on early childhood experiences, the rational-emotive therapist holds that the client is solely responsible, in the present, for his or her unhappiness or life problems. Based on this personal responsibility, the therapist explicitly points out how the client is maintaining inaccurate self-evaluations.

The goal of therapy is to teach persons to see themselves more realistically. Thus, the anorectic is required to face the eating problem and is charged with personal responsibility for his or her condition. For example, an anorectic may believe that everyone should immediately love and admire her. From this perspective, the refusal to eat and the slim appearance may be strategies to obtain love and admiration. Rational-emotive therapists use a variety of techniques to combat these illogical beliefs. The techniques include confrontation, challenge, persuasion, commands and logical argument. The therapist does not go easy on the person with an eating problem. In some cases, the therapist may give homework assignments where the anorectic must regularly participate in the evening meal. In short, a therapist with this perspective overtly attempts to influence the client.

Cognitive Therapy

Cognitive therapy is similar to the rational-emotive approach and is based on the work of Dr. A.T. Beck [26]. A major difference between cognitive and rational-emotive approaches is that confrontation or arguments over points of logic are avoided by cognitive therapists. Professionals who use cognitive therapy attempt to change the individual by making suggestions and giving advice in a friendly manner.

In a recent review of cognitive therapy and anorexia nervosa, Drs. Garner and Bemis described the rationale for treatment of patients.

> *The cognitive approach to anorexia nervosa may be distinguished by its explicit concern with beliefs, values, and assumptions. Moreover, as long as the constructs are relevant to the patient's belief system, a cognitive model does not require adherence to a unitary theory and may retain conceptual integrity while borrowing from the valuable observations of various clinical theorists. A central aim of much of the information gathering in the initial interviews is to understand the patient's belief system, which is comprised of attitudes about weight, assumptions about self-worth, values related to performance, and developmental expectations, as well as attitudes about the family. These occasions also provide the opportunity to assess the preponderance of certain types of formal reasoning errors ... and general cognitive style [27, p. 115].*

Cognitive therapists begin by establishing a trusting and close relationship with the anorectic. Once this relationship is established, therapy is directed at changing the beliefs that are thought to create anorexia. Therapists recognize that anorectics exhibit a unique set of cognitions and patterns of reasoning. The anorectic tends to see the world in black and white. Drs. Garner and Bemis call this way of viewing the world *dichotomous reasoning*. They say that this form of logic characterizes much of the anorectic's belief system and is not restricted to food and weight issues. For example, some patients see their parents as absolutely perfect while others describe them as complete failures. This same logic is said to permeate beliefs about food and exercise. Anorectics believe that they cannot eat a small portion of food without losing control and eating to excess. Also, they may think that it is not possible to miss a day of exercise without permanently stopping.

In addition to dichotomous thinking, cognitive therapists suggest that other logical errors may underlie the anorectic's reasoning. These reasoning errors include self-centered thinking, making too much of minor issues, superstitious thinking, and engaging in huge generalizations based on little evidence. In order to correct faulty thinking, cognitive therapists use a number of strategies.

1. Monitor their (anorectic's) thinking or heighten their awareness of their own thinking.

2. Recognize the connection between certain thoughts and maladaptive behaviors and emotions.

3. Examine the evidence for the validity of particular beliefs.

4. Substitute more realistic and appropriate interpretations.

5. Gradually modify the underlying assumptions that are fundamental determinants of more specific beliefs [27, p. 118].

Paradoxical intention is a cognitive technique used to change the anorectic's beliefs. This technique involves encouraging patients to do exactly what they want to do. The strategy is designed to make clients see how ridiculous their beliefs are by agreeing with their views. For example, Drs. Hsu and Lieberman treated 8 anorectics with this method. The patients were told that it was better for them to remain anorexic since prior therapy had not been completely successful. The "advantages" of anorexia nervosa were outlined by the therapists and the patients could disagree with these advantages if they wished. A male anorectic was treated by paradoxical intention and the case was described as follows:

Patient 1 was the youngest of identical triplets. Unlike his two brothers, he had always been an underachiever; he was overweight (105 kg) premorbidly. He developed anorexia nervosa at the age of 18, shortly after the death of his mother. After the onset of his illness he had intensive psychotherapy and was admitted five times in 5 years to a university psychiatric unit for feeding until he reached his target weight. He remained ill and was admitted to our hospital. His stay was stormy; on one occasion he took an overdose of drugs. After 6 months he was discharged, weighing 70 kg, but he lost weight rapidly. At this point paradoxical intention technique was used. The patient was told 1) that he should keep his illness; 2) that he seemed to gain the following benefits through his illness — he could punish his family for keeping his mother's illness from him and for blaming him later for her death, and his slimness represented a radical break with his 'bad' past and made him look more like his two slim brothers; 3) that he did not have to agree with our understanding of such 'benefits' and that he could continue to be seen by us, if he so wished, to explore other issues. In the following session he explored his guilt about his past 'bad' behavior and his anger and hatred of his family. For 6 months he attended these sessions, during which time he maintained his weight at 90% average weight. At a 4-year follow-up he was at 90% average weight (63 kg); he was working 14 hours a day as a credit controller, living with his father, and attending evening classes. He had no close friends and no interests other than reading [28, p. 651].

There are other techniques used to change the illogical beliefs of anorectics. For example, de-centering is a strategy for encouraging patients to examine specific beliefs from a new perspective. The anorectic may think that other people will notice any slight change in appearance. A patient may complain that even a slight increase in weight will be noticed. The therapist may state that many people vary in weight from week to week but this is unremarkable to others. When seen from this perspective, the belief appears illogical. Removal of such irrational beliefs is thought to promote normal eating habits.

Cognitive therapy is a recent development in the treatment of anorexia nervosa. According to Dr. Garner, "these methods are particularly appealing because they are quite compatible with other more traditional approaches to psychotherapy" [29, p. 427]. For this reason, it is likely that the cognitive approach will increase in popularity among professionals.

Evaluation of Cognitive Therapy

Cognitive psychotherapists are not concerned with interpretations of the anorectic's mental state. Therapists target specific errors in logic and reasoning as expressed in the communication of the client. Changes in styles of thinking (e.g. dichotomous thinking) are assumed to alter specific beliefs that support self-starvation. Thus, cognitive psychotherapy is more focused on the eating problem than insight approaches.

Therapists and researchers with a cognitive perspective are interested in testing the effectiveness of their methods. Specific techniques are well described and distinguished from other strategies of treatment. At the present time there are few studies that assess the effectiveness of cognitive methods. However, controlled-clinical experiments could determine which components of treatment alter erroneous thinking. Other research could show whether changes in thinking produce long term restoration of weight and adjustment to life.

In the study by Hsu and Lieberman concerning paradoxical intention (see above), there was an evaluation of treatment success. They found that seven of 8 patients (88%) treated with paradoxical intention improved. Two to four years after therapy, these 7 patients were between 76 and 90 percent of normal weight. Weights were stable and the patients were not under psychiatric care at the time of follow-up [28]. Based on the 66 percent criterion of spontaneous recovery, the treatment was a success. This suggests that some cognitive treatments may be effective. There is, however, reason for caution. This is a single study of only 8 patients and the findings may not be representative of the effectiveness of cognitive therapy. In addition, control groups were not used and because of this, it is not possible to be sure that improvements in weight were due to the treatment.

In terms of activity anorexia, we suggest that cognitive therapy focus on beliefs and assumptions related to eating, weight, and exercise. If these beliefs are changed by cognitive intervention, and are correlated with self-starvation, the activity-anorexia cycle may be interrupted. Also, a change in such beliefs could prevent a relapse following recovery of normal weight. Cognitive techniques may combat the influence of the "fitness culture" whose standards are appealing to the anorectic.

However, cognitive perspectives do not emphasize the interrelationships of food restriction and physical activity. We believe that successful therapy must directly address these relationships. Because of this, direct behavior modification seems more important to an effective long-term treatment program. Behavior therapy can be used to stop exercise induced starvation. For this reason, we suggest that cognitive therapy be combined with behavior modification techniques.

REFERENCES

Although many of these reference may be of interest, we have indicated (with an asterisk*) those that are written for the non-specialist reader.

1. Eysenck, H. J. (1952). The effects of psychotherapy: An evaluation. *Journal of Consulting Psychology*, 16, 319-324.
2. Eysenck, H. J. (1961). The effects of psychotherapy. In H. J. Eysenck (Ed.), *Handbook of abnormal psychology* (pp. 697-725). New York: Basic Books.
3. Agras, W. S. and Kraemer, H. C. (1983). The treatment of anorexia nervosa: Do different treatments have different outcomes? *Psychiatric Annals*, 13, 928-935.
4. Bliss, E. L. and Branch, C. H. H. (1960). *Anorexia nervosa: Its history, psychology, and biology*. New York: Paul Hoeber.
5. Masserman, J. H. (1941). Psychodynamics in anorexia nervosa and neurotic vomiting. *Psychoanalysis Quarterly,* 10, 211.
6. Waller, I. J. V., Kaufman, M. R. and Deutsch, F. (1940). Anorexia nervosa. *Psychosomatic Medicine,* 2, 3-40.
7. Rockwell, W. J. K. (1986). Anorexia nervosa - treatment perspectives. In F. E. F. Larocca, (Ed.), *Eating disorders : Effective care and treatment,* (pp. 1-10). St. Louis: Ishiyaku EuroAmerica, Inc.
8. Smith, D. (1982). Trends in counseling and psychotherapy. *American Psychologist,* 37, 802-809.
9. Hall, A. and Crisp, A. H. (1983). Brief psychotherapy in the treatment of anorexia nervosa: Preliminary findings. In P. L. Darby, P. E. Garfinkel, D. M. Garner and D. V. Coscina (Eds.), *Anorexia nervosa: Recent developments in research,* (pp. 427-439). New York: Alan R. Liss Inc.
10. Rampling, D. (1978). Anorexia nervosa: Reflections on theory and practice. *Psychiatry,* 41, 296-301.
11. *Bruch, H. (1978). *The golden cage*. Cambridge: Harvard University Press.
12. *Dally, P., Gomez, J. and Isaacs, A. J. (1979). *Anorexia nervosa*. (pp. 103-128). London: William Heineman Medical Books Ltd.
13. Keys, A., Brozek, J., Henschel, A., Mickelsen, O. and Taylor, H. L. (1950). *The biology of human starvation*. Minneapolis: University of Minnesota Press.
14. Smith, M. L. and Glass, G. V. (1977). Meta-analysis of psychotherapy outcome studies. *American Psychologist,* 32, 752-760.
15. Landman, J. T. and Dawes, R. M. (1982). Psychotherapy outcome: Smith and Glass' conclusions stand up under scrutiny. *American Psychologist*, 37, 504-516.

16. Eysenck, H. J. (1952). The effects of psychotherapy: An evaluation. *Journal of Consulting Psychology*, 16, 319-324.

17. Eysenck, H. J. (1963). Behavior therapy, spontaneous remission and transference in neurotics. *American Journal of Psychiatry*, 119, 867-871.

18. *Eysenck, H. J. (1966). *The effects of psychotherapy*. New York: Inter-Science Press.

19. Erwin, E. (1980). Psychoanalytic therapy: The Eysenck argument. *American Psychologist*, 35, 435-443.

20. *Minuchin, S., Rosman, B. L. and Baker, L. (1978). *Psychosomatic families: Anorexia nervosa in context*. Cambridge, MA: Harvard University Press.

21. *Minuchin, S. (1974). *Families and family therapy*. Cambridge, MA: Harvard University Press.

22. *Selvini-Palazzoli, M. (1978). *Self-starvation*. New York: Jason Aronson.

23. *Selvini-Palazzoli, M. (1974). *Self-starvation : From individual to family therapy in the treatment of anorexia nervosa*. New York: Jason Aronson.

24. Rosman, B. L., Minuchin, S., Leibman, R. and Baker, L. (1976). Input and outcome of family therapy in anorexia nervosa. In J. Claghorn (Ed.), *Successful psychotherapy*, (pp. 128-139). New York: Bruner/Mazel.

25. *Ellis, A. (1962). *Reason and emotion in psychotherapy*. New York: Lyle Stuart.

26. *Beck, A. T. (1976). *Cognitive therapy and emotional disorders*. New York: International University Press.

27. Garner, D. M. and Bemis, K. M. (1985). Cognitive therapy for anorexia nervosa. In Garner, D. M. and Garfinkel, P. E. (Eds.), *Handbook of psychotherapy for anorexia nervosa and bulimia*. New York: The Guilford Press.

28. Hsu, L. K. G. and Lieberman, S. (1982). Paradoxical intention in the treatment of chronic anorexia nervosa. *American Journal of Psychiatry,* 139, 650-653.

29. Garner, D. M. (1985). Individual psychotherapy for anorexia nervosa. *Journal of Psychiatric Research*, 19, 423-433.

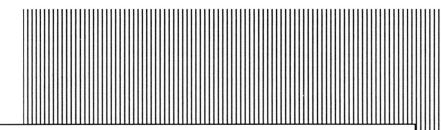

The main topics are:

● **MEDICAL THERAPY**
● **BEHAVIOR THERAPY**
● **WHERE TO FIND HELP**

Summary

• Direct treatments of anorexia nervosa focus on eating and weight gain — social adjustment is secondary.

• Medical therapy includes hospitalization, re-feeding, and drug control of behavior. Specific procedures may have negative side effects.

• Medical therapy is effective when starvation is life-threatening and is recommended by most health professionals.

• Behavior therapy is based on the principles of operant conditioning — objectives are to increase and maintain eating and body weight by arranging reinforcing consequences.

• Behavior therapy is about 90% effective in the short-term- and long-term management of eating and body weight. In terms of social adjustment, it has not been as successful.

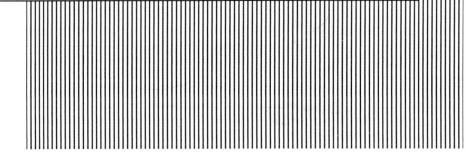

CHAPTER

Direct Treatments of Anorexia Nervosa

6

Weight gain and the resumption of normal eating are the primary objectives of *direct therapies* for anorexia nervosa. There are two basic methods of direct intervention. Medical therapy involves hospitalization, the use of drugs, and forced rest and feeding. Behavior therapy includes the use of positive and negative reinforcement for eating and weight gain. These direct methods are often combined with the indirect treatments such as insight, family or cognitive psychotherapy (see Chapter 5). Medical intervention is recommended by all therapists when self-starvation is life-threatening.

1   MEDICAL THERAPY

A person who is suffering from severe starvation requires *medical therapy* to restore health. When admitted to a hospital, anorectics are often forced to remain in bed. The first task is to ensure that sufficient nutrients are consumed. Many anorectics show disturbances of electrolyte balance (e.g. sodium, chloride, and potassium). Potassium deficiency must be immediately corrected since low levels of this electrolyte may induce cardiac arrest (i.e. heart attack).

There are several ways to accomplish re-feeding. The least intrusive method is to compliment the anorectic's diet with nutritional supplements. These supplements are provided in liquid form (e.g. Sustacal) and must be consumed by the patient. When nutritional supplements are refused, a more forceful method is implemented. A feeding tube may be forced through the nasal cavity and into the stomach. The most complex method of forced feeding is to surgically insert a catheter into a major blood vessel. Complete nutrition is provided by infusing a protein solution that includes electrolytes, minerals, glucose, and vitamins.

These methods of re-feeding must be closely monitored since too much food may be detrimental (i.e. gastric problems) to the patient who has just entered hospital. Also, patients may become dependent on these artificial feeding techniques. For this reason, it is advisable to slowly decrease nutritional supplements and increase normal eating. The patient progresses from a daily diet of 1500 calories to as much as 5000 calories a day. A feeding plan for malnourished patients has been described by Dr. Peter Dally and his co-workers.

> *Particularly if a patient is emaciated and has been literally starving herself to death, it is advisable to begin re-feeding with a bland milky diet of about 1500 calories, giving small amounts at 2-hourly intervals. ...The amount of food is gradually increased until, after 10-14 days, the patient is having a diet of between 4000 and 5000 calories a day. ...The emphasis is on carbohydrate: double helpings of potatoes, but not of meat. Snacks between main meals consist of cereal-fortified drinks, with toast, butter and jam. Toast is readily digested, as it has already been partially converted into dextrins* [1, pp. 110-111].

With good progress, a patient may be required to consume hearty meals and snacks. For example, breakfast may consist of two eggs and buttered toast, cereal with milk and sugar, juice, and sweetened tea with milk. Nurses use encouragement and persuasion to ensure that uncooperative patients eat what they are given. Patients may try to deceive the nurses by concealing or vomiting their food. For this reason, accurate measures of weight must be recorded on a daily basis.

Dieticians are used to provide advice on the serious consequences of starvation. They help plan a balanced and nutritious diet for each patient. At first, the patient may be allowed to eat any preferred food as long as the selection is reasonable. Following this period, a more formal diet is designed. Dieticians invite patients to participate in planning a long term diet. Participation in diet planning is used to increase the patient's commitment to maintain weight gains following hospitalization.

Medical Regulation of Anorexia

Patients who are afraid of gaining weight may be given a tranquilizing drug. The medical reason is to relieve anxiety and overcome fear of eating. Anorectics who appear depressed are placed on anti-depressant medication. Treatment with drugs is usually limited to the initial period of hospitalization. As the patient begins to eat, gains weight, and shows an improved attitude to treatment, medication is reduced or stopped. Chlorpromazine, a major tranquilizing drug, has been recommended by many physicians who treat anorexia nervosa. The drug is given when patients appear restless, anxious, and afraid of eating. However, since the early 1970's, the use of this drug for the treatment of anorexia has declined. When it is prescribed, the drug is often administered in three or four daily doses of 20 to 75 mg. each. The overall dosage may be increased to as much as 1000 mg. depending on the patient's tolerance for the drug. Anorectics often have low blood pressure and chlorpromazine may further reduce it. For this reason, blood pressure and dosage are closely monitored.

There are several negative side effects associated with chlorpromazine. Side effects vary from person to person and include sleepiness, dry mouth, blurred vision, jaundice, trembling and shaking, swallowing and protrusion of the tongue, and epileptic seizures. Some of these effects rarely occur and physicians argue that the benefits to a starving patient may sometimes outweigh the risks.

Many anorectic patients show signs of unhappiness and depression. Anti-depressant drugs are sometimes prescribed for this problem. A group of drugs called the 'tricyclics' are used to elevate the patient's mood. These drugs are given in small doses (e.g. 10 mg. of Amitriptyline three times a day) and are sometimes recommended for tension and anxiety reduction on an outpatient basis. When restricted to low dosage, these drugs have few side effects.

In addition to tranquilizing and anti-depressant agents, many other drugs have been used. For example, a common therapy of the 1960's combined chlorpromazine with insulin. Insulin reduces blood sugar and produces sweating, dizziness, and hunger. Anorectics responded poorly to insulin treatment. This is because severe starvation also contributes to elevated insulin levels. Too much insulin is dangerous and a few patients have died from insulin injection. Today, insulin is not used to treat self-starvation.

Attempts at control of anorexia nervosa have included more invasive medical therapies than pharmaceutical treatment. For example, electro-convulsive therapy (ECT) involves passing an electrical current through the brain of the patient. There is controversy about the effectiveness of ECT as a medical procedure. Nonetheless, some doctors use ECT to improve the patient's mood and lift depression. In contrast, Dr. Dally indicates that ECT is rarely given but is used "… not to lift depression or improve the patient's emotional state, but as an urgent life-saving means of overcoming her resistance to eating. Inevitably ECT is seen by the patient as a form of punishment. She is almost certain to have been told beforehand that if she continues not to co-operate ECT will be used" [1, p. 120-121].

Physicians view medical interventions as necessary intrusions for the long-term benefit of the patient. The anorexic individual is often reluctant and rejects medical help. The rejection of life-saving procedures is seen as part of the illness. The patient's right to reject treatment is removed as is common with other mental illnesses. Food is the medicine that is prescribed by the doctor. Many medical therapies for anorexia are designed to make the patient take the prescribed food.

Evaluation of Medical Therapy

When starvation is severe, death is imminent. Hospitalization and medical therapy may be the only way to save the person's life. Nonetheless, there are a variety of treatments that are more or less effective in restoring eating and weight. For example, tube feeding has been found to produce a weekly weight gain of 2.8 pounds. High-calorie diet and bed rest has produced a weekly gain that may be as high as 3.7 pounds. The tranquilizer, chlorpromazine, has some unpleasant side effects but has been reported to produce a weight gain of 4 pounds per week [2, p. 1097]. The physician may choose from these alternatives or may combine several treatments depending on the medical condition of the patient.

Medical research has shown that some treatments are ineffective or dangerous. As previously mentioned, during the 1960's insulin was used to encourage eating. The negative side effects were detected and this substance is no longer recommended for treatment of anorexia. A surgical technique called pre-frontal leucotomy (i.e. brain surgery) was used to treat the obsessive-compulsive symptoms that sometimes accompanied anorexia nervosa. This treatment was discontinued when long-term follow-ups indicated that initial improvements in eating and weight were temporary. Also, Dr. Dally states that depression and suicide are complications resulting from psychosurgery [1].

The treatment of anorexia is often based on clinical judgment and general medical knowledge. To illustrate, anorectics frequently have dangerously low levels of potassium due to vomiting and laxative abuse. This electrolyte must be replenished or cardiac problems will develop. Many medical decisions are based on the experience and intuition of the physician. The doctor who has treated many cases of anorexia may intuitively know how to deal with these patients. While intuition remains an important part of medical practice, it is not a substitute for research.

Chlorpromazine has been recommended to alleviate the anorectic's anxiety about weight gain and eating. This seems reasonable since chlorpromazine does reduce anxiety and anorectics do eat more. However, animals who are made anorectic also increase eating when given chlorpromazine [3]. It is not reasonable to assume that animals eat more because of reduced anxiety about weight gain. A major effect of chlorpromazine is to lower physical activity. Animals and humans *eat more when physical activity decreases* [4]. The research evidence suggests that the intuitive understanding of how this drug works may be incorrect. If this is true, it would be better to directly control physical activity rather than treat anxiety.

Our analysis of activity anorexia includes physiological mechanisms that regulate exercise and appetite. Current medical practices of hospitalization, bed rest, and re-feeding may inadvertently stop the activity-anorexia cycle. However, the medical community continues to treat anorexia as a neurotic disorder, and treatments have not been focused directly on the activity anorexia. We think this is unfortunate since more precise and effective treatments are possible with a change in perspective. Animal and human research suggests that the blocking of neural opiates may be one strategy for medical treatment [5].

2   BEHAVIOR THERAPY AS A TREATMENT METHOD

Another direct therapy for the treatment of anorexia is *behavior therapy*. Therapy is directed at the regulation of food intake by changing the rewards and costs of eating and weight gain. Behavior therapy is based on the experimental analysis of behavior that is sometimes called operant conditioning [6]. The term *operant* is used to describe behavior that *operates* upon the environment to produce consequences. Some consequences of behavior strengthen it. These consequences are called positive and negative reinforcers.

Principles of Behavior

Positive reinforcement involves the presentation of consequences that strengthen behavior. For example, social approval may be given for dieting and the approval increases the tendency to stick to the diet. *Negative reinforcement* occurs when removal of "some state of affairs" strengthens behavior. A person may stay on a diet to stop others from criticizing their weight. Positive and negative reinforcement can combine to strengthen the practice of dieting. Many other so called "voluntary" actions of people are increased by positive and negative reinforcement.

Operant behavior does not always result in continuous reinforcement. Usually, behavior is intermittently reinforced. Many characteristics of human behavior depend on the *schedule of reinforcement* A schedule of reinforcement is a description of how frequently, and on what basis, behavior is reinforced. Reinforcement may occur after a period of time or after a certain number of responses. People are not always reinforced by going to a movie; some movies are boring. Infants are not picked up by their mothers each time they cry. Persons are not immediately reinforced for calling a taxi; it takes time for the cab to arrive. Anorectics only occasionally receive reinforcement for eating small meals and reinforcement is often delayed; it takes time for people to notice weight loss. Generally, the more intermittent and unpredictable the schedule the greater the persistence of behavior. The person who sticks to a task and refuses to quit shows the effects of intermittent reinforcement.

Human behavior is often acquired, maintained, and changed by providing and withholding reinforcement. When a person's behavior no longer results in reinforcement, behavior will eventually weaken. Withdrawal of reinforcement is called *extinction*. The first effects of extinction are emotional outbursts and a momentary increase in response. These effects are short-lived and behavior gradually declines. A person usually obtains soft drinks from a vending machine by putting money in the machine (the operant). When the machine fails to work, people typically become angry (i.e. kick or bang on the machine) and initially put in more money. If the machine continues to malfunction, the person stops using it. Extinction also occurs for social behavior. An individual who repeatedly phones a friend and does not get an answer, eventually stops phoning.

Reinforcement and extinction are often combined. This procedure is called *differential reinforcement*. Although one friend may not answer the phone (extinction) others often do (reinforcement). This differential reinforcement results in a person phoning those friends who are available to talk. Differential reinforcement also accounts for why we talk to a friend about some topics but not others. The friend who is interested in politics but not religion will reinforce discussion of politics and show little interest in religious issues.

Differential reinforcement of conversational topics may explain many of the psychological symptoms of the anorectic. When the anorectic talks about issues involving distorted body image, fear of being fat, perfectionistic standards, and many other topics, the therapist encourages discussion. Topics that are considered less central to the eating problem are not given as much attention. Because of this differential reinforcement, patients often describe themselves, and their problems, in a manner that is consistent with their therapists' views. More importantly, the behavior-therapy perspective suggests that these verbal expressions are not symptoms of anorexia nervosa; they are responses acquired during therapy [7, 8].

The reinforcers that follow behavior are many and varied. Some consequences are social (e.g. other's admiration or scorn) and are provided by other people. Enjoyable activities can also strengthen behavior (e.g. dancing, swimming or eating a good meal). Other reinforcing events range from sensory stimuli such as a musical sound, to physiological reactions like the release of neural opiates. There are many different kinds of reinforcers, and whether or not an event is reinforcing depends on the biology, and learning history, of the individual. One person may be reinforced by the approval of others and another may not care what people say about them. A good steak dinner is a positive reinforcer for some people but not for vegetarians.

Other consequences weaken behavior and are called aversive. *Punishment* occurs when behavior is followed by an aversive event. A child may be spanked for playing on a busy road. The spanking may weaken this behavior. Another way to decrease an operant is to take away positive reinforcers. When a child misbehaves and a favorite television program is turned off, the annoying behavior may decrease. People use punishment because it quickly suppresses troublesome conduct, especially when accompanied by positive reinforcement of preferred behavior. Although punishment frequently occurs in everyday life, it has a variety of negative side effects.

The most significant side effects are emotional. Punishment produces crying, cowering, fear, and aggression. Research has shown that exposing an individual to random punishment can produce severe helplessness and depression [9]. When people are subjected to unfair and unnecessary punishment they learn to give up and accept their fate. Many behavior problems that are labelled neurotic, phobic and depressive may have resulted from indiscriminate use of punishment. Because of these effects, most behavior therapists use positive reinforcement and punishment is used *only as a last resort* when behavior is self-destructive or life-threatening [10].

A life-threatening case of anorexia nervosa was treated with punishment *after all other treatments had failed*. This is the *only* published report of punishment in the literature of behavior therapy and anorexia nervosa. The case involved a 15-year old girl, of average height, who was hospitalized after her weight dropped from 150 to 57 pounds. She stated that she would "die before she would ever be that fat again." Following hospitalization, she was discharged when her weight reached 88 pounds. After months of supportive psychotherapy, use of drugs, rational-emotive therapy, and positive reinforcement of weight gain, she again started losing weight. The report by Dr. Richard Blue suggests this desperate state of affairs.

Figure 6.1
The side effects of punishment. These effects are serious
and punishment should only be used as a last resort
when other treatments have failed.

1. The person who delivers punishment may become an aversive stimulus.

2. The mere presence of the punishing agent suppresses ongoing behavior whether desired or not.

3. People learn behavior that escapes or avoids the punishing agent.

4. Punishment generates emotional behavior (e.g. crying and fear).

5. Punishment may induce aggressive behavior directed at the agent or displaced to other objects or people.

6. The use of punishment increases. The punishing agent is reinforced by the removal of the upsetting conduct and tends to repeat the punishing actions.

7. The level of punishment escalates. Punishment must be increased in frequency and intensity to have the same effect. One result is the physical abuse of children or old people who cannot retaliate.

8. When aversive stimulus is used inconsistently, people may learn to quickly give up and become helpless.

...By mid-January, C's weight had dropped to 78 pounds and the family was frantic. It was decided to continue the psychotherapy and positive reinforcement on an outpatient basis. The change would be the introduction of punishment to change her maladaptive response pattern. A wooden switch was obtained from a branch and set in the parent's bedroom. Each time C. threw up her food or engaged in a temper tantrum, her mother would follow these actions with five painful hits from the switch. During the punishment nothing was said. Eating continued to be followed by 'happy talk.' Utilizing this program (for two months) ... the number of times that C. threw up decreased from a weekly high of 12 to a low of zero. In fact, after 4 weeks of punishment plus positive reinforcement she quit throwing up her food altogether. Her weight increased from 78 pounds to 94 pounds and she stopped all tantrums. Her perfectionistic standards changed from high rigidity to a more accepting level. She

went back to school and ...completed the tenth grade. Therapy was terminated during the summer months. A follow up in September ... showed that C. was doing fine: her weight was 106 pounds. She had become involved with a young man and was participating in extra-curricular activities. A follow up questionnaire sent to her concerning treatment showed that C. thought that punishment had helped more than any of the other treatments. 'It woke me up to what a crazy thing I was doing.' She also explained that everyone's 'understanding' only seemed to make her situation worse. Another follow up (6 months later) indicated C. was making a successful adjustment to both school and family life. At last follow-up her weight had remained at 105 pounds [11, p. 745].

In summarizing this case, Dr. Blue stated that punishment should not be used *until all positive-treatment procedures have been exhausted.*

In addition to changing behavior by positive or negative consequences, behavior therapists often alter those events that immediately precede behavior. The likelihood that a person will engage in a particular act may be affected by cues or signals. These cues are technically called *discriminative stimuli* that are said to "set the occasion" for behavior. Some cues "tell the person" that if I perform this action certain consequences will follow. For example, the presence of parents at the meal may set the occasion for refusing to eat. This occurs because refusing to eat has been reinforced by attention and concern from the parents. Modification of this behavior (refusing to eat) may entail having the mother and father eat with their child without providing noticeable attention or concern. Withdrawal of this social reinforcement changes the "meaning" of parental cues and thereby alters the behavior of the child. The family lunch session, arranged by family therapists (see Chapter 5), uses this kind of behavior modification.

Behavior Therapy and Anorexia Nervosa

Behavior therapy has been used to treat anorexia nervosa since the early nineteen sixties. The behavioral perspective suggests that refusing to eat is learned behavior regulated by reinforcement. Behavior therapists, in the early sixties, argued that rejection of food was maintained by positive reinforcement. They argued that anorectics received attention from others for this behavior [12].

Later research showed that withdrawal of attention for refusing to eat sometimes failed to change anorectic behavior [13]. Because of these findings, researchers suggested that refusing to eat was also maintained by negative reinforcement. The basic idea is that anorectics have been criticized for their weight and eating habits. This criticism causes fear of being fat and refusing to eat is reinforced by removal of this fear.

Behavior therapists sometimes recommend a procedure called systematic desensitization to eliminate intense fear. The anorectic is taught to relax and is presented with a series of images that approximates the feared state. Elimination of the fear presumably removes the consequences (i.e. the aversive emotional state) that maintain anorexic behavior. Improvement of weight has been reported in three cases of anorexia nervosa that were treated with systematic desensitization. [14, 15, 16] In one of these reports, Drs. Schnurer and Rubin caution that this treatment alone may only be effective for a sub-group of anorectic patients. Although systematic desensitization has been effective in treating phobic reactions (i.e. an intense fear of some object or event), it has seldom been used to treat anorexia nervosa.

Modification of anorectics' poor eating habits and low weight most often occurs in a hospital setting. Management of eating and weight is a first priority for people with severe starvation. Behavior therapy has been viewed as an effective technique for accomplishing this objective.

Treatment begins by measuring the anorectic's weight. Patients are usually weighed once a day for several days. Treatment effectiveness can be measured against this weight baseline. The anorectic may be required to stay in bed and all unnecessary objects (e.g. television, magazines, etc.) are removed from the room. Following this, a combination of positive and negative reinforcement procedures is implemented.

Positive reinforcement involves increased social activity and visiting privileges for weight gain. Negative reinforcement occurs when the anorectic increases eating and weight in order to get out of bed, go out of the room, and leave the hospital. A response prevention procedure may be used to stop patients from vomiting. The anorectic may be required to sit in a day room with a hospital attendant for an hour or so after each meal. This stops the patient from going to a washroom to throw-up.

Each patient is given an individualized treatment program. The program stipulates the required daily or weekly increase in weight and the privileges that can be earned. When target weights are not attained, privileges are removed. Behavioral contracts are often negotiated with the patient. These contracts detail the therapist's requirements for eating and weight gain and the patient's rewards for meeting the objectives. The anorectic usually has a say in setting the objectives and rewards. Perhaps the most important source of reinforcement in the contract is "getting off the program" and out of the hospital [17].

The general objectives of behavior therapy for treatment of anorexia nervosa were outlined by Dr. Halmi of Cornell University.

> ... There are four general treatment goals for an anorexic patient:
>
> 1. To have the patient return to a normal medical condition; this means that the patient must gain weight to a normal level and then maintain it, and also must stop purging behavior.
>
> 2. To have the patient resume normal eating patterns.
>
> 3. To assess and treat relevant psychological issues.
>
> 4. To counsel the anorectic's family appropriately, with emphasis on the family's effect on maintaining the anorexic state of the patient, and to assist the family in developing methods to promote the normal functioning of the patient. Behavior management is especially useful for the first two goals, but to some degree it can also be used to accomplish the third and fourth goals [18, p. 152].

When weight gains are sufficient, eating patterns are stabilized, and a positive approach to life is observed, the anorectic is allowed to leave the hospital. There is growing recognition that patients will resume disturbed eating patterns unless therapy is continued. From the behavior-therapy perspective, relapse is likely if the person is returned to the same environment (i.e. family and friends) that produced the anorexia.

Behavior therapist's are currently recommending an integrated program of insight or cognitive psychotherapy, family therapy and behavior management for weight. A behavioral contract (see above) is negotiated or imposed by the behavior therapist. Essentially, the patient is required to maintain weight and normal eating patterns in order to obtain privileges. School personnel and family members may be asked to monitor the anorectic's behavior and enforce the terms of the contract. Dr. Halmi states that "… for a high-school student who has been physically active, it is often effective to have her weighed by the school nurse every Monday and, on the Mondays that she is below her normal weight, to forbid her to participate in any school sports or in gym classes for that week "[18, p. 154]. An anorectic child may enjoy family outings, television programs, talking on the telephone, and other activities. Parents agree to use these activities as rewards for positive weight gain.

One way to involve the family is to include them as part of a behavioral contract. Such contracts insure that family members become active participants in the treatment process. However, behavioral contracts are directed at the anorectic's behavior rather than family interaction patterns. We have noted the significant impact that the families have in transmitting the cultural values of fitness to children. Direct behavioral intervention to modify the socialization practices of family members may be a more important extension of behavior therapy. From our perspective, behavior therapists are narrowly focused on weight gain and have not explored this possibility.

Evaluation of Behavior Therapy

There are approximately 24 clinical studies of the effectiveness of behavior therapy. This is a relatively large number of studies when compared with other outcome research (i.e. family therapy and psychotherapy). Behavior therapists state objective goals for treatment success (i.e. weight gain) and this provides a clear basis for evaluation. Generally, the goals are to re-establish normal body weight and train appropriate eating habits.

Most behavioral studies concentrate on measures of weight and weight gain. These behavioral objectives have been criticized as limited by other professionals [19]. The major objection has been that weight gain is only a reflection of the underlying personality disorder. Long term success requires a change in personality. Behavior therapists argue that severe weight loss creates many of the so-called personality problems. Thus, weight gain eliminates these other problems.

In our opinion, weight gain is central to any successful treatment. Also, it is impossible to evaluate behavior therapy without considering weight gain since this is the common measure used in these studies. There are two aspects of weight recovery that must be considered. First, the success of behavior therapy in restoring weight for hospitalized patients; and second, the long term maintenance of weight gains.

In our review of treatment studies, we identified 78 patients who received some form of hospital-based behavior therapy. We used studies between 1965 and 1980 and judged the amount of weight gain as successful, partially successful, or a failure. For example, a patient who went from 62 to 86 pounds was classified as a success [2]. One study reported that a woman weighed 47 pounds when hospitalized and she was 64 pounds when discharged [20]. We called this a partial success since her weight was still very low. If the patient gained little or no weight this was a treatment failure [21]. Based on this classification, 70 patients were successfully treated (90%), seven were partial successes, and only one case was a failure. These results strongly suggest that anorectics will benefit from behavior therapy in the hospital.

The effects of behavior therapy on long-term maintenance of weight gain is also important. When follow-up information was available, we classified patients as full successes, partial successes, and failures. Full success was based on the therapy maintaining weight gains without indications of poor social adjustment. Social adjustment refers to reports by patients about school or job satisfaction, relationships with friends and family, and so on. Partial success was defined as maintaining weight gains but social adjustment was not good. Failures were cases where the person was re-admitted to the hospital for any reason related to anorexia nervosa. Sixty-two patients were assessed 2 or more months after being discharged from the hospital. Of these, 44 were successfully treated (71%), twelve were partial successes, and six were treatment failures. Because behavior therapists do not emphasize social adjustment as a long term objective, we re-classified these patients only on the basis of weight maintenance. This resulted in 56 successful treatments (90%) and six failures. These results indicate that behavior therapy is an effective treatment for maintaining weight gains since this therapy well exceeds the 66 percent spontaneous recovery rate. In terms of social adjustment, which most professionals consider important, behavior therapy is not as effective.

The behavioral understanding of anorexia nervosa suggests that the disorder is acquired and maintained by social reinforcement. From our perspective, reinforcement from family and peers encourages physical exercise and dieting. However, there are other reinforcement processes that are activated when exercise and dieting are combined. The reinforcers are not social in this case; rather reinforcement is based on physiological effects within the person. Our research suggests that exercise produces brain opiates (i.e. runner's high). Release of neural opiates reinforces exercise. Under certain conditions opiates suppress appetite and this contributes to further increases in physical activity. Physiological events, therefore, work to maintain activity-based anorexia [22, 23].

3 WHERE TO FIND HELP

A self-help approach to anorexia is also available that is based on people solving their problems together. The Anorexic Aid Society was the first self help organization for eating disorders and was formed in Great Britain in 1974. This development in treatment is currently gaining momentum in the United States and Canada. The United States based Bulimia Anorexia Self Help (BASH), a non-profit organization, is particularly active. This group publishes a monthly magazine, sets up conferences, and operates a crisis telephone line.

ANOREXIA NERVOSA

1. **Bulimia Anorexia Self Help, Inc. (BASH)**
    6125 Clayton Ave., Suite 215,
    St. Louis, MO. 63139, U.S.A.
    [Crisis hot line, 24 hours daily, 1-800-762-3334]

2. **National Anorexic Aid Society**
    PO. Box 29461,
    Columbus, OH. 43229
    U.S.A.

3. **Anorexia Nervosa and Bulimia Foundation of Canada**
    P.O. Box 3074,
    Winnipeg, Manitoba,
    R3C 4E5, Canada.
    (204) 783 6786

4. **Bulimia Anorexia Nervosa Association**
    University of Windsor,
    Faculty of Human Kinetics
    401 Sunset Ave.,
    Windsor, Ontario
    N9B 3P4, Canada

5. **Anorexic Aid, National Headquarters**
    The Priory Center,
    11 Priory Rd.,
    High Wycombe Bucks, HP13 6SL
    England.

6. **Anorexic Family Aid**
    National Information Center,
    Sackville Place,
    44 Magdalen St.,
    Norwich, Norfolk, NR3 1JU
    England.

7. **Society for the Advancement of Research into Anorexia**
    Stanhope, New Pound
    Wisborough Green,
    Billingshurst, West Sussex, RH14 OEJ
    England.

DEPRESSION AND SUICIDE

8. **Rescue Inc.**
    Rm. 25, Boston Fire Headquarters
    115 Southampton St.
    Boston, MA. 02118, USA
    617-426-6600

9. **International Association for Suicide Prevention**
    Suicide Prevention Ctr.
    1041 S. Menlo Ave.
    Los Angles, CA. 90006, USA
    213-381-5111

10. **National Save-A-Life League**
    815 2nd Ave., Suite 409
    New York, NY. 10017, USA
    212-736-6191

SELECTING A THERAPIST

11. **Psychiatric Service Section**
    American Hospital Assoc.
    840 N. Lake Shore Dr.
    Chicago, IL. 60611, USA

12. **Mental Health Help Line**
    789 West End Ave.
    New York, NY. 10024, USA
    212-663-4372

13. **Psychotherapy Selection Service**
    3 East 80th Street
    New York, NY. 10021, USA
    212-861-6381

REFERENCES

Although many of these references may be of interest, we have indicated (with an asterisk*) those that are written for the non-specialist reader.

1. *Dally, P., Gomez, J. and Isaacs, A. J. (1979). *Anorexia Nervosa.* London: William Heinemann Medical Books Ltd..

2. Blinder, B. J., Freeman, D. M. A. and Stunkard, A. J. (1970). Behavior therapy of anorexia nervosa: effectiveness of activity as a reinforcer of weight gain. *American Journal of Psychiatry,* 126, 1093-1098.

3. Routtenberg, A. and Kuznesof, A. W. (1967). "Self-starvation" of rats living in activity wheels on a restricted feeding schedule. *Journal of Comparative and Physiological Psychology,* 64, 414-421.

4. Stern, J. S. (1984). Is obesity a disease of inactivity? In A. J. Stunkard and E. Stellar (Eds.), *Eating and Its disorders.* New York: Raven Press.

5. Kaye, W. H., Picker, D. M., Naber, D. and Ebert, M. H. (1982). Cerebrospinal fluid opioid activity in anorexia nervosa. *American Journal of Psychiatry,* 139, 643-645.

6. *Skinner, B. F. (1953). *Science and human behavior.* New York: MacMillan.

7. Azrin, N. H., Holz, W., Ulrich, R. E. and Goldiamond, I. (1961). The control of the content of conversation through reinforcement. *Journal of the Experimental Analysis of Behavior,* 4, 25-30.

8. Lindsley, O. R. (1969). Direct behavioral analysis of psychotherapy sessions by conjugately programmed closed-circuit television. *Psychotherapy: theory, research and practice,* 6, 71-81.

9. Seligman, M. E. P., Maier, S. F. and Solomon, R. L. (1969). Pavlovian fear conditioning and learned helplessness. In R. Church and B. Campbell (Eds.), *Aversive conditioning and learning.* New York: Appleton-Century-Crofts.

10. Repp, A. C. and Nirbhay, N. S. (in press). *Aversive and non-aversive treatment: The great debate in developmental disabilities.* Sycamore, Illinois: Sycamore Press.

11. Blue, R. (1979). Use of punishment in treatment of anorexia nervosa. *Psychological Reports,* 44, 743-746.

12. Allyon, T., Haughton, E. and Osmond, H. O. (1964). Chronic anorexia: a behavior problem. *Canadian Psychiatric Association Journal,* 9, 147-154.

13. Leitenberg, H., Agras, W. S. and Thomson, L. E. (1968). A sequential analysis of the effect of selective positive reinforcement in modifying anorexia nervosa. *Behavior Research and Therapy,* 6, 211-218.

14. Lang, P. J. (1965). Behavior therapy with a case of nervous anorexia. In L. P. Ullman and L. Krasner (Eds.), *Case studies in behavior modification.* New York: Holt, Rinehart and Winston.

15. Hallsteen, E. A. (1965). Adolescent anorexia nervosa treated by desensitization. *Behavior Research and Therapy,* 3, 87-91.

16. Schnurer, A. T., Rubin, R. R. and Roy, A. (1973). Desensitization of anorexia nervosa seen as a weight phobia. *Journal of Behavior Therapy and Experimental Psychiatry,* 4, 149-153.

17. Agras, W. S., Barlow, D. H., Chapin, H. N., Abel, G. G. and Leitenberg, H. (1974). Behavior modification of anorexia nervosa. *Archives of General Psychiatry,* 30, 279-286.

18. Halmi, K. A. (1985). Behavioral management for anorexia nervosa. In D. M. Garner and P. E. Garfinkel (Eds.), *Handbook of psychotherapy for anorexia nervosa and bulimia*. New York: The Guilford Press.

19. Kellerman, J. (1977). Anorexia nervosa: the efficacy of behavior therapy. *Journal of Behavior Therapy and Experimental Psychiatry, 8*, 387-390.

20. Bachrach, A. J., Erwin, W. J. and Mohr, J. P. (1965). The control of eating behavior in an anorexic by operant conditioning techniques. In L. Ullman and L. Krasner (Eds.), *Case studies in behavior modification*. New York: Holt, Rinehart and Winston.

21. Bhanji S. and Thompson, J. (1974). Operant conditioning in the treatment of anorexia nervosa: A review and retrospective study of 11 cases. *British Journal of Psychiatry, 124*, 166-172.

22. Pierce, W. D., Epling, W. F. and Boer, D. P.(1986). Deprivation and satiation: the interrelations between food and wheel running. *Journal of the Experimental Analysis of Behavior, 46*, 199-210.

23. Epling, W. F. and Pierce, W. D. (1988). Activity-based anorexia: A biobehavioral perspective. *International Journal of Eating Disorders, 7*, 475-485.

PART II

Activity Anorexia

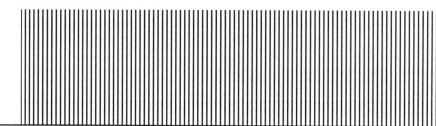

The main topics are:

- **ACTIVITY ANOREXIA IN ANIMALS**
- **ACTIVITY ANOREXIA IN HUMANS**

Summary

- Activity anorexia is more than a sub-set of anorexia nervosa. People in sports, athletics, and fitness may have eating problems due to the combined effects of food restriction and excessive training.

- Animals develop activity anorexia when food restriction generates excessive wheel-running that feeds back on food intake (Multiplier Effect).

- Activity anorexia is affected by meal schedule, the opportunity for physical activity, and adaptation to restricted feeding and change in living conditions.

- Ballet dancers and athletes develop anorexia in accord with the biobehavioral model based on animal studies.

- Diagnosed anorectics who are hyperactive and athletes who have eating problems are locked into the activity-anorexia cycle.

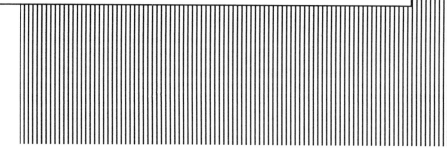

CHAPTER

Behavioral Foundations of Activity Anorexia

7

Activity anorexia is a term that describes the loss of appetite that occurs when physical activity interferes with eating. The person who contacts the activity-anorexia cycle appears to willfully self-starve. However, this form of self-starvation is not intentional. People do not voluntarily initiate the activity-anorexia cycle and they cannot easily stop it.

Motivational conditions are generated when food restriction and exercise occur together. The first effect of combining dieting and exercise is that physical activity accelerates to excessive levels. As exercise increases, the value of food declines and people eat less. Paradoxically, as food intake decreases (i.e. deprivation) the motivation to exercise increases. The person is, therefore, trapped by a feedback cycle of increasing physical activity and decreasing food consumption. The result of this motivational process is starvation and, in some cases, death.

1 ACTIVITY ANOREXIA IN ANIMALS

Activity anorexia occurs in animals. We have produced this kind of anorexia in several strains of rats and mice [1]. The laboratory rat is an ideal subject for behavioral research on eating disorders. Rats are known to eat up to 20 percent of the world's annual food supply. Like humans, rats are omnivores; they eat both plants and meat. Rats have an excellent sense of taste and in the wild are very sensitive to different kinds of food. This allows them to naturally choose a balanced food supply. In our laboratory, they are given a healthy, well-balanced diet of dried food and water is always available. When allowed

111

to eat freely, these animals typically have between 10 to 15 small meals each day. Total food intake is around 25 grams a day. Importantly, it is very difficult to make a rat stop eating.

Laboratory rats live two to three years and are sexually mature adolescents at about 50 days. Since human anorexia is most commonly reported in adolescent females, we often use young rats in our experiments. Activity anorexia occurs in both male and female animals, but occurs more rapidly in females. This is because females weigh less than male animals. This lower weight means that females reach the point of starvation more quickly. Our preference is to investigate activity anorexia with young male animals. Female rats have frequent estrus cycles and are more active during the cycle. This increase in activity presents a problem for activity-anorexia experiments. The increase in activity during estrus cannot be distinguished from activity due to food restriction.

Adolescent-male rats of about 50 days weigh approximately 270 grams; they are growing and increasing in weight. When fully grown, these animals weigh about 550 grams or a little over one pound. Young rats are typically more active than older ones. This

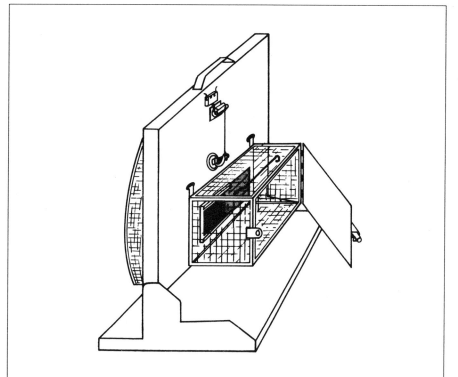

Figure 7.1 A drawing of a standard 1.1 meter Wahmann activity wheel with an attached side cage. A sliding door prevents or permits the animal to move between the cage and wheel.

difference in baseline weight and activity results in a higher incidence of activity anorexia in younger animals. Activity anorexia can be induced in older animals but not as frequently and it takes longer to develop.

In our laboratory, about 90 percent of the adolescent animals become anorexic within 8 days when exposed to the experimental procedures. When animals are 6 months old (and weight about 450 grams), around 70 percent can be made anorexic within 20 days. The original experiments demonstrated that animals will die of starvation [2]. For ethical reasons, we stop the experiment when animals reach approximately 70 percent of normal weight. This is slightly below the weight criteria used to define human anorexia [3].

The experimental procedures to induce activity anorexia have been developed over many years. Our experiments are based on procedures described in the 1960's by Drs. Routtenberg and Kuznesof [2, 4]. In our laboratory, adolescent rats are placed in a cage that is attached to a running wheel [5]. At this point, the rats are separately placed in the side-cage with the door to their wheel closed. Food is freely available in the cage and each animal can eat as much as it wants. The amount eaten is measured each day for five days. Also,

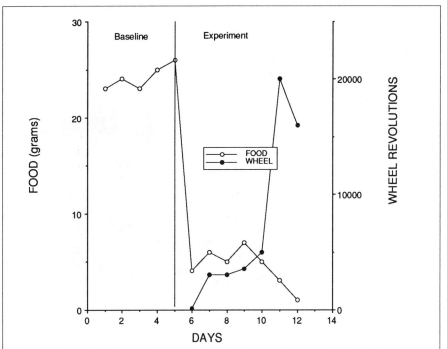

Figure 7.2   Graph of an experimental rat's food intake and wheel running. During the baseline, food intake is about 25 grams a day. At the dark line, the experimenter restricted food to one 90-minute meal and allowed the animal to run on the wheel. At day nine, wheel running starts to accelerate and food intake declines.

animals are weighed on a daily basis. The food and weight measures provide baseline or reference points for the experiment.

Half of the animals are randomly assigned to the control group and the others are in the experimental condition. The experimental procedures are designed to combine food restriction and voluntary activity. Experimental and control animals are now restricted to a single 90-minute daily feeding and during this time animals can eat as much as they want. The doors to the wheels are opened and experimental animals are allowed to run. Control animals can also enter the wheels but the wheels will not turn — they are locked.

Several procedural points are noteworthy. The animals are given access to the wheels *except* during the 90-minute feeding period. In this way, eating does not compete with running. When wheels are available (22.5 hours), there are no requirements for animals to run. They can stay in their cages, enter the wheels to rest, walk on the wheels, or do anything they want. Finally, it is important to note that the 90-minute feeding is sufficient for these animals. Control animals adapt to the feeding schedule within 7 days and easily live their lives on the daily 90-minute feeding.

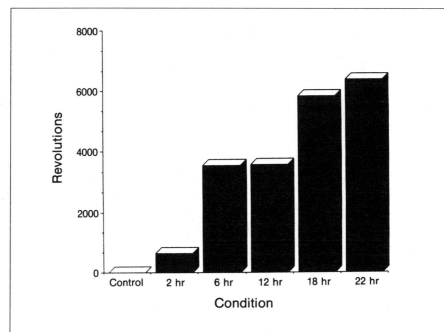

Figure 7.3 Time of access to a free-turning wheel and average number of wheel revolutions each day. Rats were given a single 90-minute meal each day and the opportunity to run was varied. The greater the time of access to the wheel the more the animals ran, although they were not required to do so.

The initial effect of placing experimental animals on one meal a day is a large drop in food consumption. This is not surprising since the animals have not experienced rapid changes in food supply and are not adapted to the new feeding schedule. When food restriction and running occur together (experimental group), a number of interesting effects result. Experimental animals begin to run on the wheels. They increase running from day to day even though there is no requirement to do so. This is an unusual response by these animals since energy expenditure is increasing at a time when food intake is limited. Within a week, running increases from several hundred revolutions a day to as many as 20,000 revolutions. This involves a massive amount of energy expenditure since an animal that weighs less than a pound is running the equivalent of 12 miles a day.

While running is accelerating to excessive levels, there is an even more surprising effect — *animals stop eating*. At first the rats try to adjust to the new feeding schedule. However, the intense running begins to interfere with eating. Food intake is suppressed and eventually begins to decline. If this process of increasing activity and declining food intake is allowed to continue, animals will stop eating. Since eating is suppressed and running is intense, body weight drops sharply and animals die of apparent self-starvation.

Self-starvation does not occur in the control animals. These animals have the same food schedule and living conditions but they cannot run. Therefore, running or physical activity is an important factor for the development of anorexia. We have conducted other experiments with additional control groups. For example, in one control group animals can run but have food all the time. These animals do not run excessively and they eat normally. Overall, our experiments demonstrate that the critical condition for activity anorexia is the simultaneous occurrence of dietary restriction and excessive physical activity. Neither the 90-minute feeding or physical activity alone will lead to anorexia. The combination of the two conditions, however, is lethal [6].

Activity and Anorexia

The process of activity anorexia occurs when physical activity is combined with conditions of dietary restriction. When food is restricted, the amount of activity will determine the chances of an animal becoming anorexic. This is in fact what happened when we controlled the amount of time that animals could run on their wheels [7].

In this study, adolescent male rats were randomly assigned to one of five activity conditions. The amount of time that animals could run on the wheels was 2, 6, 12, 18, or 22 hours a day. The only difference between the groups was the opportunity to run. As in the previous experiments, rats were freely fed and then changed to one 90-minute daily feeding.

The opportunity to run influenced the amount of activity of the animals. Generally, the more time the animals had to run the higher their daily activity. Other results showed that food intake was affected by the amount of running. As amount of running increased, food intake decreased. We were able to classify each animal on a continuum of anorexia.

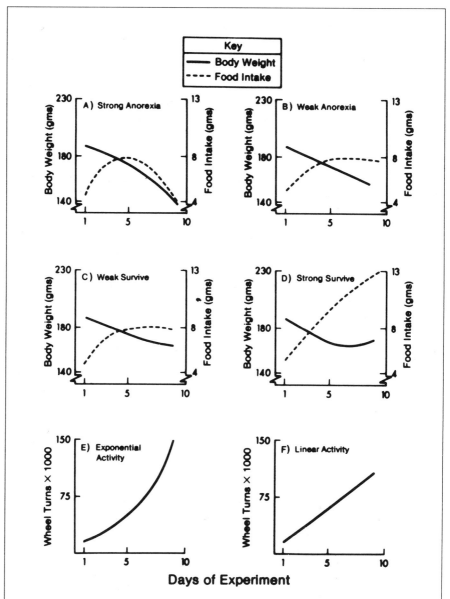

Figure 7.4   Idealized curves for body weight and food intake that allowed for the classification of two anorexic and two survival effects. Notice that the strong-anorexic effect (A) is characterized by rapidly declining food intake and body weight. This effect always occurs when physical activity exponentially increases (E). Linear activity (F) may lead to weak anorexia (B) or weak survival (C). Those animals that do not run always show the strong-survival effect (D).

Strongly-anorexic animals showed clear suppression of food intake and sharply declining body weight. When animals were given 18 hours or more to run, 78 percent became strongly anorexic. Only 14 percent of the animals with 12 hours or less opportunity to run were strongly anorexic. All cases of strong anorexia were accompanied by a specific type of activity curve.

The activity curve is a graph of the number of wheel turns that animals made each day. This curve rapidly accelerates upward on a daily basis for anorexic animals. In other words, the animals are geometrically increasing daily activity. This change in daily *rate* of activity is important for an understanding of activity anorexia. If activity slowly increases (i.e. linear) or remains the same from day to day, anorexia is much less likely. The amount of time an animal ran determined the likelihood of an accelerated activity curve; the change in daily activity then determined the occurrence of anorexia.

One implication is that people who combine dieting with *rapidly increasing* physical activity are likely to become anorexic. The athlete who substantially increases training or the sedentary person who begins a fitness program may be at risk if they are also dieting. High intensity exercise has been shown to reduce food consumption in both animals and humans (see Chapter 8). Under conditions of food deprivation, such high intensity exercise may induce anorexia.

Adaptation Effects

In a 1962 report, Drs. Spear and Hill commented on the excessive loss of weight by rats living in activity wheels [8] ... This observation was the basis for a series of experiments by Drs. Routtenberg and Kuznesof on self-starvation in laboratory rats. These researchers established that self-starvation was a reliable effect and showed that adaptation to the food schedule and living environment played a role in the self-starvation process [2, 4] ... Our activity-anorexia procedures (see above) were based on these early experiments. Rats were given free access to running wheels and were fed 1 hour each day. Animals ran more and more, ate less, and died. Those animals who were fed on the same food schedule but could not run increased eating and survived.

Once the basic effect was established, the researchers became interested in conditions that influenced self-starvation. Further experiments showed that the change in feeding schedule (free food to 1-hour meal) contributed to starvation effects. Routtenberg called this factor "deprivation stress." In order to reduce this stress, animals were given experience with the 1-hour feeding schedule before being placed in running wheels. This "stress inoculation" resulted in 3 out of 4 animals surviving [4].

Although experience with the restricted feeding schedule is important, we do not agree with Routtenberg's concept of deprivation stress. Rather than infer "stress" caused by deprivation, we prefer to discuss how animals adapt to food restriction. The point is that adjusting to the feeding schedule is more descriptive of what animals actually do. Stress is not directly measured and is only inferred from the food-restriction procedures.

In our laboratory, adaptation to the feeding schedule allows animals to regulate their eating. When eating adjusts, body weight stabilizes and this reduces wheel running. The reason that starvation is reduced is that adaptation results in less food restriction. Anorexia only occurs when food restriction is sufficient to induce excessive wheel running. Adaptation to the feeding schedule interferes with one of the necessary conditions for self-starvation (i.e. food restriction).

Adaptation to the running wheel was also suggested as a way to reduce self-starvation. Routtenberg argued that "novelty stress" occurred when animals were abruptly moved from the home colony to running wheels. This sudden change of environment was expected to disrupt eating. In fact, this was the case. Food intake was lower when animals were rapidly shifted to running wheels rather than slowly adapted. Contrary to expectations, however, the number of animals that self-starved was not affected by novelty stress.

In Routtenberg's critical experiment, half of the animals were initially adapted to running wheels and the other half were not. Animals in the adapted condition were allowed to run for 3 hours a day for two weeks. Other animals were not given this experience. Adapted and non-adapted animals were then placed on the 1-hour feeding schedule (i.e. food restricted). Some of the animals in each adaptation group were allowed to run while others were not. Adaptation to the running wheels did not affect the number of animals that starved. The majority of wheel-running animals starved in both the adapted and non-adapted conditions. Thus, adaptation to wheels had no effect on incidence of anorexia. Also, all animals without wheels survived. Physical activity rather than novelty stress was the important factor for self-starvation.

Abrupt changes in living conditions disrupt eating but do not determine self-starvation. If novelty stress contributes to anorexia, it does so indirectly. Our interpretation is that novelty stress may reduce food intake. Lower intake augments the food restriction imposed by the 1-hour feeding schedule. Food restriction lowers body weight and increases physical activity. Higher activity further reduces food intake. Thus, physical activity and food restriction are the major determinants of anorexia.

Meal Frequency

Previously, we noted that free-feeding rats eat between 10 and 15 small meals a day. Total eating time is about 1 to 2 hours but meals are distributed throughout the day. This is the same amount of eating time (1 to 2 hours) provided in the activity-anorexia experiments. The major difference is that in the experiments eating is confined to a specific period of time imposed by the experimenter. Since rats eat in bouts, a single 1-hour meal creates a problem. The animals may continue to eat in bouts of 1 to 3 grams of food separated in time. However, since the imposed feeding schedule requires that food be removed after an hour the animals can only engage in two of three bouts of eating before food is removed. This means that total food intake may be severely depressed, especially when animals are rapidly shifted (as opposed to gradually introduced) to the 1-hour feeding schedule.

Food restriction therefore arises, in part, from the fact that animals eat infrequently during the 1-hour meal period. If total eating time remained the same (i.e. 60 minutes) but the number of meal periods increased (e.g. from one 1-hour period to four 15-minute periods), less food restriction may occur. For example, an animal may eat three times during a single 1-hour meal. The same animal may eat twice if the meal period is 15 minutes. When four 15-minute meal periods are scheduled, the total time is the same as the 1-hour feeding, but the number of eating bouts is 8 rather than three. Assuming the animals eat 3 grams of food each bout, four 15-minute meals yields a total intake of 24 grams while a 1-hour meal only yields 9 grams. This analysis suggests that increasing the number of meal periods may alleviate the food restriction that is critical to self-starvation.

An important experiment by Drs. Kanarek and Collier investigated the effects of meal frequency on self-starvation [9]. In this experiment, four groups of rats were exposed to the activity-anorexia procedures. Animals in these groups were placed in wheels (active conditions) and the number of meal periods was varied. One group received the usual 1-hour feeding; a second group was fed two 30-minute meals; a third received four 15-minute meals and the fourth group had continuous access to food. Another four groups of rats received the same feeding schedules but did not have wheels (inactive conditions).

Regardless of activity, animals ate least on the 1-hour feeding. Two 30-minute meals produced greater food intake than a 1-hour meal but not as much as four 15-minute feedings. Generally, lower food intake occurred for animals that had activity wheels. Food intake was reduced most when activity combined with the 1-hour feeding schedule. This "multiplier effect" (activity X feeding schedule) is critical for activity anorexia.

Feeding schedule determined the amount of wheel running. The more frequent the meal periods the less the animals ran. Accelerated and excessive running characterized the group that was fed 1 hour a day. This finding is in accord with other studies of self-starvation and activity anorexia. Two 30-minute feedings produced a gradual, linear increase in running. We have found that a low daily increase in running can combine with food restriction to produce anorexia but many animals survive [7]. The group with four 15-minute meal periods did not run more than free-feeding animals and did not significantly increase daily activity.

Body weight was also affected by meal frequency and activity. Active animals lost more weight than inactive ones. Also, as the number of meal periods decreased (holding total eating time constant at 1 hour) so did the weight of the animals. The most dramatic decrease in weight occurred when animals were fed for one hour and allowed to run. Our interpretation of this result is that meal frequency determines amount eaten and activity level. Activity further suppresses eating. Thus, meal frequency combines with activity to affect body weight. As Drs. Kanarek and Collier have recognized, body weight and running are correlated. Body weight loss may therefore contribute to an increase in running when food is restricted.

There was no report of the number of anorexias that occurred under each feeding schedule. The researchers stated that one of five animals died in the group that had wheels and was fed a single 1-hour meal. Another animal in this group appeared close to death and at this point the experiment was terminated. All inactive animals were gaining weight at the end of the experiment. This was also the case for the active animals that were freely fed or given four 15-minute meals. The animals that received two 30-minute feedings and had activity wheels are difficult to assess. Their weights were low and stable but activity was increasing when the experiment was stopped.

In summary, the research on meal schedules shows that scheduling meal periods affects the level of physical activity. This effect of meal schedule occurs even when total eating time remains the same. In humans, social obligations, work requirements, and so on may alter meal patterns. This change in food schedule may affect the chances that people will become anorexic.

Modification of Activity Anorexia

The research by Kanarek and Collier focused on the development of self-starvation. We have been interested in the modification of activity anorexia. In our laboratory two students, Holly Day and Tammi Kwan, investigated the effects of changing the feeding schedule and stopping activity when animals were strongly anorexic. In these experiments rats were placed on a single 90-minute feeding and allowed to run on activity wheels. When animals reached 75 percent of their free-feeding weight, two modification procedures were started. Some animals continued to be fed once a day but their wheels were locked (i.e. activity was stopped). Other animals could continue to run but they were given free access to food (i.e. the feeding schedule was changed). The animals who were returned to free feeding *immediately* stopped running, started eating, and survived. Wheel running stopped even though body weight had not increased. Excessive activity is induced by the restricted feeding schedule and reinstatement of food supply stops it. When the animal stops running, the activity-anorexia cycle is disrupted and food intake recovers.

When animals were continued on the 90-minute feeding schedule but activity was prevented, they continued to eat less and lose weight. Apparently, animals cannot adjust to the restricted-feeding schedule when starvation is severe. Control animals given the same 90-minute feeding, but not starving, quickly adjust to the schedule.

In other experiments, we have found that starvation occurs more quickly when animals are on food restriction and activity is allowed to continue . This is because excessive running interacts with the feeding schedule to further suppress food intake. Prevention of physical activity at less severe levels of starvation reduces the incidence of anorexia — but the same procedure is not effective when starvation is pronounced [7].

Implications of Animal Experiments

The animal experiments are based on the assumption that the underlying process of anorexia can be identified, described, and generalized. For this reason, activity anorexia in animals is a biobehavioral model of human anorexia that is usually classified as anorexia nervosa. The diagnostic label, anorexia nervosa, is assigned when there is no apparent rational cause for refusing to eat. In contrast, political prisoners have starved themselves to death to draw attention to their objectives. Since the reasons for starvation are clear, these individuals are not labelled neurotic. When the reasons for starvation are not clear, people cannot understand why the person is refusing to eat. The person is therefore diagnosed as neurotic when the causes of unusual behavior are inconspicuous. Animal experiments identify the causal process and make anorexia understandable.

The animal model of activity anorexia shows how physical activity and food restriction combine to produce starvation. There is no need to infer that starving rats are neurotic. The rat is simply responding to the environmental arrangements of the experiment. The animal model helps to identify critical features that establish, maintain, and eliminate anorexia. For example, since rats do not have the mental capabilities of humans, anorexia cannot be attributed to complex distortions in thought. Distorted thinking may accompany anorexia in humans, but the animal model suggests that such distortions are not fundamental reasons for starvation.

In our view, activity anorexia is one functional category or type of anorexia [10]. Currently, all cases of so called willful self-starvation are given the diagnostic label of anorexia nervosa. There may be several distinct forms of anorexia with different determinants. To illustrate, Drs. Mrosovsky and Sherry have described animal anorexias in several species that occur when biologically significant activities (e.g. defense of territory, care of young, times of sexual reproduction, etc.) interfere with obtaining and eating food [11]. While these natural anorexias may not extend to humans, there may be other types that do. At the very least, psychiatrists and psychologists should consider the possibility that human self-starvation is not a single diagnostic category (i.e. anorexia nervosa).

The most prominent feature of self-starvation in animals is excessive physical activity. For this reason, we use the descriptive term "activity anorexia" as a convenient label. The problem is that the anorexia process is more complicated than the term implies. Activity must combine with food schedules that cause suppression of eating. It is the interaction or *multiplier effect* that is critical for activity anorexia. A change in food schedule (i.e. frequency and duration of meals) may result in lower food intake and body weight. Activity increases as food intake decreases. As this occurs, physical activity accelerates and this prevents animals from adjusting to the food schedule.

Activity anorexia in animals is usually generated by imposing a restricted feeding schedule. Following this change in food schedule, the animals are given the opportunity to run. Anorexia may also be induced by changes in physical activity. There is evidence that physical activity can independently suppress food intake in free-feeding animals (see Chapter 8). The greater the intensity and duration of exercise the greater the suppression of food intake. Physical activity also changes the pattern and number of meals eaten each day [12]. Thus, physical activity directly contributes to anorexia by suppressing food intake and altering food schedules.

2 ACTIVITY ANOREXIA IN HUMANS

Hyperactivity and excessive physical exercise are a common features of anorexia nervosa (see Chapter 4). The presence of excessive physical activity strongly suggests that many cases of anorexia nervosa are, in fact, instances of activity anorexia. In such cases, hyperactivity is not a secondary symptom. Physical activity is the major determinant of this kind of self-starvation.

When starvation is extreme, physical activity usually becomes less excessive because the individual is too sick to continue. This could make it difficult to distinguish between activity anorexia and other forms of self-starvation. Only a detailed case history focused on the person's involvement with sports, exercise, and physical activity (e.g. walking long distances) can distinguish activity anorexia from other types of anorexia.

At the present time, anorexia nervosa is the only diagnostic category for so called willful self-starvation. We argue that activity anorexia occurs in a significant number of patients who exhibit notable hyperactivity. However, *activity anorexia is more than a subset of anorexia nervosa*. This form or anorexia extends to many undiagnosed instances of human self-starvation. Currently, there is concern for athletes and ballet dancers who start dieting but cannot stop. A study by Drs. Garner and Garfinkel found a high incidence of anorexia among ballet dancers [13]. Dancers far exceeded the highest previously reported rate of one percent for girls at an English boarding school [14]. This is an interesting result because ballet students are occasionally required to combine severe dieting with intense training. According to the animal studies of activity anorexia, this combination promotes anorexic behavior.

The Garner and Garfinkel study compared ballet dancers, fashion models, anorectic patients, competitive music students, and normal weight university students, on various measures of anorexia. Fashion models and ballet dancers have more cases of diagnosed anorexia than the other groups. This is not surprising since thin women are likely to enter these professions. Also, 94 percent of the anorectics, 38 percent of the dancers, 25 percent of the models, and 10 percent of the normal weight students, showed disturbed eating attitudes. Dancers are required by their profession to be more active than models and this may contribute to greater disturbance of eating attitudes.

A more important finding concerned the development of anorexia during professional training. Ballet dancers are required by their profession to be very physically active while models are not. Both groups share the pressure to diet and maintain a thin appearance. Only ballet dancers are required to combine dieting and exercise. This implies that ballet dancers are more susceptible to activity anorexia than models. The results showed this was the case. Six percent of the ballet dancers developed anorexia during training and only 3.5 percent of the models did. None of the music or university students became anorexic.

The ballet students came from three national-calibre dance schools. Two of these schools were entirely devoted to ballet training. One school included an academic program and students were required to attend classes. The full-time ballet schools were more competitive and presumably required more intense physical exertion from students. Higher physical exercise should result in more cases of anorexia. Again this was the finding. Only 3.8 percent of the less competitive dancers developed anorexia during training while 7.6 percent of the more competitive dancers became anorexic. The overall pattern of results is consistent with the activity-anorexia cycle found in the animals.

Athletes may also suffer from activity anorexia when they combine dieting and exercise. There is increasing concern about anorexia in competitive athletes. This concern has been expressed by Dr. Nathan Smith in a comment published in the medical journal, *Pediatrics*.

Increasing numbers of young people are seriously committed to highly competitive sports programs, while coaches and athletes are increasingly aware of the advantage of reducing fatness for optimal athletic performance in almost all sports. This urgency to minimize body fat may lead to excessive voluntary weight reduction associated with a pathologic degree of food and fatness aversion. The degree of body wasting experienced by these starving young athletes is often so severe as to satisfy the major diagnostic criteria of primary anorexia nervosa. Excessive weight loss and food aversion in athletes differs from that usual in anorexia nervosa [15, p. 139].

The most important difference that Dr. Smith finds between these athletes and diagnosed anorectics is the absence of "deep seated" personal problems in athletes. This distinction is not helpful from our point of view. In our laboratory, animals also refuse to eat when food restriction is combined with exercise. When animals, athletes and anorectics increase activity and decrease food intake, they are suffering from activity anorexia.

A well-known study by Dr. Yates and her colleagues compared obligatory runners with anorexia nervosa patients [16]. In this study, the researchers interviewed 60 male marathon runners and speculated about their personality characteristics. The traits of these runners were compared to the "typical obsessive patient with anorexia as described in the literature and observed in our clinic." Male long-distance runners were said to resemble anorectic women in terms of family background, socioeconomic status and a variety of personality characteristics. The researchers suggested that both of these groups inhibited anger, had high self-expectations, tolerated physical discomfort, denied having serious physical problems, and were often depressed. The investigators concluded that runners and anorectics were similar because they shared an "attempt to establish an identity."

The matching of personality characteristics from subjective reports is open to severe criticism. One distinct possibility is that the similarities reflect the biases of the researchers. That is, in an uncontrolled study where researchers are looking for common characteristics, they are likely to find them. In our view, searching for trait similarities and identities misses the point. The most obvious comparison between runners and anorectics is in terms of dieting and exercising. Interestingly, Yates and her colleagues mentioned this in passing, but failed to recognize its importance. They state that "the typical obligatory runner is a diet-conscious man, whereas the typical anorexic is an exercise-conscious woman." If runners and anorectics do share any common attributes, it may be due to the effects of excessive exercise and food restriction.

Athletic anorexias are best understood as part of the more general category, activity anorexia. Comparison of eating problems in athletes with activity-induced starvation makes it clear that a search for underlying personality disturbance is unnecessary. The onset of activity anorexia depends on combining exercise and dieting in a way that initiates the feedback cycle. When anorectics and athletes report on the frequency and order of their symptoms, dieting occurs first and increasing exercise follows [17]. This activity-anorexia pattern is clearly seen in the self-report of a young woman runner who was eventually diagnosed as having anorexia nervosa. This case was reported in the British magazine *Athletics Weekly* by Cliff Temple, a respected athletics coach.

It all began in February 1987 when my coach told me in a very unfeeling way that I needed to lose weight — 'You've got a fat arse.' 'Go away and lose some of it'. This I did literally. I lost two and a half stones (31.5 pounds) of my overlarge posterior. What my coach did not do was tell me how to lose the weight sensibly, so naturally I did it my way.

To begin with I ate normally, cutting down the amount of sweet things I ate and stopped putting sugar in my tea. As a result my weight dropped to eight stones (112 pounds) and my running improved.

By mid March I clocked up a healthy seven stones twelve (110 pounds) and consequently my running improved. This along with the fact that my coach was still convinced that I had lost no weight, encouraged me to go on dieting and what started off as a healthy diet to lose a few pounds soon became an obsession and overtook me completely.

We will comment on the development of activity anorexia throughout this case presentation. The young woman was a competitive athlete who was not neurotic when she began dieting. Social pressure from her coach initiated dieting and she remarked that her running "improved." As the intensity of her running increased so did her dieting and her body weight dropped. At this point she had locked into the activity-anorexia cycle.

My whole life revolved around my diet. The amount I ate soon became less and less until I avoided meal times completely. I would go back to my boyfriend's house after college which enabled me not to eat as I would tell my parents I was eating there. I could get away with eating nothing at his house.

The thought of food scared me. All food was bad. If I had to either start eating or become ill I would rather have become ill.

I managed to avoid eating at home for a number of weeks. It was easy for me to miss lunch as I was at college. I would lie, saying I had eaten when I hadn't. I felt almost scared to eat.

Every time my mum questioned me about my eating habits I confirmed that I had eaten at my boyfriend's house, and when she asked him, he also said I had, as not to betray my trust. Despite this, however, when my weight dropped to seven and a half stone (105 pounds), my mum took me to see my GP. This was in April and he told me that I was perfectly healthy and I was not that much under weight for somebody of my age and height. He added that I could afford to lose another half stone (7 pounds) without it affecting my running.

The next few months saw me stopping eating completely. I had a total personality change. I lost interest in everything except my diet. I got very depressed and apathetic. I grew a covering of very fine hair all over my stomach and back. I felt cold all the time even when I was sitting in front of an open fire.

My face was drawn and pale and my eyes looked hollow and lifeless. It gradually got harder and harder for me to train, although I would never miss a run and the combination of eating nothing and running six miles would obviously make me lose weight.

I became hyperactive. I always had to be doing some form of exercise. If I woke up during the night I would weigh myself, not just once but I would get on and off the scales for about half an hour in the hope that I would get lighter.

One day, late in April me and my boyfriend had one almighty row, triggered off by my illness. This resulted in him going home very upset. His mother, when hearing the cause of his distress, drove around to our house that afternoon and told mum that I hadn't been eating there and that I was, in her opinion anorexic.

After the onset of the activity-anorexia cycle and starvation, she reported a fear of food and avoidance of eating. In this case, fear and avoidance of food resulted from the combination of excessive exercise and her dieting. This fact clearly shows that psychological factors follow from the biobehavioral process and are not the underlying causes of anorexia. The account was written after she had been treated for anorexia nervosa. Her description of fear may have been the result of her therapy. A prominent view of anorexia nervosa is that it is a weight phobia. Whether her fear of food was truly felt, or a learned description of her illness, is not the critical point. In either case, fear follows rather than precedes the anorexia. Because of this temporal sequence, fear of food is not an adequate explanation of her anorexia.

A "total personality change" also followed, rather than preceded, the development of her anorexia. This is interesting because anorexia is often explained as the outcome of personality disturbance. In this case, the most obvious reason for the personality change is starvation. In other words, starvation is the cause of the behavioral, attitudinal, and emotional changes. A famous study by Dr. Keys and his associates showed that young, healthy, and psychologically normal, male volunteers became emotionally disturbed as a result of forced food restriction and starvation [18]. For example, like the young woman in this case, some of the starving men reported long periods of depression.

The report also suggests that food was no longer of value to her. This decline in value is similar to recent laboratory findings with animals. Experiments show that reinforcing effectiveness of food declines with increasing exercise [19]. Other experimental evidence indicates animals will stop eating when exercise is excessive [7]. A change in the reinforcing value of food is indicated by her comment "all food was bad." In Chapter 8, we will provide more details about the motivational basis of activity anorexia.

Even though her weight was spiralling downward her physical activity continued to increase. She said "I became hyperactive. I always had to be doing some form of exercise." At this point, her dieting and exercise were out of control.

> By the time mum approached me, some two or three days late, I had started to make myself sick, even though I was eating virtually nothing anyway. I denied it when I was asked if I had lied about eating at my boyfriend's house. Although I had said this, she still took me back up to see the GP. He weighed me and I was seven stone two (100 pounds). He said I was very healthy and my diet was just a fad. He told me that my dieting was being rewarded by the successful racing results which I had achieved over the last few weeks.

> When my running hit a low, he said I would stop dieting and start eating — I didn't.

Her physician did not recognize the potentially lethal implications of the activity-anorexia cycle. This is not surprising because the negative effects of dieting and training have not been emphasized by the medical profession. From his point of view, she was dieting and running because of her success at racing and she could stop when she wanted. This was a serious mistake. The motivational conditions of the cycle make it unlikely that she will be able to stop.

> It all came to a head when my sister, a student psychiatric nurse, came home for the weekend. She was very alarmed at the amount of weight I had lost and she questioned me about it. I confided in her, telling her I that I ate nothing and when I did eat I made myself sick because I couldn't stand the conscience which I got when I ate. She persuaded me into allowing her to tell my parents. That evening we sat and talked it out. I was persuaded to go back and see the GP the following day and tell him that I had been making myself sick. The next morning dad went up and told him what had been happening and arranged for me to go up that afternoon. This I did, but he was still convinced there was no problem.

> He said however, that he would arrange for me to see a specialist. The waiting list, the doctor informed us, was until August, so we asked him to arrange an appointment for a private consultation. It took two weeks before we heard from the doctor and during this period I gradually began to eat less and less and drank nothing — I was in a state of complete starvation.

It is rather incredible that her physician missed the obvious physical signs of starvation and the onset of vomiting. This failure to diagnose anorexia may be based on the fact that she was an athlete. The doctor could account for the excessive exercise and extreme dieting by pointing to her training requirements. Many cases of activity anorexia in athletes may be missed for similar reasons.

Her report that "…when I did eat I made myself sick because I couldn't stand the conscience which I got when I ate" is characteristic of starving people. Some of the men in the Keys' starvation study also vomited after eating and reported pangs of conscience. One man lost his willpower and ate some food that was forbidden by the rules of the study. He immediately felt emotionally upset and sick to his stomach. Following this, he vomited and felt remorse [19, p. 887]. Activity anorexia generates starvation and starvation produces a variety of behavioral, physical, and psychological effects that are reversed when weight is restored. The young woman was finally seen by a psychiatrist who diagnosed anorexia nervosa and admitted her to hospital. She was treated with medical therapy (see Chapter 6) and discharged after four weeks. She reported that she still has problems with eating but her weight has recovered. In summarizing her experience she stated that:

> Anorexia Nervosa is a growing problem in women's athletics. Coaches no longer have to look out for shin splints and stress fractures, but they have to look out for anorexia, and they should know what to look out for, and I do not think many of them do.
>
> It has, at the moment, ruined my athletics and me as a person. Something has to be done, and fast before it does the same to more and more people [20, pp. 12-13]. *

This case clearly illustrates the development and progression of activity anorexia. We recognize that this is an interpretation of this young woman's anorexia and alternative interpretations are possible. However, the onset and progression of anorexia in this woman are strikingly similar to activity anorexia in animals. Because experiments with humans are not possible or desirable, parallels between animal research and human case studies are important for testing the generality of the activity-anorexia process.

REFERENCES

Although many of these references may be of interest, we have indicated (with an asterisk*) those that are written for the non-specialist reader.

1. Epling, W. F., Pierce, W. D. and Stefan, L. (1981). Schedule-induced self-starvation. In C. M. Bradshaw, E. Szabadi and C. F. Lowe (Eds.), *Quantification of Steady-state operant behaviour*, (pp. 393-396). Amsterdam: Elsevier/North Holland Biomedical Press, 1981.
2. Routtenberg, A. and Kuznesof, A. W. (1967). "Self-starvation" of rats living in activity wheels on a restricted feeding schedule. *Journal of Comparative and Physiological Psychology, 64*, 414-421.
3. Feighner, J. P., Robins, E., Guze, S. B., Woodruff, R. A., Winokur, G. and Munoz, R. (1972). Diagnostic criteria for use in psychiatric research. *Archives of General Psychiatry, 26*, 57-63.

---

4. Routtenberg, A. (1968). Self-starvation of rats living in activity wheels: adaptation effects. *Journal of Comparative and Physiological Psychology*, 66, 234-2 38.

5. Epling, W. F., Pierce, W. D. and Stefan, L. (1983). A theory of activity-based anorexia. *International Journal of Eating Disorders*, 3, 27-46.

6. Epling, W. F. and Pierce, W. D. (1989). Excessive activity and anorexia in rats. In K. M. Pirke, W. Wuttkeand U. Schweiger (Eds.), *The menstrual cycle and its disorders: Influences of nutrition, exercise and neurotransmitters*. New York: Springer-Verlag.

7. Epling, W. F. and Pierce, W. D. (1984). Activity-based anorexia in rats as a function of opportunity to run on an activity wheel. *Nutrition and Behavior*, 2, 37-49.

8. Spear, N. E. and Hill, W. T. (1962). Methodological note: Excessive weight loss in rats living in activity wheels. *Psychological Reports*, 11, 437-438.

9. Kanarek, R. B. and Collier, G. H. (1983). Self-starvation: A problem of overriding the satiety signal? *Physiology and Behavior*, 30, 307-311.

10. Epling, W. F. and Pierce, W. D. (1988). Activity-based anorexia: A biobehavioral perspective. *International Journal of Eating Disorders*, 7, 475-485.

11. Mrosovsky, N. and Sherry, D. F. (1980). Animal anorexias. *Science*, 207, 837-842.

12. Levitsky, D. (1974). Feeding conditions and intermeal relationships. *Physiology and Behavior*, 12, 779-787.

13. Garner, D. M. and Garfinkel, P. E. (1980). Sociocultural factors in the development of anorexia nervosa. *Psychological Medicine*, 10, 647-656.

14. Crisp, A. H., Palmer, R. L. and Kalucy, R. S. (1976). How common is anorexia nervosa? A prevalence study. *British Journal of Psychiatry*, 218, 549-554.

15. Smith, N. J. (1980). Excessive weight loss and food aversion in athletes simulating anorexia nervosa. *Pediatrics*, 66, 139-142.

16. Yates, A., Leehey, K. and Shisslack, C. M. (1983). Running — an analogue of anorexia? *New England Journal of Medicine*, 308, 251-255.

17. Beumont, P. J. V., Booth, A. L., Abraham, S. F., Griffiths, D. A. and Turner, T. R. A (1983). Temporal sequence of symptoms in patients with anorexia nervosa: a preliminary report. In P. L. Darby, P. E. Garfinkel, D. M. Garner and D. V. Coscina (Eds.), *Anorexia Nervosa: Recent Developments in Research*, (pp. 129-136). New York: Alan R. Liss, Inc.

18. Keys, A., Brozek, J., Henschel, A., Nickelsen, O. and Taylor, H. L. (1950). *The biology of human starvation*. Minneapolis: University of Minnesota Press.

19. Pierce, W. D., Epling, W. F. and Boer, D. P. (1986). Deprivation and satiation: The interrelations between food and wheel running. *Journal of the Experimental Analysis of Behavior*, 46, 199-210.

20. *Temple, C. (1987). Athletics nervosa. *Athletics Weekly*, Oct. 15.

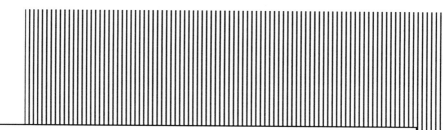

The main topics are:

- EFFECTS OF FOOD SUPPLY ON PHYSICAL ACTIVITY
- EFFECTS OF PHYSICAL ACTIVITY ON FOOD INTAKE
- APPETITE AND SATIETY
- MOTIVATIONAL INTERACTIONS OF EATING & EXERCISE

Summary

- Men in starvation experiments show excessive exercise. This is evidence that food restriction generates physical activity in humans.

- Substantial research indicates that physical activity reduces food intake in humans.

- People (and animals) usually adjust their food intake to match energy requirements. This is not the case if food is restricted at the same time that exercise is increasing.

- Physical activity affects eating by reducing meal size (satiety) and meal frequency (appetite).

- Experiments show that the reinforcing effectiveness of physical activity increases with food deprivation. Also, the reinforcing effectiveness of food declines with a change in exercise level. These two relations provide a behavioral account of activity anorexia.

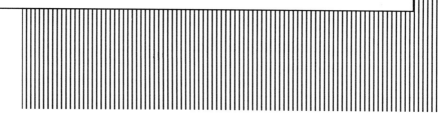

CHAPTER

Motivational Basis of Activity Anorexia

8

An adequate behavior analysis of activity anorexia must account for the suppression of eating as physical activity becomes excessive. In addition, the account must show how accelerated physical activity is the result of food restriction and deprivation. In order to document these effects, it is necessary to review studies concerned with the relationship between physical activity and food intake.

Some studies show that physical activity decreases food intake and the amount of decline is regulated by intensity of exercise. Other research demonstrates that deprivation of food increases physical activity. Food deprivation often arises from changes of meal schedule. The frequency and duration of meals appear to contribute to excessive exercise. Finally, there are studies that demonstrate the motivational link between eating and running.

1 EFFECTS OF FOOD SUPPLY ON PHYSICAL ACTIVITY

The starvation experiment by Dr. Keys and his colleagues showed the effects of food deprivation on human behavior. This study is important because food deprivation was imposed by the researchers and they could document the resulting physiological and behavioral changes in the men (see Chapter 4). We have discussed the progressive increase in exercise, sports and physical activity that occurs when food is restricted. We have also pointed to the eventual decline in physical activity as starvation becomes severe. It is interesting to ask whether these relationships were observed in the Keys' study.

The ideal food-deprivation experiment would have allowed the men ample opportunity to exercise, walk or run without requiring this activity. This was not the case in the Keys' study since the men were *required* to engage in moderately strenuous exercise. The men had to do a physical activity program, hike 22 miles a week, and walk an additional 2 or 3 miles per day (i.e. to go from their barracks to the mess hall). Each man was also required to do a weekly 30-minute work out on a motor-driven treadmill at 3.5 miles an hour on a 10 percent grade. These requirements would tend to mask the effects of food deprivation on physical activity. This is because the men were doing so much activity that the extra effects of food reduction would be hard to detect.

Because the men in the starvation experiment were forced to exercise, the researchers focused on the decline in fitness and activity during starvation. During the starvation period, Keys and his associates noted that "...most of the men felt weak and tired easily .... The marked reduction in strength was periled by a general curtailment of self-initiated, spontaneous activities" [1, p. 828].

Although it is difficult to be certain, there is some evidence that food deprivation did engender excessive physical activity. Even though daily physical exertion was required, some men exceeded the requirements. Keys and his colleagues reported that "...some men exercised deliberately at times. Some of them attempted to lose weight by driving themselves through periods of excessive expenditure of energy ..." [1, p. 828]. The researchers said that the excessive exercise of these men was an attempt to lose weight in order to get more food. In order to protect the subjects, the researchers were obligated to give more food if weight loss was too severe. Although the Keys' interpretation cannot be ruled out, the results are consistent with animal experiments that demonstrate an increase in physical activity when food is restricted. That is, food deprivation itself may have caused the excessive expenditure of energy that the researchers observed.

Human studies suggest that increased body weight and food consumption are associated with inactivity [2, 3]. That is, obese people are less physically active than individuals of normal weight [4, 5]. On the other hand, low body weight and food intake generate physical activity. Increased mobility and arousal have been described for the "starving poor" in 19th century England [6]. A similar effect was observed for malnourished German school children during World War One [7], and starving people in post World-War-Two Germany. Although these reports are interesting, the evidence is anecdotal and circumstantial. Stronger evidence for the effects of food intake on activity can be found in animal research concerned with diet and exercise.

Deprivation, Food Supply and Activity

In an early study by Dr. Finger, rats increased wheel running when deprived of food [8]. The animals were separated into two groups that went either 24 or 72 hours without food. Small increases in wheel running occurred after 24 hours. The animals that were food deprived for 72 hours showed a 94 percent increase in wheel running. In our laboratory, Douglas Boer deprived rats of food until they reached 75 percent of their normal weight.

Animals that have food continuously available typically run less than 1000 wheel turns a day. The deprived animals increased their daily running and at the peak were 10 times more active than free-feeding animals. Generally, food deprivation alone generates high levels of physical activity.

Although food deprivation and body-weight loss increase physical activity [9], the control of wheel running over long periods of time is more complicated. After high levels of running are induced by deprivation and weight loss, running is regulated by food supply. Drs. Russell and Amy have conducted research with Douglas Boer and ourselves on induction of prolonged running by rats [10]. When rats were given access to running wheels and fed a fixed amount of food, their weights stabilized and they ran about 8,000 meters a day. The results showed that long-term running was not controlled by loss of weight. This suggested to us that prolonged exercise was due to the amount of daily food we provided.

A subsequent study by our research team indicated that after running was established by weight loss, it was controlled by food supply. We could make animals increase or decrease running by programming small changes in the amount they were fed each day. Even though the changes in food supply did not affect their weights, the animals' running was sensitive to daily food ration. Running went up when food supply decreased and went down when food increased [11].

Overall, these findings suggest that the excessive exercise of anorectic patients may initially arise from rapid loss of weight. Following this, physical activity may be closely regulated by daily food intake. The animal evidence suggests that forced or voluntary changes in food consumption will produce rapid alterations in physical activity. A person at low weight may considerably increase the risk of activity anorexia by slight modifications in food intake.

In addition to deprivation, weight loss, and the size of food ration, the scheduling of meal periods contributes to excessive running by animals. For this reason, meal schedules are important to an understanding of the activity-anorexia cycle.

Meal Schedules and Physical Activity

Researchers have noted excessive physical activity that occurs as a "side effect" of delivering food to a hungry animal [12]. In a typical experiment, a rat is reduced to 80 percent of normal weight and small amounts of food are presented every now and then. For example, the animal may receive a food pellet (45 mg.) every 180 seconds. When the animal has a running wheel available it runs on the wheel between the food periods.

An early experiment by Drs. Levitsky and Collier showed that wheel running was due to the periodic delivery of food [13]. When rats could press a lever and get food each time, they did not run on the wheel. A shift to a periodic food schedule generated considerable wheel running (325 turns per hour). Wheel running immediately followed food delivery and continued throughout the interval between food presentations. When lever pressing no longer produced food (i.e. extinction) wheel running declined (as did lever pressing). The study suggests that periodic food schedules induce running when food deprivation is held constant (80 percent body weight).

The effects of food schedules on activity were reported by Dr. White in a recent study [14]. Rats were allowed to run on a wheel for 30 minutes and food was delivered every 60 seconds. This condition was compared to a 30-minute session where animals received the same amount of food but it was given to them at the start of the session. Generally, the animals ran at a higher rate (number of wheel turns per minute) when food was delivered on a schedule than when food was given all at once. Dr. White concluded that wheel running was a *schedule-induced* behavior. That is, wheel running is produced by the scheduled delivery of food.

There is some dispute about the conclusion that running is induced by food presentation. Drs. Penney and Schull argued that:

Simple periodic food schedules may have at least two different effects. First, they may increase the probability of behavior that normally occurs in 'food getting' situations. Second, periodic food presentations may serve as time markers initiating intervals that must elapse before food again becomes available, and under stimulus conditions signaling the temporary absence of food animals may seek alternative sources of reinforcement [15, p. 277].

There were several phases in the Penney and Schull experiment but we will describe only the critical procedures.

Rats were given a signal light every 60 seconds for one hour. When a signal occurred, a single lever press turned the light off and 50 percent of the time produced a food pellet. Thus, only half of the signals were accompanied by food. The rats were allowed to wheel run throughout the experimental session. More wheel running occurred when the signal was not accompanied by food than when it was. Drs. Penny and Schull interpreted this finding as support for the idea that food served as a "time marker." Such a conclusion follows from the observation that most of the wheel running occurred when food was absent. This suggests that running is not generated by the presentation of food; rather, it is the time between food presentations that is critical.

In the natural environment, the "marker" for food availability is the rate of occurrence of food items. As the density (food items per unit time) of food decreases animals become more mobile. As density increases mobility decreases. When the time between eating bouts becomes very long, physical activity dramatically increases and will not stop until high rates of food items are again contacted. This response to food supply is likely due to the evolutionary history of the species. Mobility during food shortage (as indicated by declining density of food) would be favoured if those animals who travelled contacted food, survived, and reproduced.

The time between food presentations in the animal studies is so short that the effects reported are not directly applicable to most human situations. However, excessive activity in humans could be generated over longer time intervals with relatively larger portions of food. The self-starvation studies reviewed in Chapter 7 involve the presentation of an entire meal once a day. Under these conditions, large and excessive increases in wheel running are generated.

A rat may obtain single food pellets after brief intervals or an entire meal after many hours. In both cases it is important to note that excessive physical activity is generated and maintained. There is evidence that suggests these effects have a common motivational basis. When small food pellets are periodically delivered, animals develop ritualized patterns of wheel running [16]. During the interval between pellet presentations, animals begin by drinking water, then run on their wheels, and finally orient toward the food cup in order to obtain the next food pellet.

A ritualized pattern of running also develops when entire meals are presented once a day. Excessive running often occurs after a 1-hour meal and lasts for approximately six hours. During the next 11 hours there is very little activity. Approximately 6 hours before the next meal, animals again show excessive activity [17, 18]. In our laboratory, we have noted a similar pattern when animals are fed a daily 90-minute meal. This distribution of running suggests that excessive physical activity is related to meal schedule.

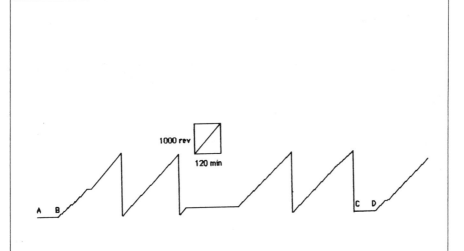

Figure 8.1 Cummulative record of wheel running over a 24-h period showing that running is organized by presentation of meals. The points A and B depict the 90-min feeding period. When the wheel is opened, the animal runs at a steady rate for several hours, stops for a period, and runs again before the next meal (C and D).

Drs. Wallace, Sanson and Singer showed that periodic presentation of small amounts of food increased the physical activity level of adult humans. These researchers also reported that people place themselves on food schedules when food is freely available [19]. In another article, Dr. Foster suggested that side effects of reinforcement schedules have importance for many clinical problems.

> *Potential candidates for human (induced behavior) range from (a) 'normal' time-filling or 'fidgety' patterns such as playing, idle conversing, finger tapping, and beard-stroking, through (b) 'neurotic' obsessive-compulsive or 'nervous-habit' patterns such as nail biting, snacking, and hand-washing, to (c) 'psychotic patterns' such as self-stimulating rituals, manic episodes, and rage outbursts. Potential candidates for human 'inducing' schedules include home, office, classroom, and ward routines, whose time, effort, and consequence properties have long been suspected of side effects by lay and professional people* [20, p. 545-546].

Because these behaviors are exaggerated, persistent, and occur at high rates they appear similar to the pronounced physical activity of many human anorectics. Of equal importance is the possibility that many of the neurotic symptoms of anorexia nervosa may be inadvertently induced by changes in food allocation or other schedules of reinforcement.

2 EFFECTS OF PHYSICAL ACTIVITY ON FOOD INTAKE

There is evidence that humans and other animals reduce food intake when physical activity becomes excessive. We have called this a *paradoxical* effect because caloric intake decreases at a time when energy output is substantially increasing [21]. From an energy balance viewpoint, food intake should match energy requirements. In fact, this matching of food intake to physical activity is the usual biological response. This occurs when physical activity is moderate or when intense activity stabilizes.

Long distance runners typically increase mileage and speed in moderate and progressive steps. Such a training strategy results in increased food intake and higher energy efficiency. In this way the athlete meets the caloric demands of the new level of running. If this were not the case, athletes would be far more susceptible to activity anorexia.

The paradoxical effect of decreasing food intake with intense exercise occurs during transition to a new level of physical activity. When exercise is increasing relative to a former level of training, suppression of food intake is the response. The runner may report a loss of appetite during this period. Reduction of food intake and loss of appetite continue as long as the rate of change in daily activity is substantial [22]. When there is little change in daily output, people begin to adjust caloric intake and energy expenditure. A similar process occurs for sedentary people who take up a fitness program. The loss of appetite experienced by these individuals corresponds to the intensity of their training. Again, the reduction of food intake is usually transitory *except* when severe dietary restriction is forced or self-imposed.

Exercise and Caloric Intake

A study by Dr. Stevenson and his colleagues showed that rats who were forced to run on a treadmill ate less on exercise days than on days when they did not exercise [23]. Additionally, the animals ate less following irregular bouts of swimming. There are many animal studies that show decreased food consumption following short periods of high intensity exercise [24, 25, 26]. Such effects are found for rats who are sedentary except for the exercise requirements of the study. The implication is that appetite is suppressed when exercise is imposed upon a sedentary baseline. This suppression extends well beyond the point of recovery from physical exertion. To illustrate, it is likely that a person who jogs before breakfast does not eat as much for lunch or supper.

The intensity of exercise is an important determinant of loss of appetite. Dr. Katch and his associates varied the intensity of exercise for rats and held total energy output constant. The researchers found that animals who were given short-duration exercise of high intensity ate less than animals who received long-duration exercise of low intensity. Importantly, both exercise groups ate less than a non-exercising group of animals [27]. These findings further support the loss of appetite that occurs when exercise is imposed on sedentary animals. The results also suggest that the intensity of training has an effect on food intake. For example, the person who runs 5 kilometers in 25 minutes should experience a greater suppression of appetite than one who covers a greater distance at a slower pace.

Research evidence shows that physical activity reduces appetite in humans. Dr. Edholm and coworkers reported that cadets eat less on days of military drilling than they do on days of less physical exertion. That is, caloric intake on drilling days was significantly depressed when compared with other days [28]. Other researchers have found that obese school children voluntarily reduce their food intake following a pre-lunch exercise period. In a well known study of factory workers in India, researchers found that people who performed light or medium physical tasks ate less than sedentary employees [29].

A study of college women also indicated that food intake declines with increasing exercise. In this experiment, 15 previously inactive college women participated in one hour of tennis or two hours of swimming on a daily basis. Both the swimmers and tennis players showed a moderate decline in caloric intake [30]. A subsequent study of college women confirmed the findings of the earlier study. Women who engaged in 30 minutes of programmed exercise a day decreased their caloric intake. The women averaged 1751 calories a day before going on the exercise program. After ten weeks of daily exercise, the women dropped to 1584 calories [31].

Men also reduce their food intake when they engage in programmed physical activity. In one study, programmed exercise reduced food intake in 15 middle-aged men who were previously sedentary [32]. A decline of approximate 200 calories a day was produced by endurance calisthenics and 2 to 4 miles of daily running. A later study showed that 30 middle-aged men who were recovering from heart attacks reduced caloric intake from 2867 to 2088 calories a day over twelve weeks of programmed exercise [33]. Generally, people and other animals reduce food intake when activity increases.

Reduction of food intake when physical activity is increasing appears to contradict common sense. The everyday understanding of energy balance suggests a positive relationship between activity and food intake. That is, as energy output increases caloric intake should also go up in order to meet the new demand. In fact, there are studies that report an increase of food intake with greater physical activity.

One study found that animals who were required to run on a treadmill increased food intake when the exercise exceeded 2 hours a day [34]. The study of factory workers in India (see above) included men who performed very heavy labor (e.g. coal-men, carriers, etc.). These people ate more than sedentary, office workers [29]. This suggests that these laborers had adjusted to the energy requirements of their jobs.

A recent study by Dr. Tokuyama and associates reported that animals would eventually adjust food intake to energy level [35]. In this study, sedentary rats were allowed to run on activity wheels and eat as much as they wanted. These animals ate more than an inactive control group. However, the adjustment to physical activity took a period of time. During the transition from sedentary to physically active, the animals reduced their caloric intake.

A similar effect has been reported by Dr. Wheeler for a sub-set of males who volunteered for a training program in long-distance running [36]. The study measured a number of behavioral and physiological changes over the 6-month program. In terms of food intake, 6 of ten males in the training group showed a reduction in caloric consumption as their running increased. The greater the increase in weekly mileage the more the reduction. However, as mileage leveled off food intake recovered, suggesting that rate of change in weekly mileage was a critical factor in food suppression. Importantly, males with low rates of change in running did not show any food reduction, a finding that coincides with animals studies of activity and self-starvation [22].

As we have indicated, some studies report that food intake decreases with exercise while other research suggests an increase. This discrepancy can be explained by considering the effects of physical activity during transition periods. Whenever physical activity is *increasing* against a prior level of exertion, appetite decreases. The studies that find a decline in caloric intake with exercise are showing this transitional effect. When a new level of exercise is reached and maintained, caloric intake goes up to meet the increased energy output. Thus, during stable periods of physical activity food intake and energy expenditure are positively related.

These results suggest that, given enough time, animals and humans adjust food intake to activity level. This adjustment occurs *when food is not restricted*. Food restriction that is either imposed or chosen (i.e. going on a diet) may interfere with this adjustment.

In terms of activity anorexia, the decline in food intake when physical activity is changing (i.e. transition period) is important. At this time, dieting or a restricted-food schedule induces even greater levels of activity. Since the rate of change in physical activity is increasing, food consumption continues to decrease. The result is a cycle of declining food intake and increasing exercise. One major implication is that dieting to lose weight or exercising to keep fit have positive benefits when they occur independently. It is the combination of these two practices that may lead to activity anorexia.

The person who begins an exercise program and who later adds dieting to increase weight loss is probably safe. In this case, physical activity is stable and does not suppress appetite. In contrast, when a person increases physical exertion and at the same time decides to diet, the probability of activity anorexia increases. As the severity of dieting and the intensity of exercise increase, activity anorexia becomes more likely.

Taken together, studies of physical activity and food intake show that increased exercise reduces food consumption in humans. This is a general effect that occurs in workers, college women, children, and middle-aged men. This effect is similar to the effects of physical activity on food ingestion in animals. These findings considerably strengthen the extension of animal studies of activity anorexia to humans. As we have noted in Chapter 7, ethical constraints prevent the experimental investigations of activity anorexia with human subjects. Because of this limitation, our theory partially relies on showing similar effects in animals and humans. In terms of the effects of physical activity on food intake such similarity is apparent.

3   APPETITE AND SATIETY

We have argued that a cycle of increasing exercise and decreasing food intake is the basis of activity anorexia. There are several ways that physical activity could decrease food intake and body weight. A common sense interpretation is that exercise burns calories. This account is not satisfactory because it fails to explain the effects of physical activity on food intake. Another possibility is that exercise alters the tendency to eat meals when they are available (i.e. appetite). In other words, a person may skip one or more meals each day. On the other hand, exercise may affect the person's tendency to stop eating during a meal (i.e. satiety).

Drs. Kanarek and Collier have suggested that satiety is the major reason for activity anorexia [37]. They argue that physical activity interferes with the amount eaten at any single meal. In other words, exercise makes the animal stop eating even though it has sufficient time to consume much more food. Briefly, they found that animals exposed to the procedures would eat a sufficient amount of food if they were fed four 15-minute meals rather than the usual 1-hour feeding (see Chapter 7 for a more complete description of this experiment).

In this view, the animal gives up eating after a short period of time even though it has an hour or more to feed. In everyday language, the animal eats a small amount of food, feels full, and stops eating. Survival depends on the animal adapting to the meal schedule by increasing the amount eaten during the feeding period. Wheel running interferes with the animals ability to adjust to the single daily feeding. Thus, it is the particular combination of this feeding schedule and physical activity that produces self-starvation in animals. The implication is that less restrictive feeding schedules (e.g. four 15-minute meals) will not result in activity anorexia.

This explanation of activity anorexia rests on the assumption that physical activity interferes with food intake *only* when the feeding schedule is severely restrictive. These are highly specific circumstances and appear to limit the generality of activity anorexia.

The implication is that other feeding schedules would permit the animal to adapt (i.e. eat enough to survive) even though physical activity remained excessive.

Unfortunately, Kanarek and Collier failed to note that the change in feeding schedule controlled the amount of activity that animals exhibited. To illustrate, on the eighth day of the experiment the animals given one meal ran approximately 3,000 revolutions; those fed four times only completed 1,000 wheel turns. Thus, the increased food intake of the animals with four brief meals may be due to less exercise rather than the change in feeding schedule. The data suggest that the feeding schedule did not override the satiety effects of exercise; rather, the more frequent feeding reduced physical activity and this allowed food intake to recover.

Another line of evidence also opposes a satiety account of activity anorexia. According to the satiety hypothesis, physical activity prevents an animal from adjusting to a restricted-feeding schedule. This assumption means that exercise somehow regulates eating *during* a meal. However, Dr. Levitsky has shown that wheel running does not affect the duration or size of a meal (i.e. satiety) in free-feeding animals [38]. The major effect of physical activity is to decrease the initiation or frequency of meals (i.e. appetite). The satiety hypothesis does not explain how activity affects appetite in free-food situations and satiety in the restricted-food condition.

The effects of activity on satiety and appetite undoubtedly play an important role in activity anorexia. However, we think it is premature to conclude that activity only contributes to anorexia by interfering with the animal's ability to adjust to the food schedule. Physical activity directly reduces food intake by altering the reinforcement value of eating. The motivational interaction of eating and exercise provides an alternative account of the effects of physical activity on appetite and satiety.

4 MOTIVATIONAL INTERACTION OF EATING AND EXERCISE

One way to understand the activity-anorexia cycle is to consider how deprivation for food affects the reinforcing value of physical activity. On the other hand, it is important to consider how engaging in exercise changes the reinforcing value of eating. The person who performs strenuous exercise may not feel like eating. The reported loss of appetite reflects a decline in the reinforcing value of food. It is also likely that an individual who diets to lose weight begins to feel energetic. The feeling reflects an increase in the reinforcing value of physical activity. Based on this analysis, the person with activity anorexia may become obsessed with exercise and disinterested in eating.

Changes in the reinforcing value of food and exercise produce changes in behavior as well as feelings. When the reinforcing value of food declines, food-related behavior weakens. People may eat less, have smaller portions, take fewer meals, reduce snacking, and perhaps choose low calorie foods. One important implication is that the person will not expend much effort to obtain food. Since the reinforcing value of food is low, eating and obtaining food are no longer maintained. A similar, but opposite, effect occurs when the reinforcing value of exercise increases. In this case, exercise-related behavior becomes more likely. People may increase active sports, join fitness facilities, organize their life around a daily workout, and choose to walk rather than drive or ride. Since the reinforcing value of physical activity is high, behavior that produces it is strengthened and maintained. Our motivational analysis of eating and exercise suggests that these activities are interrelated. Depriving an animal of food should increase the reinforcing value of exercise. Rats who are required to press a lever in order to run on a wheel should work harder when they are deprived of food. Additionally, engaging in exercise would be expected to reduce the reinforcing value of food. Rats who are required to press a lever for food pellets should not work as hard following a day of exercise. We designed two experiments to test these ideas [39].

Reinforcement Value of Exercise

We asked whether food deprivation increased the reinforcing effectiveness of wheel running. Although it was well known that food restriction induced physical activity, the reason for this was not known. One major explanation was that food deprivation produced general arousal that resulted in spontaneous activity [40]. Food-deprived rats who increased wheel running were said to show the effects of general arousal.

This account is not satisfactory to us because it fails to explain the interrelations between eating and running. An account based on changes in reinforcement effectiveness has several advantages. It explains the relationship between eating and exercise without inventing mechanisms like "general arousal." If animals work harder for an opportunity to exercise when deprived of food, this would show that running had increased in its capacity to support behavior. Also, such an increase in the reinforcement effectiveness of running could be directly related to changes in food allocation.

Our analysis suggested that depriving an animal of one reinforcer (i.e. food), changed the reinforcing value of a different reinforcer (i.e. running). This was an intriguing implication because increased reinforcement effectiveness is usually achieved by withholding the reinforcing event. That is, when a long-distance runner sustains an injury that prevents running, the reinforcing value of this activity increases. The increased effectiveness of this reinforcer is observed when the runner attempts different remedies, runs despite the pain, and "hangs around" watching others run. Surprisingly, our analysis predicted similar changes in behavior by withholding *food* rather than running.

We used 9 young rats of both sexes to test the reinforcing effectiveness of wheel running as food deprivation changed. The animals were trained to press a lever to obtain 60 seconds of wheel running. When the animal pressed the lever a break was removed and the running wheel was free to turn. After 60 seconds, the break was again activated and the rat had to press the lever to obtain more time to run.

Once lever pressing for wheel running was consistent, each animal was tested when it was food-deprived (75 percent of normal weight) and when it was at normal weight. Recall that the animals were expected to work harder for exercise when they were food-deprived. The next step in the experiment was to test the reinforcement effectiveness of wheel running.

In order to measure the reinforcing effectiveness of wheel running, the animals were required to press the lever more and more for each opportunity to run. Specifically, the rats were required to press 5 times to obtain 60 seconds of wheel running, then 10, 15, 20, 25 and so on. The point at which they gave up pressing for wheel running was used as an index of the reinforcing effectiveness of exercise.

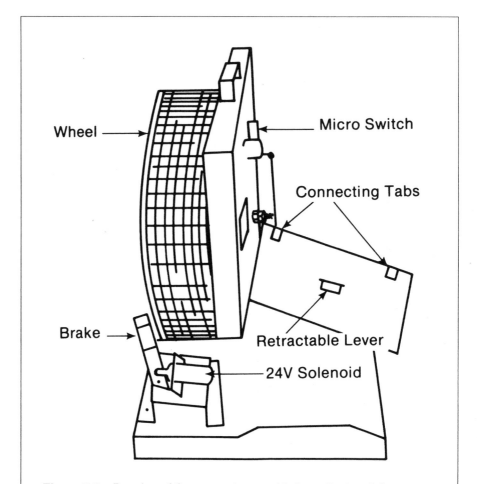

Figure 8.2 Drawing of the apparatus used to investigate reinforcement effectiveness of running. Portrayed is the retractable lever that was mounted on a metal plate that fit over the enterance to the wheel. Also shown is the break that was controlled by 24-V continuous-operate solinoid. Republished from Pierce, W. D., Epling, W. F., and Boer, D. P. [1986[. Deprivation and satiation: The interrelations between food and wheel running. *Journal of the Experimental Analysis of Behavior*, 46, 199-210. Permission granted by the Society for the Advancement of Behavior Analysis (SABA).

The results showed that all animals lever pressed for wheel running more when food deprived than when at normal weight. In other words, animals worked harder for exercise when they were hungry. Further evidence indicated that the reinforcing effectiveness would go up and down when an animal's weight was made to increase and decrease. For example, one subject pressed the bar 1567 times when food deprived, 881 times at normal weight, and 1882 times when again food deprived. This indicated that the effect was reversible and was tied to the level of food deprivation.

Although reinforcing effectiveness of running increased with level of food deprivation, there was a point where exercise began to decrease in value. When body weight was 70 percent or less, animals would not work as hard as they did with less deprivation.

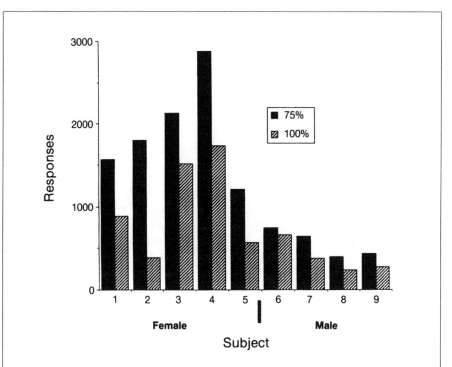

Figure 8.3   Maximum number of bar presses (responses) completed by 5 female and 4 male rats on a progressive-ratio schedule. The animals pressed the lever to obtain 60 seconds of wheel running. Subjects were tested at 75 or 100 percent of free-feeding body weight. All animals work harder for exercise when food deprived. Female rats show a greater response to deprivation than males. Republished from Pierce, W. D., Epling, W. F., and Boer, D. P. [1986]. Deprivation and satiation: The interrelations between food and wheel running. *Journal of the Experimental Analysis of Behavior*, 46, 199-210. Permission granted by the Society for the Advancement of Behavior Analysis (SABA).

This suggested to us that the lethargic behavior of starving people and anorectics may reflect a decline in the reinforcement value of exercise. Of course, it is also true that as starvation becomes extreme the individual may be too weak to exercise. Both of these effects may contribute to the loss of motivation to exercise.

Reinforcement Value of Food

In a second experiment, we investigated the effects of exercise on the reinforcing effectiveness of food [40]. Four male rats were trained to press a lever for food pellets. When lever pressing reliably occurred, we tested the effects of exercise on each animal's willingness to work for food. In this case, we expected that a day of exercise would *decrease* the reinforcement effectiveness of food on the next day.

Test days were arranged to measure the reinforcing effects of food. One day before each test, animals were placed in their wheels without food. On some of the days before a test, the wheel was free to turn and on other days it was not. When the wheel was free to turn, animals could choose to exercise or remain in an attached cage. Three of the four rats ran moderately in their activity wheels on exercise days. One rat did not run when given the opportunity. This animal was subsequently forced to exercise on a motor-driven wheel. All animals were well rested (3 to 4 hours of rest) before each test. This insured that the effects were not due to fatigue.

Reinforcement effectiveness of food was assessed by counting the number of lever presses for food as food became more and more difficult to obtain. To illustrate, an animal had to press 5 times for the first food pellet, 10 for the next, then 15, 20, 25 and so on. As in the first experiment, the "giving up" point was used to measure reinforcement effectiveness. Presumably, the more effective or valuable the reinforcer (i.e. food) the harder the animal would work for it.

When test days were preceded by a day of exercise, the reinforcing effectiveness of food decreased sharply. Animals pressed the lever more than 200 times when they were not allowed to run but no more than 38 times when running preceded test sessions. Food no longer supported lever presses following a day of moderate wheel running, even though a lengthy rest period preceded the test. Although wheel running was moderate, it represented a large change in physical activity since these animals were previously sedentary. As we have noted earlier, it is the change from one level of exercise to another that reduces the value of food reinforcement. Prior to each test the animals had spent an entire day without food. Because of this, the reinforcing effectiveness of food should have increased [41]. Exercise, however, seems to override the effects of food deprivation since responding for food went down rather than up. Other evidence from these experiments suggested that the effects of exercise were similar to feeding the animal. This finding is important for activity anorexia since exercise appears to substitute for eating.

The rat that refused to run also showed a sharp decline in lever pressing for food after forced exercise. Exercise was again moderate but substantial relative to the animal's sedentary history. Because the reinforcement effectiveness of food decreased with forced exercise, we concluded that both forced and voluntary physical activity produce a decline in the value of food. This finding suggests that people who increase their physical activity due to occupational requirements (i.e. ballet dancers, military recruits, etc.) may value food less.

5   CONCLUSION

Our research on the motivational interrelations between exercise and eating has several implications for the understanding of activity anorexia. Food deprivation *increases* the reinforcement effectiveness of physical activity (i.e. running). Spontaneous or forced activity *decreases* the reinforcement effectiveness of food. These two relationships explain the occurrence of activity anorexia.

Dieting to lose weight increases deprivation for food. As food deprivation goes up, exercise becomes more valued (in the sense of supporting behavior that produces it). This leads to an overall increase in physical activity and ritualized patterns of behavior related to exercise. A change in level of exercise produces a decline in the value of food. When food is low in reinforcement value, eating is depressed and food-related behavior declines. The interaction of these two relationships is the behavioral basis of the activity-anorexia cycle.

In our view, these motivational interrelations have a basis in natural selection. Natural selection may have favored those animals that increased locomotor activity in times of food scarcity. The adaptive value of a decline in the reinforcement value of food when energy expenditure is increasing requires an in depth analysis. Chapter 9 explores the evolutionary and physiological foundations of the link between physical activity and food regulation.

REFERENCES

Although many of these references may be of interest, we have indicated (with an asterisk *) those that are written for the non-specialist reader.

1.   Keys, A., Brozek, J., Henschel, A., Mickelson, O. and Taylor, H. L. (1950). *The biology of human starvation*. Minneapolis, Minnesota: University of Minnesota Press.
2.   Bloom, W. L. and Edix, M. F. (1967). Inactivity as a major factor in adult obesity. *Metabolism*, 16, 679-684.
3.   Mayer, J. (1965). Inactivity as a major factor in adolescent obesity. *Annals of the New York Academy of Sciences*, 131, 502-506.
4.   Chirico, A. M. and Stunkard, A. J. (1960). Physical activity and human obesity. *New England Journal of Medicine*, 263, 935-940.
5.   Jeffrey, D. B. and Knauss, M. R. (1981). The etiologies, treatments, and assessments of obesity. In S. N. Haynes and L. Gannon (Eds.), *Psychosomatic disorders: A psychophysiological approach to etiology and treatment*, (pp. 269-319). New York: Praeger.

6.   Howard, R. B. (1839) *An inquiry into the morbid effect of deficiency of food chiefly with reference to their occurrence amongst the destitute poor.* London: Simpkin, Marshall & Co.

7.   Blanton, S. (1919). Mental and nervous changes in children of the Volkschulen of Trier, Germany, caused by malnutrition. *Mental Hygiene,* 3, 343-386.

8.   Finger, F. W. (1951). The effect of food deprivation and subsequent satiation upon general activity in the rat. *Journal of Comparative and Physiological Psychology,* 4, 557-564.

9.   Collier, G., Hirsch, E. and Kanarek, R. (1977). The operant revisited. In W. K. Honig and J. E. R. Staddon (Eds.), *Handbook of operant behavior,* (pp. 28-52). Englewood Cliffs, NJ: Prentice-Hall.

10.   Russell, J. C., Epling, W. F., Pierce, D., Amy, R. M. and Boer, D.P. (1987). Induction of voluntary prolonged running by rats. *Journal of Applied Physiology,* 63, 2549-2553.

11.   Boer, D. P. (1989). *Determinants of excessive running in activity anorexia.* Ph.D. dissertation, Department of Psychology, The University of Alberta.

12.   Falk, J. L. (1977). The origin and functions of adjunctive behavior. *Animal Learning and Behavior,* 5, 325-335.

13.   Levitsky, D. and Collier, G. (1968). Schedule-induced wheel running. *Physiology and Behavior,* 3, 571-573.

14.   White, J. M. (1984). Schedule-induced wheel-running: effects of exposure to the schedule. *Physiology and Behavior,* 34, 119-122.

15.   Penney, J and Schull, J. (1977). Functional differentiation of adjunctive drinking and wheel running in rats. *Animal Learning and Behavior,* 5, 272-280.

16.   Staddon, J. E. R. (1977). Schedule-induced behavior. In W. K. Honig and J. E. R. Staddon (Eds.), *Handbook of operant behavior,* (pp. 125-152). Englewood Cliffs, NJ: Prentice-Hall.

17.   Epling, W. F., Pierce, W. D. and Stefan, L. (1983). A theory of activity-based anorexia. *International Journal of Eating Disorders,* 3, 27-46.

18.   Woods, D. J. (1969). *The effects of age and chlorpromazine on self-starvation in activity wheels.* M. A. Thesis. Department of Psychology, Northwestern University.

19.   Wallace, M., Sanson, A. and Singer, G. (1977). Adjunctive behavior in humans on a food delivery schedule. *Physiology and Behavior,* 20, 203-204.

20.   Foster, W. S. (1978). Adjunctive behavior: An under-reported phenomenon in applied behavior analysis. *Journal of Applied Behavior Analysis,* 11, 545-546.

21.   Epling, W. F. and Pierce, W. D. (1988). Activity-based anorexia: A biobehavioral perspective. *International Journal of Eating Disorders,* 7, 475-485.

22.   Epling, W. F. and Pierce, W. D. (1984). Activity-based anorexia in rats as a function of opportunity to run on an activity wheel. *Nutrition and Behavior,* 2, 37-49.

23.   Stevenson, J. A. F., Box, B. M., Feleki, V. and Beaton, J. R. (1966). Bouts of exercise and food intake in the rat. *Journal of Comparative and Physiological Psychology,* 21, 118-122.

24.   Oscai, I. B. and Holloszy, J. O. (1969). Effects of weight changes produced by exercise, food restriction, or overeating in bodily consumption. *Journal of Clinical Investigation,* 48, 2124-2128.

25.   Ahrens, R. A., Bishop, C. L. and Berdanier, C. D. (1972). Effect of age and dietary carbohydrate source on the response of rats to forced exercise. *Journal of Nutrition,* 102, 241-248.

26. Crews, E. L., Fuge, K. W., Oscai, L. B., Holloszy, J. O. and Shank, R. E. (1969). Weight, food intake, and bodily composition: Effects of exercise and of protein deficiency. *American Journal of Physiology,* 216, 275-287.

27. Katch, F. I., Martin, R. and Martin, J. (1979). Effects of exercise intensity on food consumption in the rat. *American Journal of Clinical Nutrition,* 32, 1401-1407.

28. Edholm, O. G., Fletcher, J. G., Widdowson, E. M. and McCance, R. A. (1955). The energy expenditure and food intake of individual men. *British Journal of Nutrition,* 9, 286-300.

29. Mayer, J., Roy, P. and Mitra, K. P. (1956). Relation between caloric intake, body weight, and physical work: Studies in an industrial male population in West Bengal. *American Journal of Clinical Nutrition,* 4, 169-175.

30. Katch, F. I., Michael, E. D. and Jones, E. M. (1969). Effects of physical training on body composition and diet of females. *Research Quarterly,* 40, 99-104.

31. Johnson, R. E., Mastropaolo, J. A. and Wharton, M. A. (1972). Exercise, dietary intake, and body composition. *Journal of the American Dietetic Association,* 61, 399-403.

32. Holloszy, J. O., Skinner, J. S., Toro, G. and Cureton, T. K. (1964). Effects of a six month program of endurance exercise on the serum lipids of middle-aged men. *American Journal of Cardiology,* 14, 753-760.

33. Watt, E. W., Wiley, J. and Fletcher, G. F. (1976). Effect of dietary control and exercise training on daily food intake and serum lipids in post-myocardial infaraction patients. *American Journal of Clinical Nutrition,* 29, 900-904.

34. Mayer, J., Marshall, N. B., Vitale, I. J., Christensen, J. H., Masyeki, M. B. and Stare, F. J. (1954). Food intake and body weight in normal rats and genetically obese adult mice. *American Journal of Physiology,* 177, 544-548.

35. Tokuyama, K., Saito, M. and Okuda, H. (1982). Effects of wheel running on food intake and weight gain of female rats. *Physiology and Behavior,* 23, 899-903.

36. Wheeler, G. D. (1989). *The effects of endurance training on cardiovascular, anthropometric, psychological and endocrine factors in healthy men and women.* Doctoral dissertation, Department of Physical Education and Sports Studies, The University of Alberta.

37. Kanarek, R. B and Collier, G. H. (1983). Self-starvation: A problem of overriding the satiety signal? *Physiology and Behavior,* 30, 307-311.

38. Levitsky, D. A. (1970). Feeding patterns of rats in response to fasts and changes in environmental conditions. *Physiology and Behavior,* 5, 291-300.

39. Pierce, W. D., Epling, W. F. and Boer, D. P. (1986). Deprivation and satiation: The interrelations between food and wheel running. *Journal of the Experimental Analysis of Behavior,* 46, 199-210.

40. Teghtsoonian, R. and Campbell, B. A. (1960). Random activity of the rat during food deprivation as a function of environmental conditions. *Journal of Comparative and Physiological Psychology,* 53, 242-244.

41. Clark, F. C. (1958). The effect of deprivation and frequency of reinforcement on variable-interval responding. *Journal of the Experimental Analysis of Behavior,* 1, 221-228.

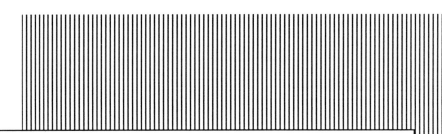

The main topics are:

- **PRINCIPLES OF EVOLUTION**
- **EVOLUTION AND BEHAVIOR**
- **EVOLUTION AND ANOREXIA**
- **EVOLUTION AND ACTIVITY ANOREXIA**
- **PHYSIOLOGICAL BASIS OF ACTIVITY ANOREXIA**

Summary

- The principles of evolution and natural extinction are reviewed.

- Behavioral characteristics are shown to be a complex interplay between evolution and environment.

- Anorexia confers adaptive advantage when alternative behavior is important for survival (e.g. molting, defence of territory, etc.)

- Activity anorexia has been adaptive for those organisms who experience unpredictable changes in food supply. When food becomes scarce, most animals travel to a new location and become anorexic during this period.

- Physiological processes involving brain opiates ensure that the reinforcing effectiveness of food declines as the reinforcing effectiveness of physical activity (e.g. travel) increases.

- Exercise-induced opiates may disrupt menstrual cycle. The mechanism is independent of the effects of exercise on the lean-to-fat ratio.

- Based on the physiological effects of physical activity on food intake and menstrual cycle, it appears that athletes and many anorexic women are suffering from activity anorexia — not anorexia nervosa.

CHAPTER

Biological Basis of
Activity Anorexia

9

In the previous chapter, we explored the behavioral relationships between eating and physical activity. This analysis revealed that activity anorexia has a distinct motivational basis. Changes in food deprivation affect the reinforcing value of exercise and increasing amounts of exercise reduce the value of food reinforcement. These changes in reinforcing value contribute to an overall decline in food intake. People who exercise to excess may eat less frequently (appetite) and may not eat as much at any one meal (satiety). Importantly, as intake declines food deprivation increases and physical activity spirals upward. The person is trapped by the activity-anorexia cycle.

The relationships that govern activity anorexia arise from the evolutionary history of species [1]. That is, the relationships between eating and physical activity have evolved. Generally, natural selection favoured those individuals who became active during severe food shortages. Those animals that travelled to a new location contacted food, survived and reproduced. Thus, the interrelations between food and exercise must be understood within a biological context.

In order to account for activity anorexia from a biological perspective, it is helpful to review the concepts and principles of evolution as they apply to the behavior of organisms. Following a discussion of evolution and behavior, we argue that activity anorexia is an outcome of natural selection. Genetic selection produces changes in anatomy and physiology. Physiological process, in turn, contribute to the regulation of behavior. The final part of this chapter outlines some of the physiological mechanisms that control the activity-food-intake cycle.

1 PRINCIPLES OF EVOLUTION

The theory of evolution is not based on speculation. From a scientific viewpoint, the major principles are not in question. In this sense, the theory of evolution is a factual account of the origin of species. Although scientists agree on the basic processes of evolution, there are debates over the details. To illustrate, some biologists claim that very rapid evolution can occur while others emphasize the gradual elaboration of species characteristics. Other debates concern the unit of selection. Some scientists argue that the unit of selection is the gene itself rather than the individual organism. In this view, the organism is the gene's way of "getting into the next generation" [2]. All of these positions are compatible with the major principle of natural selection. Thus, disputes over *how* evolution works do not challenge the fact of evolution [3].

Natural Selection

The evolutionary history of a species (or phylogeny) is the result of natural selection. In 1859, Darwin described how organisms change as a result of this process [4]. Detailed observations of a variety of species led Darwin to conclude that reproductive success was the "driving force" of nature. Those individuals that produce offspring transmit their characteristics to the next generation and this is what is meant by "reproductive success."

Darwin described differences among the members of sexually reproducing species. With the exception of identical (monozygotic) twins, all individuals in a population are different from one another. Some of these individuals are more successful than others in producing offspring. Differences in reproductive success occur when some individuals possess characteristics that make them more likely to survive and reproduce. Because some individuals produce more offspring than others, their genetic traits are increased in the next generation. This process of differential reproductive success is called natural selection and the change in genetic constitution of a species is evolution [3].

In the *Origin of Species*, Darwin discussed "survival of the fittest." This phrase has often been misunderstood. A common interpretation is that nature is characterized by violent competition for scarce resources such as food. In fact, survival of the fittest simply refers to reproductive advantage. Aggressive animals may be maimed or mortally wounded in combat and because of this fail to reproduce — in this case, more complacent animals gain reproductive advantage and are the "fittest." The ultimate test for fitness is the frequency of offspring from generation to generation. An important consideration is that any physical or behavioral trait may confer reproductive advantage at one time but become non-adaptive if living conditions change. Thus, the fitness of a trait can vary from one generation to the next.

Evolutionary biologists make an important distinction between phenotype and genotype. An organism's *phenotype* refers to all characteristics observed during the lifetime of an individual. For example, an individual's size, color, and shape are structural aspects of phenotype. Behavioral characteristics include taste preference, aggression, shyness, and so on. Different characteristics and behavior of individuals may, or may not, reflect underlying genetic variation. The *genotype* refers to the actual genetic makeup of the organism. Some observable characteristics are largely determined by genotype, other features are strongly influenced by experience, but most result from an *interaction* of genes and environment. For example, the height of a person is determined by genes and by nutrition. Evolution only occurs when the phenotypic differences among individuals are based upon differences in genotype. If differences in height, or other characteristics, do not result from differences at the genetic level, selection for tallness (or shortness) cannot occur. This is because there are no genes for height to pass onto the next generation. People who engage in body-building by lifting weights may substantially increase muscle size (phenotype) but this characteristic will not be passed to their children. Natural selection can only occur when there is genetic variation. There are two major sources of genetic variation — sexual recombination of existing genes and mutation. Genetic differences among individuals arise from sexual reproduction. This is because the blending of male and female genes produces an enormous number of combinations. Although sexual recombination produces variation, the number of genetic combinations is constrained by the existing gene types. In other words, there are a finite number of genes in a population and this determines the amount of variation due to sexual reproduction.

Mutation occurs when the genetic material (e.g. genes or chromosomes) of an individual is changed. These changes are accidents that affect the genetic code carried by ovum or sperm. For example, naturally occurring background radiation may alter a gene site or a chromosome may break during the formation of sex cells or gametes. Such mutations are passed to the offspring who display new characteristics. In most instances, mutations produce characteristics that work against an organisms survival and reproductive success. However, on rare occasions they produce traits that improve reproductive success. The importance of mutation is that it is the source of new genetic variation. All novel-genetic differences are ultimately based on mutation.

2 EVOLUTION AND BEHAVIOR

Darwin recognized that the behavior of organisms was a heritable characteristic [5]. Animals of the same species often show differences in behavioral characteristics and these differences contribute to greater (or lesser) reproductive success. For example, the care and attention provided to young varies within a species. Careful parenting may increase the chances that the offspring survive. To the extent that these offspring in turn reproduce, attentive caretaking is selected. Selection does not always favour the attentive parent. If a parent sacrifices its life guarding the young, the offspring may not survive. In this case, careful parenting is selected against. The behavior of organisms is always a phenotypic expression of genes and environment. Some behavioral characteristics are closely regulated by genes and in such instances the environment plays a subsidiary role. To illustrate, in some species defense of territory occurs as a ritualized sequence of behavior called a fixed-action pattern [6]. The behavior pattern is based on a "genetic blueprint" and the environment simply initiates the sequence. Other examples of behavior that are strongly determined by genes include instinctual responses, reflexes, and so on. The environment plays a greater role in the regulation of other forms of behavior.

When organisms were faced with unpredictable and changing environments, natural selection favoured those individuals whose behavior was flexible. Behavioral flexibility is often called learning, intelligence, or knowledge. We use behavioral flexibility to mean any change in behavior that results from environmental experience. Such experiences include watching what others do, the effects produced by one's actions, and exposure to new information.

Behavioral flexibility reflects an underlying structural change of the organism. To illustrate, the size and complexity of the central nervous system is associated with an organisms ability to change it's behavior on the basis of experience. Such structural changes are ultimately based on genes. Genes code for proteins and many of these proteins are enzymes. Enzymes act as catalysts that control developmental processes. These processes interact with each other and with the external environment to produce the physiology of the organism [7]. Thus, differences in structure, based on genetic variation, give rise to differences in behavioral flexibility. Flexibility, in turn, leads to greater (or lesser) reproductive success and the propagation (or attenuation) of the genes underlying this capacity.

The evolution of behavioral flexibility had an important consequence. Behavior that was closely tied to survival and reproduction could be influenced by experience. Behavior related to survival and reproduction is typically regulated by specific physiological processes. However, for behaviorally-flexible organisms, this control by physiology may be modified by experiences during the lifetime of the individual. The extent of such modification depends on the amount and scope of behavioral flexibility [8, 9]. For example, sexual behavior is closely tied to reproductive success and is regulated by distinct physiological processes. In humans, however, sexual behavior is also influenced by socially-mediated experiences. These experiences dictate when sexual intercourse will occur, how it is performed, and who can be a sexual partner. Powerful religious or social control can even make people abstain from sex. This example illustrates that the biologically-relevant behavior of humans is often determined by physiology and experience.

3 EVOLUTION AND ANOREXIA

An important class of biologically-relevant behavior is concerned with obtaining, preparing, and consuming food. The survival value of eating is obvious; the survival value of not eating is less obvious. There are, however, anorexias that occur in many species that have resulted from natural selection.

There are animals that substantially decrease food intake and lose weight even when food is abundant. In these animals, anorexias often occur when the organism is engaged in other biologically-relevant behavior or when food supply shows seasonal variation. Drs. Mrosovsky and Sherry have discussed animal anorexias and state that:

... Bull seals go without feeding for several weeks while they defend their territory and harem; to feed would entail their going into the water and leaving their territory unprotected. Fasting also occurs in association with incubation, migration, molting, and hibernation, even though food is sometimes readily available. Such fasting can be distinguished at the outset from the fasting of sick animals because it occurs regularly, at specific stages of the life cycle [10, p. 837].

The survival value of anorexia during significant life events is apparent. Eating competes with biologically important activity.

In addition to anorexias that occur during important life events, some anorexias have evolved as adaptations to regular fluctuations in food supply. Animals who evolved in environments with periodic food shortages hibernated and conserved energy or migrated to a reliable food source. During these periods, animals frequently refuse to eat. For example, ground squirrels hibernate during the winter and will not eat when aroused [11, 12]. The survival value of anorexia during hibernation is less obvious than anorexia induced by competing activities. However, anorexia during hibernation apparently contributes to energy efficiency. During a period of hibernation, body temperature decreases and the kidneys do not function well. The kidneys remove waste products from the blood stream and the animal must remain awake for efficient kidney function. Staying awake is energy expensive because the animal must heat it's body to normal temperature. Thus, refusal to eat during hibernation may relate to the energy cost of waking. In fact, the more squirrels eat the sooner they come out of hibernation [11].

Anorexias that result from hibernation or competing activities seem to involve a lowering of "set point" body weight. Set point refers to the body weight that an animal defends. When body weight is stable, a period of fasting results in decreased weight and increased appetite. If food is reinstated, the animal eats voraciously and returns to its previous baseline weight. This return to set point is followed by a decline in appetite and body weight stabilizes.

Natural anorexias appear to involve a slow and progressive decline in set point [10]. In this situation, animals defend a lower body weight rather than attempt to regain normal weight. According to our view, this decline in set point insures that the reinforcing effectiveness of food is decreasing at a time when the animal must engage in other activities (i.e. sexual intercourse). Also, during a period of hibernation an animal may refuse food because the reinforcement value of eating is low relative to hibernating.

The lowering of set point and decline in the reinforcing effectiveness of food may have resulted from evolution and natural selection. For some animals a reduction in food consumption, during biologically significant life events, led to greater reproductive success. Birds that remained on their nests (and gave up eating) during incubation insured the survival of their offspring. Similarly, male deer that guarded their female conquests at the expense of eating had more offspring. In these cases (and others), declining set point and reduced reinforcement value of food improved fitness. Anorexias that occur in response to seasonal variation in food supply, molting, defence of territory and harem, and incubation of eggs are not obviously related to human self-starvation. However, these anorexias demonstrate how "voluntary" reduction of food intake had survival value.

As we have documented, activity anorexia is a type of self-starvation that occurs in humans and other animals. We contend that this form of anorexia also had survival value and is therefore an important variant of evolutionary-based anorexia. In this view, the interrelationships between physical activity and food intake are based on evolved structural features of organisms. Although activity anorexia seems to reflect an underlying genotype (i.e. physiological and neurological characteristics) the phenotypic expression (i.e. self-starvation of individuals) involves a complex interplay between organism and environment.

4   EVOLUTION AND ACTIVITY ANOREXIA

Activity anorexia results from the interrelationships of (1) deprivation and food schedule on physical activity, and (2) activity on food consumption. Briefly stated, strenuous locomotor activity works to suppress appetite. This decrease in the value of food reinforcement serves to affect food schedule and/or deprivation that further increases activity [13]. These factors, excessive physical activity and food restriction, appear to be a sufficient set of conditions for producing activity anorexia.

An evolutionary account of eating and activity points to the survival value of such behavior. During times of food scarcity, organisms can either stay and conserve energy or become mobile and travel to another location. The particular strategy adopted by a species depends on natural selection. Thus, if travel lead to reinstatement of food supply and remaining resulted in starvation, then those animals that travelled would gain reproductive advantage. This means that locomotion induced by changes in food supply became a major evolutionary adaptation of some species.

Many species (e.g. rats, mice, gerbils, guinea pigs, etc.) increase locomotion when food-deprived [14, 15, 16, 17]. In terms of primates, Dr. James Loy observed a colony of free-ranging rhesus monkeys who inhabited an island off the southeast corner of Puerto Rico. During early July of 1968, a severe food shortage occurred. The island was covered with heavy vegetation and the monkey's supplemented their diet by eating plants and an occasional insect. However, their main source of food was commercial monkey chow that was distributed at several feeding stations around the island. Unfortunately, the food shipment for June was delayed and the animals experienced a severe famine.

These monkeys showed a marked reduction in social behavior. For example, monkeys spend a considerable time grooming one another. This behavior and sexual activity substantially decreased during the famine. Most importantly, Dr. Loy reported that there was a dramatic increase in food-directed physical activity. He stated that:

> ... *There was a great increase in the amount of time spent foraging from the vegetation cover. Some monkeys, especially the young, appeared to lose weight.*

A few of the monkeys that subsequently died appeared lethargic immediately before they were missed from their group. These same monkeys foraged constantly *up to their death or disappearance* [18, p. 265; emphasis ours].

The increase in foraging is interesting and consistent with the physical activity observed in laboratory animals exposed to food shortage. Like foraging, the apparently spontaneous running of laboratory animals is controlled by food allocation (see Chapter 8); and this suggests that wheel running is displaced food-seeking behavior.

There are other primates who show increased locomotion when food supply decreases. Drs. Devore and Hall have studied the ecology of baboons living in different regions of the African continent. They have studied the movement and range of baboon troops as related to food supply. These researchers noted that:

Studies in southern Africa, Kenya, and on hamadryas in Ethiopia all indicate the average distance travelled by baboons during a day is three miles. This measures the shortest distance from the sleeping place in the morning, along the route travelled during the day, and back to a sleeping place in the evening. The distance the group

Figure 9.1   A troop of baboons who are foraging on the African savannah.

or any individual baboon walks is much greater, since feeding activity is meander-ing. There is also considerable latitude in the distance travelled on any particular day. This varies from only a few yards (when a Kenya group sleeps in a fig tree and feeds in and under the tree throughout the following day) to a maximum distance of 12 miles (observed once for a group of 65 in South-West Africa). The contrast in available food between a heavily laden fig tree and the sparse vegetation of the study in South-West Africa suggests that available food is the single most important factor affecting length of day range. *This is supported by observations at different seasons, which show that during the seasons when suitable vegetable foods are most plentiful average day ranges are shorter ... A second reason for the longer average day range in the dry season (Kenya) or winter (Cape) is that a group is more likely to shift* to a new core area ... *during these seasons. It is likely that this shifting is also related to the available food supply, representing movement to a new locus of foraging activity after reduction of the available food in the former locus* [19, pp. 31-32, emphasis ours].

These observations of baboon behavior make it clear that there are two aspects to food-seeking behavior. Within a foraging area, these animals will travel up to 12 miles a day to obtain food. However, when the regional food supply drops below some optimal level the baboons may travel large distances to another foraging area. Again, these findings are consistent with the excessive increase in wheel running of laboratory animals deprived of food.

Apparently, many species have adapted to food shortages by increasing physical activity. When food supply decreases, travel to another location may be necessary. Travel may be set off by decreasing contact with food, reduction in the caloric value of food items, and by internal cues associated with loss of body weight (see Chapter 8). Current evidence suggests that internal cues associated with weight loss play a major role in initiating locomotor activity [20].

In our laboratory, animals show large increases in wheel running at several depletion points (typically between 85 and 75 percent body weight). Interestingly, approximately 10 percent of the animals do not display excessive activity. This finding suggests that the tendency to travel when food is depleted is distributed in the population. Some animals leave when weight loss is minimal, some at more severe levels, and some stay and do not travel. These differences in behavioral characteristics make evolutionary sense.

When food is becoming scarce, natural variation insures that some animals leave the location and travel to another area. This same variation guarantees that other members of the species remain in the same location. Those individuals who travel may, or may not, find a new supply of food. If food is contacted then these individuals are more likely to survive and reproduce. Thus, the tendency to travel during a famine increases in the population. On the other hand, the best strategy may be to stay since the food shortage could be temporary. Also, the amount of food in the location may now be sufficient for those few animals that remain. If staying leads to survival and reproductive success then this tendency is selected. With both kinds of selection operating, it is likely that a range of variation in the tendency to travel will be maintained in the population.

A major problem for an evolutionary analysis of activity anorexia is to account for the decreased appetite of animals who are travelling to a new food patch. The fact that increasing energy expenditure is accompanied by decreasing caloric intake seems to violate common sense. From a homeostatic (i.e. energy balance) perspective, food intake and energy expenditure should be positively related.

In fact, as previously noted, this is the case if an animal has the time to adjust to a new level of activity and food supply is not greatly reduced [21]. However, during aperiodic depletion of food sources travel should not stop when food is infrequently contacted, or is difficult to acquire, since stopping to eat would be negatively balanced against reaching a more abundant food patch. Increasing contact with food would signal a replenished food supply and reduce the tendency to travel. Our research indicates that the distance covered in a day is regulated by the amount of food consumed rather than by improvement in body weight [22]. Apparently, the decision to travel is related to weight loss and the decision to stop is regulated by food consumption.

Daily food consumption depends on the density and size of the food items contacted. In this regard, it is important to recall that the reinforcing value of food is low when physical activity is high. This process had selective advantage since animals that found food less attractive would travel more quickly to a place where food was more plentiful.

A decline in the reinforcing value of food means that animals will not work hard for nourishment. When food is scarce, considerable effort may be required to obtain it. For this reason, animals ignore food and continue to travel. However, as food becomes more plentiful and the effort to acquire it decreases the organism begins to eat. Food consumption and increasing body weight lower the reinforcement value of physical activity and travel stops. On this basis, animals who expend large amounts of energy on a trek or migration become anorexic.

The evolutionary processes that produced anorexia during a famine-induced travel were probably important to early man. It is difficult to be sure, but human tribes of hunters and gatherers likely reacted to sudden food shortages in the same way as other primates. The primate evidence suggests natural selection favoured travel in times of food scarcity (see above).

Modern humans possess the genetic compliment that favours physical activity in times of food shortages. Most humans in Western culture do not experience natural famines. However, a culture that encourages dieting and exercise may inadvertently trigger the activity-anorexia cycle. That is, in humans sociocultural factors (see Chapter 10) can produce and maintain conditions of food depletion even though food is readily available. Thus, anorectics may not experience increased contact with food, activity continues to spiral upward, and food consumption remains low or declines.

An evolutionary analysis provides one type of understanding of activity anorexia. However, the explanation is based on ultimate causation and the genetic history is indirectly inferred. Another kind of biological explanation is based on proximate causation involving specific physiological mechanisms that link eating and physical activity.

5 PHYSIOLOGICAL BASIS OF ACTIVITY ANOREXIA

Recent evidence points to the role of endogenous opiates as mediators of the relationship between eating and physical activity. Endogenous opiates are natural substances produced in the central nervous system (e.g. pituitary gland, cell bodies of medial basal hypothalamus, etc.) that have effects similar to drugs like heroin or morphine. In fact, heroin and other opioid drugs bind to the same neurological receptors as the naturally occurring, or endogenous, opiates. Interestingly, endogenous opiates are addictive when externally administered and produce euphoria (feeling of well-being), analgesia (pain relief), and a variety of other responses.

Activity and Endogenous Opiates

In a review article, Drs. Herz and Dum suggested a link between the endogenous opiates and motivation for food [23]. In another review, Drs. Marrazzi and Lubi proposed that anorexia nervosa was the result of addiction to endogenous opiates. They state that:

> ... Opioid systems in the brain are assumed to play a fundamental role in adaptation to starvation and the down-regulation of metabolic set points. There is now substantial evidence that opioids are mobilized in states of prolonged food deprivation, and we are hypothesizing that they are the substrate for an auto-addictive process responsible for the relentlessness of chronic anorexia nervosa [24, p. 191].

In terms of activity anorexia, the endorphins are the most interesting of these opiates.

We suggest that beta endorphin (ß-endorphin), and perhaps other brain opiates, mediate(s) the relationship between increasing physical activity and decreasing food intake. Generally, declining body weight stimulates an increase in physical activity. Physical activity increases production of ß-endorphin and this increase reinforces exercise (i.e. runners high) [25]. In terms of activity anorexia, it is significant to note that, ß-endorphin reduces the inclination to eat when daily exercise is increasing or when body weight remains low. Finally, ß-endorphin, appears to be involved in the control of menstrual cycle and problems of menstruation are a prominent symptom of anorexia in women.

In order to investigate the role of endorphins, researchers typically use one of several primary techniques: Opiates such as morphine are administered; substances that stimulate brain opiates are given; the amount of endogenous opiates is measured by assay; and finally, drugs that block the effects of opiates are injected or given orally. All of these techniques are designed to identify the effects of neural opiates.

There is evidence that ß-endorphin and other brain opiates have opposite effects on appetite depending on body weight. At normal or obese weight, a variety of animals will decrease eating when an opiate-blocking agent is injected [26]. Since naloxone blocks

---

Table 9.1
Methods Used to Research Endogenous Opiates

---

1. Drugs like morphine or heroin are injected. Recall that these drugs bind at the same receptors as endogenous opiates and have similar effects.

2. Stimulating substances are given that activate the production of neural opiates. One stimulant, 2-deoxy-D-glucose, is used to increase the secretion of β-endorphin.

3. The concentration of endorphins in the blood or central nervous system is measured by radio-immunoassay. Brain concentrations must be measured after sacrificing the animal but plasma endorphins, or endorphins in cerebrospinal fluid, can be measured in the intact organism. Most studies of exercise and endorphins use assays of blood samples before and after training.

4. Substances that block the effects of opiates are injected. These blockers bind to the opiate receptors and prevent binding by the endogenous opiates. Naloxone is one type of blocking agent that has been used to investigate the effects of β-endorphin. Injections of this drug often produce behavioral effects that are the opposite of those produced by opiates.

---

endogenous opiates, this research suggests that the opiates stimulate eating when animals are at normal weight or higher. On the other hand, research indicates that opiates may *suppress* appetite when exercise is intensive or when body weight is low.

In terms of the suppressive effects of endogenous opiates, Dr. Davis and his co-workers found that exercise trained rats ate less when given an injection of an opiate stimulant [27]. In addition, Drs. Sanger and McCarthy found that rats who were food deprived for 24 hours ate less when injected with morphine [28]. Since morphine is similar to the endogenous opiates, this suggests that opiates reduce appetite *under conditions of food deprivation* [29]. A similar effect seems to occur in humans who are starving. A recent study found that the β-endorphin stimulus (2-deoxy-D-glucose) increased judgments of hunger in normal-weight people but *decreased* hunger in anorexic patients [30].

As we have frequently noted, hyperactivity is a characteristic feature of anorexia nervosa. There is evidence that intense physical exercise increases endorphin levels. Research has shown that intense exercise by humans resulted in elevated levels of plasma ß-endorphin [31, 32]. Other researchers have found that runners had a higher concentration of endorphins after completing a marathon [33]. Endorphin levels remained elevated for up to 2 hours after the race. Dr. McMurray and his co-workers investigated the effects of exercise intensity on release of ß-endorphin [34]. Twenty men and women in good health volunteered to ride a stationary bicycle. The "workload" on the bicycle was increased from low to high intensity. Blood samples were obtained before and after each exercise session. ß-endorphin increased when exercise levels were at 80% of the individual's maximum output. Generally, the evidence is clear that intense exercise produces increases in plasma ß-endorphin.

According to the activity-anorexia hypothesis, physical activity suppresses food intake. We have shown that under starvation conditions endorphins reduce food intake in animals and decrease reports of hunger in humans. In addition, strenuous physical activity increases blood concentrations of ß-endorphin. If activity anorexia is mediated by endorphins then anorectics should show increased levels of endogenous opiates. In fact, elevated opiate levels have been measured in diagnosed anorectics.

Dr. Kaye and his associates found higher than normal levels of endogenous opiates in the cerebrospinal fluid of anorexia nervosa patients [35]. These elevated levels were found in patients who were severely under weight but not in patients who were close to normal body weight. This finding is somewhat controversial since Drs. Gerner and Sharp carried out a similar study and found that ß-endorphin levels were normal for anorectic patients [36]. Unfortunately, the weight status of the patients in this study was not reported. The discrepancy between the two studies may therefore be due to the difference in patients weights.

There is some evidence that endogenous opiates function to suppress appetite in anorexic patients. A study by Dr. Moore and his colleagues found that weekly-weight gain was substantially increased when anorexia patients were given a constant intravenous infusion of the opiate blocker, naloxone [37]. Although food intake was not measured in this study, it is difficult to see how a 10 fold improvement in weight gain could be accomplished without a substantial increase in eating. Nonetheless, a possibility is that endorphins affect the conservation of nutrients and lower energy expenditure [38]. An opiate blocker would therefore contribute to weight gain in the absence of increased food intake. However, Drs. Reid and Wideman failed to confirm the conservation hypothesis in starving rats [39]. This suggests that the opiate blocker resulted in more eating by anorexic patients. Finally, recall that anorectics reported less hunger when given an opiate stimulant. Overall these findings are consistent with an opiate-induced suppression of eating in anorexic patients.

We have previously noted that the release of endogenous opiates may function as reinforcement for physical activity. The reinforcement hypothesis suggests that injection of an opiate blocker will decrease the intense wheel running of anorexic animals. This is because the euphoric effects of opiates are diminished by blocking the receptors. In our laboratory, research by Dr. Douglas Boer has explored the effects of naloxone on the anorexic running of six male rats [40]. In this study animals were made anorexic by feeding them for 90 minutes a day and providing a running wheel. Once wheel running exceeded 5,000 revolutions per day (5 km) each animal was given a small dose of naloxone (0.5 ml) or saline (0.5 ml) on alternative days. Saline is salt water and is often used in physiological experiments as a placebo control. Average number of wheel revolutions were approximately 5,800 for saline days and 4,800 on days when the animals were injected with the opiate blocker (naloxone). Importantly, each animal showed less running on the days when naloxone was given. These findings provide preliminary evidence for the hypothesis that anorexic running is strengthened and maintained by opiate release.

At this point, it is useful to summarize the evidence for activity-anorexia mediated by endogenous opiates. Starvation and loss of weight increase physical activity. Physical activity produces an increase in endogenous opiates. One important property of opiates is their "euphoric" or reinforcing effects. Because of these effects, physical activity increases and this produces a further elevation in endogenous opiates. Importantly, when body weight is reducing due to food restriction high levels of opiates decrease appetite. Notably, anorexic patients are hyperactive and show high levels of endogenous opiates. These patients also gain weight when endogenous opiates are blocked and do not feel hungry when opiates are stimulated.

Anorexia, Exercise and Fertility

In chapter four, we outlined problems of menstrual cycle in anorectic women and female athletes. There appears to be two physiological processes that regulate female fertility. One process involves estrogen changes due to declining body fat. Dr. Frisch has accumulated substantial evidence that menstrual cycle is regulated by the relative amount of fat or adipose tissue [41]. From this perspective, physical activity affects menstrual cycle because exercise contributes to lean-body mass. We are essentially in agreement with Dr. Frisch's account of female fertility; however, there is evidence that a second process contributes to menstrual problems of anorectics and women athletes [42]. This process involves the effects of exercise on the release of endogenous opiates that, in turn, affect menstrual cycle. Problems of menstruation during activity anorexia are apparently due to both of these processes.

The most prominent feature of anorexia is starvation. According to Dr. Frisch, problems of menstruation usually occur when a woman becomes too lean. Evolution has insured that reproduction will not occur at times when food is scarce. Dr. Frisch states:

It is not surprising that the reproductive function ... falters when a women becomes too lean. Such a response would have given our female ancestors a selective advantage by insuring that they conceived only when they could complete a pregnancy successfully. Reproduction, after all, requires energy, or calories: some 50,000 to 80,000 calories to produce a viable infant and then from 500 to 1,000 calories a day for lactation... In ancient times, when the food supply was scarce or fluctuated seasonally and when breast milk was a newborn's only food, a woman who became pregnant when she lacked an adequate store of body fat — the most readily mobilized fuel in her body — could have endangered both her own life and that of her developing fetus and newborn infant [41, p. 88].

The central idea is that women must attain a sufficient lean-to-fat ratio in order to menstruate. A brain structure called the hypothalamus releases gonadotropin-releasing hormone (GnRH) that starts the process of menstruation and ovulation. At the present time, it is not clear how the lean to fat ratio affects the release of GnRH. Loss of body fat may lower body temperature or change metabolism and this may signal the hypothalamus. Dr. Frisch favours an account based on changes in estrogen level resulting from loss of body fat. When the amount of fat declines relative to leanness, a particular kind of estrogen (the female sex hormone) increases. Presumably, these changes in estrogen signal the hypothalamus to stop the release of GnRH. Since GnRH regulates the onset of menstrual cycle, a disruption produces irregularity, delay, or cessation of the monthly cycle.

In terms of activity anorexia, Frisch's model of fertility suggests that physical activity contributes to fat reduction that, in turn, leads to menstrual problems. In this regard, Dr. Frisch indicates that:

Several recent studies, including our own, have shown that dieting is not the only way women become lean enough to impair their hypothalamic function and disrupt menstruation. Well-trained athletes of all kinds, such as runners, swimmers and ballet dancers, have a high incidence of delayed menarche, irregular cycles, and amenorrhea. This pattern implies that exercise could be the cause — presumably by building muscles and reducing fat, thus raising the ratio of lean mass to fat [41 p. 93].

From this perspective, the hyperactivity of anorectics may contribute to problems of menstruation by altering the lean to fat ratio. However, there is evidence that a second process may be involved. This process occurs when physical activity increases the release of endogenous opiates.

In chapter four, we noted that physical activity can produce problems of menstruation for women athletes. Olympic and college track and field athletes often experience delayed onset of menstrual cycle [43, 44]. Ballet dancers who are very active may also have delay of menstruation [45]. The earlier young women begin training the greater the chance of delayed menarche [46]. Importantly, research findings show that almost 50% of exercising women with amenorrhea are not excessively lean [47]. Taken together, the evidence suggests that physical activity can affect menstrual cycle *independent* of the lean-to-fat ratio.

We have already documented the increase in endogenous opiates that occurs during intense exercise. Drs. Cumming and Rebar suggest that opiate release could be involved in exercise-associated problems of menstruation [48]. Opiate levels are known to affect the release of luteinizing hormone through their action on the hypothalamus and GnRH [49,

50]. Luteinizing hormone (LH) plays a major role in the control of menstrual cycle. Opiates seem to decrease the release of LH in women who exercise excessively [51].

The direct effect of exercise on LH release has been investigated by Dr. Cumming and his associates [52]. These researchers compared LH levels of female long-distance runners to sedentary women of similar height and weight. All women were experiencing normal menstrual cycles at the time of the study. Blood samples were collected from an intravenous catheter every 15 minutes for six hours. The number of LH pulses and total amount of LH was lower in the runners. Since none of the women had exercised for 24 hours before the study, training seems to have a long lasting effect on LH release.

The opiate hypothesis suggests that LH suppression is due to increased levels of endogenous opiates generated by exercise. One test of this idea is to give the opiate blocker, naloxone, to exercising women. An opiate blocker should increase LH levels in these women. In fact, Drs. Cumming and Rebar conducted such a study and found that LH levels did not improve in women with exercise-induced amenorrhea [47]. In contrast, Dr. McArthur and her co-workers found that naloxone produced the expected increase in LH levels [53].

These contrasting findings may have occurred because of the conditional effects of naloxone. Dr. Petraglia and associates studied the LH response times in 18 healthy women [54]. Twelve young women were given naloxone at different times in their menstrual cycle. Six of the older women were postmenopausal and were also given the opiate blocker. The effects of naloxone on LH depended on age and phase of cycle. Naloxone only increased LH level in normally menstruating women during the luteal phase of the cycle. Since naloxone produces variable effects in healthy women, it is also likely that the drug has inconsistent effects in women with exercise associated amenorrhea. Thus, the opiate hypothesis of menstrual problems is difficult to test by administering opiate blockers.

A more direct test of the opiate hypothesis involves the administration of opiate drugs. Recall that an opiate agent, such as morphine, binds at the same receptors as the endogenous opiates. For this reason, morphine and natural opiates should produce similar effects on LH levels. In the study by Dr. Petraglia, the same women were given the opiate drug morphine. Interestingly, as expected, morphine decreased LH in these women. This decrease in LH did not depend on age or phase of cycle. The findings suggest that increases in endogenous opiates produce decreases in LH levels. Unfortunately, there are no studies of the effects of opiate drugs on LH levels of exercising women. Such a study would provide a stronger test of the opiate account of menstrual problems during activity anorexia.

In summary, menstrual problems during activity anorexia can be attributed to two major processes. The most obvious process is that starvation produces lean body mass. When women are excessively thin estrogen level changes and this affects menstrual cycle. Physical activity may also affect the lean-to-fat ratio. As women become more fit due to exercise, the proportional amount of body fat decreases and this again affects estrogen level and menstrual cycle. A second process occurs when exercise increases the release of endogenous opiates. These natural opiates are known to decrease lutenizing hormone (LH) and this hormone is involved in the regulation of menstrual cycle. In this case, physical activity directly influences menstruation and does not depend on changes in body weight. Thus, women who are diagnosed anorexic on the basis of menstrual problems and who show high levels of activity are likely suffering from activity anorexia.

6 CONCLUSION

In this chapter, we have shown that activity anorexia is a natural response to unexpected food shortage. When food is depleted, natural selection has insured that most individuals leave their territory and travel to another location. This same selection pressure guarantees that some individuals stay behind. When travelling is the dominant tendency, research suggests that the "decision to go" is a response to significant loss of weight. Once travel has begun, animals refuse to eat — they become anorexic. This refusal is apparently due to the declining value of food reinforcement. We have shown that this decline insures that travel continues until the individual contacts an abundant food supply. As food density increases the animal begins to eat and the reinforcing value of travel declines. Many species, including humans, seem to have evolved this kind of response to unpredictable food shortages.

These evolutionary tendencies are regulated by specific physiological processes. Starvation and loss of weight increase physical activity and physical activity stimulates the release of brain opiates. Brain opiates reinforce the continuation of physical activity. Because of these effects people show increases in exercise, sports, and fitness that further increases brain opiates. When body weight is low opiates decrease appetite. Notably, anorexic patients are hyperactive and show high levels of brain opiates. Drugs that block the opiates cause anorectics to gain weight. These patients also indicate they do not feel hungry when opiates are stimulated.

The relationship between exercise and brain opiates appears to account for the loss of normal menstrual function in female anorectics. Exercise contributes to increased opiate release that, in turn, affects hormones which regulate menstrual cycle. Thus, women who are diagnosed as having anorexia nervosa as a result of extreme thinness and menstrual problems are apparently exhibiting activity-based anorexia.

REFERENCES

Although many of these references may be of interest, we have indicated (with an asterisk *) those that are written for the non-specialist reader.

1. Epling, W. F., Pierce, W. D. and Stefan, L. (1983). A theory of activity-based anorexia. *International Journal of Eating Disorders*, 3, 27-46.
2. *Dawkins, R. (1976). *The selfish gene*. London: Oxford University Press.
3. *Barash, D. P. (1982). *Sociobiology and behavior*. New York: Elsevier.

4. *Darwin, C. (1859). *On the origin of species by means of natural selection*. London: John Murray.
5. *Darwin, C. (1871). *The descent of man, and selection in relation to sex*. New York: Appleton.
6. Fantino, E. and Logan, C. A. (1979). *The experimental analysis of behavior: A biological perspective*. San Francisco: W. H. Freeman.
7. Wispe, L. G. and Thompson, J. N. (1976). The war between the words: Biological versus social evolution and some related issues. *American Psychologist, 31*, 341-348.
8. Baum, W. M. (1983). Studying foraging in the psychological laboratory. In R. L. Mellgren (Ed.) *Animal cognition and behavior*. Amsterdam: North Holland Press.
9. Pierce, W. D. and Epling, W. F. (1988). Biobehaviorism: Genes, learning and behavior. *Center for Systems Research*, Working Paper 88-95, University of Alberta.
10. Mrosovsky, N. and Sherry, D. F. (1980). Animal anorexias. *Science, 207*, 837-842.
11. Mrosovsky, N. and Barnes, D. S. (1974) Anorexia, food deprivation and hibernation. *Physiology and Behavior, 12*, 265-270.
12. Torke, K. G. and Twente, J. W. (1977). Behavior of spermophilis lateralis between periods of hibernation. *Journal of Mammalogy, 58*, 385-390.
13. Epling, W. F. and Pierce, W. D. (1984). Activity-based anorexia in rats as a function of opportunity to run on an activity wheel. *Nutrition and Behavior, 2*, 37-49.
14. Vincent, G. P. and Pare, W. P. (1976). Activity-stress ulcer in the rat, hamster, gerbil and guinea pig. *Physiology and Behavior, 16*, 557-560.
15. Epling, W. F., Pierce, W. D. and Stefan, L. (1981). Schedule-induced self-starvation. In C. M. Bradshaw, E. Szabadi and C. F. Lowe (Eds.), *Quantification of steady-state operant behaviour*, (pp. 393-396). Amsterdam: Elsevier/North Holland Biomedical Press.
16. Cornish, E. R. and Mrosovsky, N. (1965). Activity during food deprivation and satiation of six species of rodent. *Animal Behaviour, 13*, 242-248.
17. Collier, G. (1969). Body weight loss as a measure of motivation in hunger and thirst. *Annals of the New York Academy of Sciences, 157*, 594-609.
18. Loy, J. (1970). Behavioral response of free-ranging rhesus monkeys to food shortage. *American Journal of Physical Anthropology, 33*, 263-272.
19. Devore, I. and Hall, K. R. L. (1985). Baboon ecology. In I. Devore (Ed.), *Primate behavior: Field studies of monkeys and apes*. New York: Holt, Rinehart and Winston.
20. Kanarek, R. and Collier, G. H. (1983). Self-starvation: A problem of overriding the satiety signal? *Physiology and Behavior, 30*, 307-311.
21. Tokuyama, K., Saito, M. and Okuda, H. (1982). Effects of wheel running on food intake and weight gain of male and female rats. *Physiology and Behavior, 23*, 899-903.
22. Russell, J. C., Epling, W. F., Pierce, D., Amy, R. M., Boer, D. P. (1987). Induction of voluntary prolonged running by rats. *Journal of Applied Physiology, 63*, 2549-2553.
23. Dum, J. and Herz, A. (1987). Opioids and motivation. *Interdisciplinary Science Reviews, 12*, 180-189.
24. Marrazzi, M. A. and Luby, E. D. (1986). An auto-addiction opioid model of chronic anorexia nervosa. *International Journal of Eating Disorders, 5*, 191-208.
25. Shainberg, D. (1977). Long distance running as mediation. *Annals of the New York Academy of Science, 301*, 1002-1009.

26. Sanger, D. J. (1981). Endorphinergic mechanisms in the control of food and water intake, appetite. *Journal of Intake Research*, 2, 193-208.

27. Davis, J. M., Lamb, D. R., Yim, G. K. and Malvern, P. V. (1985). Opioid modulation of feeding behavior following repeated exposure to forced swimming exercise in male rats. *Pharmacology and Biochemistry of Behavior*, 23, 709-714.

28. Sanger, D. J. and McCarthy, P. S. (1980). Differential effects of morphine on food and water intake in food deprived and freely-feeding rats. *Psychopharmacology*, 72, 103-106.

29. Epling, W. F. and Pierce, W. D. (1988). Activity-based anorexia: A biobehavioral perspective. *The International Journal of Eating Disorders*, 7, 475-485.

30. Nakai, Y., Kinoshita, F., Koh, T., Tsujii, S. and Tsukada, T. (1987). Perception of hunger and satiety induced by 2-deoxy-D-glucose in anorexia nervosa and bulimia nervosa. *International Journal of Eating Disorders*, 6, 49-57.

31. Farrell, P. A., Gates, W. K., Muksud, M. G. and Morgan W. P. (1982). Increases in plasma ß-endorphin/ß-lipotropin immunoreactivity after treadmill running in humans. *Journal of Applied Physiology*, 52, 1245-1249.

32. Colt, E. W. D., Wardlaw, S. L. and Frantz, A. G. (1981). The effect of running on plasma ß-endorphin. *Life Science*, 28, 1637-1640.

33. Appenzeller, O., Standefer, J., Appenzeller, J. and Atkinson, R. (1980). Neurology of endurance training: Endorphins. *Neurology*, 30, 418-419.

34. McMurray, R. G., Forsythe, W. A., Mar, M. H. and Hardy, C. J. (1987). Exercise intensity-related responses of ß-endorphin and catecholamines. *Medicine and Science in Sports and Exercise*, 19, 570-574.

35. Kaye, W. H., Picker, D. M., Naber, D. and Ebert, M. H. (1982). Cerebrospinal fluid opioid activity in anorexia nervosa. *American Journal of Psychiatry*, 139, 643-645.

36. Gerner, R. H. and Sharp, B. (1982). CSF ß-endorphin immunoreactivity in normal schizophrenic, depressed, manic and anorexic patients. *Brain Research*, 237, 244-247.

37. Moore, R., Mills, I. H. and Forester, A. (1981). Naloxone in the treatment of anorexia nervosa: Effect on weight gain and lipolysis. *Journal of the Royal Society of Medicine*, 74, 129-131.

38. Margules, D. L. (1979). ß-endorphin and endoloxone: Hormones of the autonomic nervous system for the conservation or expenditure of bodily resources and energy in anticipation of famine or feast. *Neuroscience and Biobehavioral Reviews*, 3, 155-162.

39. Reid, L. D. and Wideman, J. (1982). Naltrexone has no effects on body weights of starving rats. *Bulletin of the Psychonomic Society*, 19, 298-300.

40. Boer, D. P., Epling, W. F., Pierce, W. D. and Russell, J. C. (1990). Suppression of food deprivation-induced high-rate wheel running in rats, *Physiology and Behavior*, in press.

41. *Frisch, R. E. (1988). Fatness and fertility. *Scientific American*, 258, 88-95.

42. Pirke, K. M., Wuttke, W. and Schweiger, U. (1989). *The menstrual cycle and its disorders: Influences of nutrition, exercise and neurotransmitters*. New York: Springer-Verlag.

43. Malina, R. M., Harper, A. B., Avent, H. H. and Campbell, B. E. (1973). Age at menarche in athletes and non-athletes. *Medical Science Sports and Exercise*, 5, 11-13.

44. Cumming, D. C. and Rebar, R. W. (1983). Exercise and reproductive function in women. *American Journal of Industrial Medicine, 4*, 113-125.

45. Frisch, R. E., Wyshank, G. and Vincent, L. (1980). Delayed menarche and amenorrhea in ballet dancers. *The New England Journal of Medicine, 303*, 17-19.

46. Frisch, R. E., Gotz-Welbergen, A. V., McArthur, J. W., Albright, T., Witschi, J., Bullen, B., Birnholtz, J., Reed, R. B. and Herman, H. (1981). Delayed menarche and amenorrhea of college athletes in relation to age of onset of training. *Journal of the American Medical Association, 246*, 1559-1563.

47. Lutter, J. M. and Cushman, S. (1982). Menstrual patterns in female runners. *Physiology and Sports Medicine, 10*, 60-72.

48. Cumming, D. C. and Rebar, R. W. (1985). Hormonal changes with acute exercise and with training in women. *Seminars in Reproductive Endocrinology, 3*, 55-64.

49. Quigley, M. E., Sheehan, K. L., Casper, R. F. and Yen, S. S. C. (1980). Evidence for increased dopaminergic and opioid activity in patients with hypothalamic hypogonadotropic amenorrhea. *Journal of Clinical Endocrinology and Metabolism, 50*, 949.

50. Ropert, J. F., Quigley, M. E. and Yen, S. S. C. (1981). Endogenous opiates modulate pulsatile luteinizing hormone release in humans. *Journal of Clinical Endocrinology and Metabolism, 52*, 583-585.

51. Warren, M. P. (1983). Effects of undernutrition on reproductive function in the human. *Endocrine Reviews, 4*, 363-377.

52. Cumming, D. C., Vickovic, M. M., Wall, S. R., Fluker, M. R. and Belcastro, A. N. (1985). The effect of acute exercise on pulsatile release of luteinizing hormone in women runners. *American Journal of Obstetrics and Gynecology, 141*, 482-485.

53. McArthur, J. W., Bullen, B. A., Beitins, I. Z., Pagano, M., Badger, T. M. and Klibanski, A. (1980). Hypothalamic amenorrhea in runners of normal body composition. *Endocrine Research Communications, 7*, 13-25.

54. Petraglia, F., Porro, C., Facchinetti, F., Cicoli, C., Bertellini, E., Volpe, A., Barbieri, G. C. and Genazzani, A. R. (1986). Opioid control of LH secretion in humans: Menstrual cycle, menopause and aging reduce effect of naloxone but not of morphine. *Life Sciences, 38*, 2103-2110.

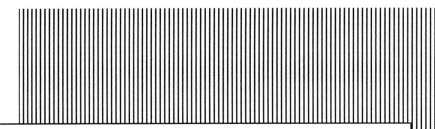

The main topics are:

● **CULTURE AND ACTIVITY ANOREXIA**
● **CULTURE, BIOLOGY AND ACTIVITY ANOREXIA**

Summary

• Activity anorexia is a complex interplay of biology, behavior, and culture.

• In terms of culture, social practices of Western society have promoted the values of thinness and fitness.

• Women (more than men) alter their appearance toward the ideal standard of beauty — thin and fit.

• Numerous studies indicate that Western culture arranges reinforcement contingencies based on appearance that increase the chances that women will combine stringent dieting with excessive eating.

• Based on this cultural conditioning, women are more likely to diet and exercise in a way that initiates the biobehavioral process of activity anorexia.

• Activity anorexia is therefore a biobehavioral process activated by cultural requirements for thinness and fitness.

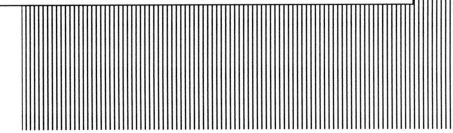

CHAPTER

The Social Context of
Activity Anorexia

10

Activity anorexia occurs in a social context. The biobehavioral processes of activity anorexia only occur when food supply is suddenly, and substantially, reduced. As we have noted in the previous chapter, many animals respond to famine by travelling to a new location and they do not eat at this time. We have shown that this strategy had survival value for several species, including early man. Modern man has inherited these tendencies even though activity anorexia has no functional value in affluent Western societies. When food is abundant and easily obtained, as in North America and Europe, anorexia should not occur. However, we will show that contemporary Western culture creates pressures to diet and exercise and because of this many people experience the activity-anorexia cycle.

1   CULTURE AND ACTIVITY ANOREXIA

In our view, culture refers to the common, everyday, practices of people. Such practices are often called customs in the sense that they are usual or customary responses of many individuals. An important aspect of culture involves teaching people to value particular ideals, symbols and standards. For example, in the United States children are taught to value freedom, the flag, and a high standard of living. Children learn to talk about, and actively pursue, these values. The socialization of values occurs when an individual receives approval for acceptable behavior and censure for unacceptable conduct. This social conditioning insures that most people behave in accord with, and uphold, the values of the community.

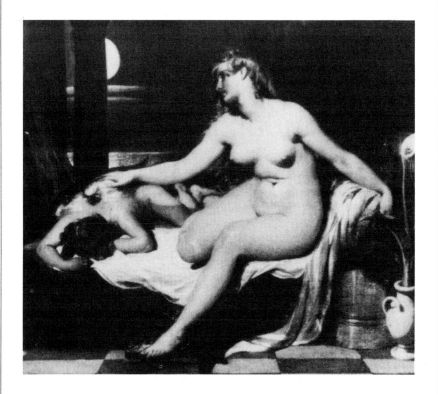

Figure 10.1 This picture shows a representative idealization of beauty in Western art from the mid-nineteenth century. This particular example is called *Venus and Cupid,* by William Etty, *circa* 1840, and is reprinted here with permission of the Russell Cotes Art Gallery and Museum, Bournemouth, England. In comparison, by today's standards someone with the appearance shown in this painting would be more likely to appear in an advertisement for a dieting system, rather than as a romantic example of womanly standards. Other variations in ideal body types can be found throughout earlier eras of history, and across a wide variety of cultures.

In Western culture, a thin and fit woman represents the ideal beauty standard [1]. Social rewards are given when women attempt to achieve this cultural standard by dieting or exercising. A thin woman is told that she looks attractive and she receives a number of social rewards that are not given to other women. Females who weigh more than the ideal standard are criticized and may be told they need to lose a few pounds. Promotions at work, being asked out on a date, reactions from friends and family, and many other social rewards are given to women who take care of their appearance. These rewards and sanctions encourage many women to alter their appearance toward contemporary standards of beauty.

Social contingencies of reinforcement (see Chapter 2) regulate the customary practices of women with regard to beauty. This means that young girls and mature women learn self-descriptions based on the reactions of others. Adolescent girls of normal weight for height often describe themselves as too heavy [2]. Most authorities of anorexia nervosa point to the distorted perceptions of such women. These researchers recognize the social pressure to be thin, but prefer to talk about the person's perceptions as determinants of "the relentless pursuit of thinness." From our point of view, both the perceptions (i.e. self-descriptions) and the active attempts to achieve the beauty standard are caused by social contingencies of reinforcement. Because of these contingencies many women combine dieting and exercising and are susceptible to the biobehavioral processes of activity anorexia.

The cultural practices of Western society also affect the behavior of men. Although there are no clear standards of beauty for men, there is evidence that obesity is not acceptable [3]. In addition, men are expected to be physically fit. Women respond positively to an athletic appearance that involves thin legs, a slim waist, and broad shoulders [4]. Thus, social approval and sexual interest are some of the rewards obtained by men who attain a physically-fit appearance. These social reinforcement contingencies induce many men to exercise but the pressure to diet is not as extreme as for women. For this reason, exercise is less often combined with food restriction and the incidence of activity anorexia is less for men.

Standards of beauty and fitness have changed over the centuries. For example, ancient statues of Venus and Aphrodite portray ideal women who are somewhat plump by today's standards. At other times the idealized woman has been depicted as almost fat. In our present culture, only women who are thin and fit are beautiful. At the turn of the century, however, women were expected to be somewhat chubby and during the nineteen forties and fifties a curvaceous figure was in vogue. Today a beautiful woman is tall and thin.

One indicator of the American beauty standard is the measurements of beauty-queen contestants. Since 1940, the average height of Miss America contestants has increased and their average weight has decreased. A similar trend has been reported for Miss U.S.A. contest finalists for 1983 and 1984. At this time, the average finalist weighed 120 pounds and was 68 inches tall. Twenty years earlier, Miss America contestants also weighed 120 pounds but were two inches shorter. Statistics from insurance companies show that for maximum life span a woman who is 64 inches tall should weigh 124 to 138 pounds. According to these health standards, both Miss U.S.A. and Miss America contestants are very thin and unhealthy [5]. Drs. Lakoff and Sherr have written about societal standards of beauty and the conditions that produce and change such ideals [6]. These authors point to the large-scale economic factors that affect the values of beauty. They state that:

> *Why are different (body) types in vogue at different times? Is the choice governed by larger social forces? It has been pointed out that in periods when starvation is a real threat, and only the wealthy can look plump and well-fed, large women tend to be idealized: in a period when the Madonna represents the feminine ideal, the large-bellied look of pregnancy — whether or not the woman is in fact pregnant — is most desirable: and at a time when it is easier to be sedentary, and food, especially of a calorific kind, is readily available to almost everyone, only the wealthy can afford the time and money required to be slim and/or athletic, and therefore these looks will be 'in' … (pp. 63-64)*

In this passage, Drs. Lakoff and Sherr suggest that changes in beauty standards follow from the practices of the wealthy class. When food is scarce the wealthy still eat well, become fat, and fatness is a symbol of prosperity. When food is abundant, the wealthy separate themselves from the common mass by pursuing thinness. Only the wealthy have the leisure time and money to attend health clubs, buy special low-calorie foods, and exercise during the time when most people are working. Under these conditions, thinness is associated with money, power, and status and, for these reasons, becomes a valued state.

Although this analysis is interesting, it is difficult to be sure that food abundance and wealth are the only factors contributing to changes in beauty standards. There are probably other economic and social conditions that influence beauty trends. Dr. Mazur suggests that standards of beauty in Western society are influenced by the fashion industry. He states that "the Great War ended an epoch in fashion as waistlines were let out and hemlines rose … Dresses of the 1920's and the ideal bodies underneath, became curveless, almost boylike [5]. More recently, high fashion models have become extremely thin to match clothing designs that require a slender body. Many women read fashion magazines and attempt to emulate the appearance of these models.

There is also a huge sports, fitness, and health industry that pushes, and may help create, the values of thinness and fitness. This industry produces billions of dollars and requires consumers who are concerned with fitness, health and slimness. Although there are considerable benefits for those who follow such a fitness standard — for instance, reduced chances of heart disease — it is important to realize that this standard increases the chances of activity anorexia in Western society.

In the remainder of this chapter, we document the preoccupation of Western culture with thinness and fitness. Initially, we describe the rise of the fitness culture and the emphasis on exercise, sports and long distance running. Following this section, we discuss the relationships between beauty, dieting and social approval. In the final section of this chapter, we attempt to explain how biology, behavior, and culture produce differential susceptibility to activity anorexia.

The Value of Fitness

The value of exercise and physical fitness is supported by people in Western societies. This is an unusual and recent development. Historically, the effects of strenuous exercise have been disputed. Before the birth of Christ, the Greek physician, Hippocrates, argued that physical exercise and competition shortened the lifespan of athletes [7]. This view of exercise was commonly held until the mid-nineteenth century. As recently as 1911, the Surgeon General of the United States Navy attempted to discourage recruits from participation in sports by suggesting that "the prolonged rigorous course of physical exercises necessary to excellence in physical sports is believed to be dangerous in its after effects upon those who indulge in athletic sports sufficiently to excel therein" [7]. Over the last 20 years this view has been replaced by a zealous concern with the benefits of physical fitness.

An article in the July 25, 1988 issue of Time magazine documents the widespread concern with physical fitness in the United States. During the 1970's, Americans spent a little over 5 million dollars a year on exercise equipment. Over the last ten years, there has

Figure 10.2　The obsession with running is illustrated in this picture. These joggers were photographed in the middle of winter.

been a phenomenal increase in the sale of this equipment. In 1987 Americans spent over 700 million dollars on weights, exercise bikes, treadmills, and exercise benches. Additionally, in this same year, young-adult Americans spent 5 billion dollars on health club fees.

A cultural obsession with fitness is reflected in the enormous popularity of long distance running. In recent years, the Boston marathon has attracted over 30 thousand enthusiasts. These runners come from all walks of life and may travel long distances to participate in the marathon. The 26 miles covered in a marathon is a remarkable distance to run. The original run to Marathon was accomplished by a Greek soldier who was sent to warn his comrades of an impending attack. The stress of this run was so great that the runner dropped dead of exhaustion after delivering his message.

The Boston marathon is only one of hundreds of such races held each year in North America and Europe. This running "craze" has resulted in large scale sales of athletic clothing. For example, in 1987 Americans spent over 6 billion dollars on high quality running shoes. This means that roughly 60 million pairs of athletic shoes were purchased by American consumers. Taken together, this evidence shows the pervasive value of fitness through exercise in contemporary Western culture.

The number of cases of anorexia has increased along with the rise of the fitness culture. From our perspective this makes sense; in a 1983 paper we argued that excessive physical activity would predispose people to anorexia. This suggestion was based on our research on activity anorexia in animals. Clinical researchers have now documented this effect in humans. Dr. Katz has based his research on our theory and has described two patients "... in whom participation in long-distance running clearly preceded the appearance of anorexia nervosa and appeared to play a role in its onset ..." [8]. In order to illustrate the serious implications of excessive long distance running for the development of anorexia, we present one of the cases reported by Dr. Katz.

(The patient), a 32 year-old physician, reported having begun to jog four years earlier when he felt that he was not getting enough physical activity during a postresidency fellowship he had undertaken. As he began to increase his jogging up to about 35 miles per week, he began to lose weight: from a 'husky' but stable weight of 175 pounds ... His weight dropped to 135 pounds over a period of about five months. During this period, he noted for the first time an increasing obsession with his weight, caloric intake, and diet. He became fascinated with his wife's gourmet cooking course, while concurrently becoming essentially a vegetarian for the first time.

By the completion of his fellowship one year later, his weight was down to 125 pounds and he was now very closely monitoring his caloric intake versus his caloric output via running. For the first time, binging (with vomiting) had occurred on rare occasions (about once a month) during the preceding year. With difficulty temporarily following the fellowship in securing a satisfactory position in his speciality, he further increased his jogging to about 50 miles per week, while now subsisting mainly on salads and coffee or diet soda; his weight now dropped to 115 pounds but he actually felt fat and constantly asked his wife for reassurance that he was not. At the same time the patient was first seen in consultation, recent hip pain, presumably a consequence of the increased running had forced a curtailment of his running, which he was trying to compensate for by extensive walking and bicycling. In association with his forced reduction in running, the patient became even more obsessed with controlling his weight and diet; he also now began to binge regularly every one to two weeks.

The patient had recently begun to feel significantly depressed. He consciously associated this with frustration over his professional situation and family problems, but it was evident, on further probing that he was principally worried about his weight increasing. He was sleeping satisfactorily but was aware of diminished libido (decreased sexual desire) for the first time. There had been no prior personal history of depressive episodes although the patient described himself as having been a compulsive and competitive, but indecisive, individual. Both parents were quite obese, with the father often dieting because of hypertension, but a family history of depression was denied.

During the ensuing months, the patient began to experience increasingly frequent and distressing episodes of bulimia; this occurred in conjunction with continued forced decrease in his jogging, particularly after he entered a new and demanding professional position (p. 75).

This case study illustrates the development of the classic symptoms of anorexia nervosa after excessive activity had reduced food intake in this patient. It is clear that the symptoms follow from the self-starvation induced by long-distance running and are not the causes of the person's anorexia.

The patients initial involvement with jogging appears to have resulted from his acceptance of the cultural value of physical fitness. We have previously shown that the reinforcement value of food declines with increasing physical activity (see Chapter 8) In humans, the social environment encourages and reinforces people who engage in strenuous exercise. Many people who begin a program of long-distance running become part of a sub-culture that is even more concerned with nutrition and exercise. This sub-culture selectively reinforces increasing weekly mileage, speed, and training techniques used to enhance performance.

Dr. David Garner and his associates have suggested that the growing emphasis on fitness has different implications for women than for men [9]. As we have noted, women are subjected to the cultural standards of beauty involving a thin appearance. In our culture women exercise for different reasons than men. For women, fitness is associated with achieving a thin and curveless body shape. According to Dr. Garner, a 1984 survey by Glamour magazine found that 95% of the female respondents had used exercise for the sole purpose of weight control. In contrast, men usually exercise for sports or cardiovascular fitness. An important implication of this difference, is that women are more likely to combine exercise with dieting. For this reason, women may be more susceptible to anorexia than men.

Thinness as A Beauty Standard

As we have stated, "thin and trim" is the contemporary beauty standard for women. There has been much discussion of the unrealistic nature of such a standard and the pressures to achieve it. The media constantly promotes the message that personal success and happiness come to those women who are thin. Dr. Bruch has suggested that movies, magazines and television promote the idea that "one can be loved and respected only when slender" [10, p. viii]. The implication is that the media are fabricating a message that has little basis in reality. Another interpretation is that the media presents an exaggerated reflection of social reactions to beauty in our culture. In other words, there are many social rewards given to women who fit the ideal beauty standard - these rewards include love, respect, success, and happiness.

Physical attractiveness has a strong impact on our social relationships. When men and women meet socially, the attractiveness of the other person affects the behavior of both sexes [11]. Dr. Green and coworkers found that attractive women were more likely to be chosen as dates [12, p. 197]. Men and women report that people who meet the cultural standards of beauty are also sociable, independent, interesting, poised, exciting, and sexually warm [13]. Unattractive people are judged to be socially deviant in a number of ways - they are seen as mentally ill, politically radical, and homosexual [14, 15]

These reactions of others to physical appearance affect an individual's behavior. People who are seen as attractive, learn positive self-evaluations and tend to be confident in a variety of social settings. Attractive people expect to do well in social situations and they generally do [16, 17] On the other hand, those who are judged as unattractive learn negative self-evaluations. To illustrate, one study showed that unattractive college students believed that they were more likely to become mentally ill in the future [18].

Obesity is a physical feature that is currently viewed as unattractive by both men and women. This prejudice begins at an early age; grade-school children judge obese people as stupid, dirty, sloppy, lazy, mean, and ugly [19, 20, 21]. In a comprehensive review, Dr. Wooley and coworkers found that professional mental-health workers, including psychiatrists, psychologists and social workers, judged obese persons as less desirable than normal-weight individuals [22]. These findings support Dr. Fitzgerald's contention that the stigma of obesity is one of a few socially accepted prejudices based solely on appearance [23].

The social rewards for beauty and sanctions for unattractiveness teach women to modify their appearance. Drs. Umberson and Hughes who are social psychologists found that attractive people do better in school; attractive individuals also have higher incomes and more occupational prestige than less attractive persons [24]. There is no biological basis for the connection between physical appearance and achievement. This fact strongly suggests that in our culture academic and work performance is selectively reinforced on the basis of appearance. Selective reinforcement based on beauty is clearly seen when the more attractive cocktail waitress receives higher tips for her service than other waitresses.

As attractiveness leads to rewards, unattractiveness leads to punishment. In medieval times, if two people were accused of the same crime, the uglier person was regarded as more likely to be guilty [25, p. 243]. This overt discrimination does not exist today, but more subtle forms of sanctions continue. Thus, Dr. Efran found that unattractive people who were accused of cheating on an exam or committing a burglary were less liked, seen as more guilty, and given more severe punishment [26].

The negative treatment of people who are judged as unattractive extends to many other social contexts. For example, obese people are frequently denied housing, jobs, promotions and educational opportunities [27, 28, 29]. Also, children who do not meet social standards of beauty are teased and ostracized by other children and may not receive as much

Figure 10.3 Women alter their appearance by applying cosmetics that make them more attractive to others. Cosmetic surgery is used to alter breasts, abdomen and thighs in accord with Western standards of beauty.

positive attention from parents and other adults. Of course, not every unattractive person encounters these social sanctions; many parents, teachers, judges and others have a more enlightened view of people than this analysis suggests. Nonetheless, the prejudice against unattractiveness is a pervasive fact of our culture.

The social benefits of beauty affect women more than men. Women less often judge men on the basis of appearance. They are more likely to emphasize personality and social position [30, 31]. In contrast, men are more interested in the appearance and body shape of women. The pornography industry primarily caters to a male audience and men are more aroused than women by visual images of the opposite sex. One implication is that women reward men for their behavior and acquired status, and men reward women on the basis of appearance. Dr. Mazur states that this sex bias may arise from either biology or socialization. In either case, it has profound implications for women [5].

...Whether because of genetic differences ... or a persistent bias in socialization, men are reliably more visually interested than are women in the bodies of the other sex. As a result, women are under more pressure than men to conform to an ideal of beauty because they quickly learn that their social opportunities are affected by their beauty, and a sense of beauty (or lack of it) becomes an important facet of a young women's self-concept (p. 282).

The arrangement of rewards and sanctions based on a woman's beauty has resulted in many women conforming to current conceptions of physical appearance. In the past, women have modified their appearance by increasing or decreasing bust size, by wearing corsets to give an "hour glass" appearance, and by altering facial appearance with cosmetics. Today, the ideal beauty standard is a very thin and athletic body type. The acceptance of this standard is reflected by evidence on breast enlargement and reduction through cosmetic surgery. Drs. Biggs, Cukier and Worthing reported the yearly number of breast enlargement surgery at their clinic [32]. This clinic is one of the largest and best known in the United States. From the early 1960's through the late 70's, these operations steadily increased but recently have declined. Other evidence indicates that the decline in breast enlargement has been accompanied by operations to reduce the size of breasts, hips, thighs and buttocks.

The acceptance of the thin standard of beauty by women has resulted in an excessive concern with weight regulation. Dr. Garner and his coworkers reviewed six women's magazines for the years 1959 to 1978. They found a 70 percent increase in articles concerned with dieting over the last ten years of their review. The acceptance of thinness as beautiful has also resulted in many normal-weight women describing themselves as overweight and many thin women failing to recognize that they are underweight [33, 34].

The value of thinness is clearly seen in a study of British school girls. Drs. Davies and Furnham found that 47 percent of the girls in their study considered themselves overweight although only 4 percent were heavier than normal [2]. The concern with weight increased as the girls reached maturity. At all ages, at least 80 percent of the girls who described themselves as overweight had thought about dieting and 36 percent of these girls were actually doing so. Surprisingly, about 10 percent of the youngest girls (12-14 years) were dieting even though they thought their weight was "just right." In the oldest category (18 years), 11 percent of the women who saw themselves as underweight were on diets. Most women in this age group (59%) perceived themselves as overweight and 35 percent of these women were dieting. These findings are not unusual and are replicated in numerous studies [35, 36, 37].

In this same study, the researchers reported on the girls' use of exercise to control weight. Within the youngest age group, 40 percent of the girls who thought their weight was "just right" had at one time considered exercise as a method of weight loss and 54 percent were currently exercising. In this same age group, 75 percent of the girls who saw themselves as overweight had previously considered exercise for weight loss and 83 percent were on an exercise program. More girls were using exercise to lose weight than would admit a desire to be thin. By age eighteen, 81 percent of the women who felt they were "just right" had considered exercise as a method of weight control and 27 percent were actually exercising. Ninety-six percent of the 18 year olds who thought they were overweight had contemplated using exercise for weight control; 74 percent were currently exercising.

In terms of activity anorexia, it is notable that these young women were frequently combining dieting with exercise. The severity of the diet and the intensity of exercise was probably quite variable; however, we would expect that the chances of anorexia are higher in this population. In fact, Dr. Crisp reported that 1 in 100 adolescent British-school girls were suffering from anorexia nervosa (see Chapter 3). This figure is the highest reported incidence of the disorder in the general population. The high incidence of anorexia, in the context of dieting and exercise, suggests that girls in this population are experiencing activity anorexia not anorexia nervosa.

2   CULTURE, BIOLOGY AND ACTIVITY ANOREXIA

The most convincing evidence for activity anorexia comes from laboratory research with animals (Chapters 7 and 8). In the laboratory situation, the experimenter controls food allocation and access to activity. In contrast, humans seem to self-regulate food intake and exercise. Given this difference, many researchers in the field of anorexia nervosa have questioned the generality of the animal model. Recently, Dr. Mrosovsky has challenged the activity-anorexia model of human self-starvation and has stated that "since (in the animal experiments) the experimenter, not the rat, imposes the 1-hour feeding regimen, the term self-starvation is silly. To the extent that the phenomenon has a human counterpart, the patient herself adopts the role of the experimenter in setting the eating patterns. The animal analogy offers no insight into why she does this" [38, p. 26].

Dr. Mrosovsky's mistake is to assume that the patient freely chooses to starve to death. In both animals and humans food restriction is imposed. The patient is not the experimenter; rather, social contingencies of reinforcement encourage and maintain dieting to lose weight. In this sense, the diet and exercise culture is the experimenter.

As we have shown, Western culture has evolved standards of beauty and fitness that favour a thin and trim appearance. Because of these standards, women are reinforced for behavior directed at achieving or maintaining a slim-body type. Women who attain a slim and trim appearance are more likely to be successful in life and interact more frequently with the opposite sex. In contrast, women who fail to meet the ideal standard receive social disapproval and are less likely to attain a high social position. These social contingencies of reinforcement regulate the behavior of women and produce the extreme concern with diet and exercise to lose weight. Thus, women choose to combine dieting and exercise because of the social reactions of others.

The person who is subjected to these social consequences does not willfully restrict food intake. Although food is abundant in Western society, a cultural famine is arranged for many women. For example, a young woman can easily go to the refrigerator and eat what she wants. However, repeated choices to eat may result in weight gain and social disapproval. On this basis, young women frequently choose to restrict their food intake.

Although it is tempting to attribute anorexia to cultural pressures to be thin, this is not an adequate explanation. The culture establishes the preconditions to diet and exercise but does not directly cause loss of appetite and severe starvation. In laboratory animals food is also restricted but animals do not die from this imposed reduction. Only those animals that exercise excessively become anorexic. Activity anorexia in humans is the result of a similar process.

Activity anorexia is a biobehavioral process initiated by unusual cultural practices. The culturally imposed "famine" increases the tendency to engage in locomotor activity that is channelled into exercise in our culture. That is, people who are dieting become active due to biological processes and this activity is expressed in socially appropriate ways. The wheel running of animals and the exercise of anorexic humans are both examples of displaced food-seeking behavior. Of course, humans also exercise on the basis of the value of fitness and health. This may contribute to anorexia because exercising is socially reinforced and can become excessive independent of food restriction.

An evolutionary account of activity anorexia points to the survival value of such behavior. During famine, organisms can either stay and conserve energy or they can become mobile and travel to another location. As we have noted in Chapter 9, the particular strategy adopted by a species depends on natural selection. Thus, if travelling to a new location lead to food and remaining to starvation, then those animals that travelled would reproduce and increase the likelihood of this behavior in the next generation. Remaining in the same location could also have survival value. The food shortage may be temporary or the food supply may be sufficient for the few animals that remain behind.

The tendency to travel or remain is probably correlated with body weight. Animals of low weight can not afford to wait until food supply is replenished. These animals should respond quickly to food reduction by becoming mobile. On the other hand, animals at higher body weights may survive by metabolizing their body fat. For these animals, waiting out a famine may be the best strategy. Thus, the tendency to become active as a result of food shortage is distributed in the population and is selected by variation in body weight.

This suggests that an animal's baseline body weight or set point is a predictor of the tendency to become active when food deprived. In fact, we have found that heavier animals are less likely to run when food is withheld.

An evolutionary analysis suggests that animals who travel during food shortages should become anorexic. This loss of appetite occurs because stopping to eat small and infrequent meals is negatively balanced against reaching a more plentiful food supply. Animals that stopped were less likely to survive and reproduce. Those animals who kept going until they reached an abundant food patch were more reproductively successful. This kind of selection has resulted in physiological mechanisms that decrease the reinforcing value of food when physical activity is high. The same selection pressure has lead to other physiological processes that increase the reinforcing value of locomotor activity when food is depleted.

Natural, or culturally imposed, famines set off the biobehavioral processes that we have called activity anorexia. These processes are the result of natural selection. At the behavioral level, food deprivation increases the motivational value of exercise and excessive activity decreases the motivation to eat. These relationships are mediated by complex physiological processes involving the endogenous opiate system. Thus, activity anorexia may be viewed as a normal response to food depletion. Western culture has arranged an environment that triggers this response in many young women.

REFERENCES

Although many of these references may be of interest, we have indicated (with an asterisk *) those that are written for the non-specialist reader.

1. *Orbach, S. (1986). *Hunger strike*. London: Faber & Faber.
2. Davies, E. and Furnham, A. (1986). The dieting and body shape concerns of adolescent females. *Journal of Child Psychology and Psychiatry*, 27, 417-428.
3. Harris, M. B., Harris, R. J. and Bochner, S. (1982). Fat, four-eyed, and female: Stereotypes of obesity, glasses, and gender. *Journal of Applied Social Psychology*, 12, 503-516.
4. Beck, S. B., Ward-Hull, C. I. and McLear, P. M. (1976). Variables related to women's somatic preferences of the male and female body. *Journal of Personality and Social Psychology*, 34, 1200-1210.
5. Mazur, A. (1986). U.S. trends in feminine beauty and overadaptation. *The Journal of Sex Research*, 22, 281-303.
6. *Lakoff, R. T. and Scherr, R. L. (1984). *Face value: The politics of beauty*. Boston: Routledge and Kegan Paul.
7. Montoye, H. J. (1967). Participation in athletics. *Canadian Medical Association Journal*, 96, 813-820.
8. Katz, J. L. (1986). Long distance running, anorexia nervosa, and bulimia: A report of two cases. *Comprehensive Psychiatry,* 27, 74-78.
9. Garner, D. M., Rockert, W., Olmsted, M. P., Johnson, C. and Coscina, D. V. (1985).

Psychoeducational principles in the treatment of bulimia and anorexia nervosa. In Garner, D. M. and Garfinkel, P. (Eds) *Handbook of psychotherapy for anorexia nervosa and bulimia,* (pp. 513-572). New York: The Guilford Press.

10. *Bruch, H. (1978). *The golden cage.* Cambridge, MA: Harvard University Press.

11. Hatfield, E. and Sprecher, S. (1986). *Mirror, mirror... the importance of looks in everyday life.* Albany, NY: State University of New York Press.

12. Green, S. K., Buchanan, D. R. and Heuer, S. K. (1984). Winners, losers, and choosers: A field investigation of dating initiation. *Personality and Social Psychology Bulletin,* 10, 502-511.

13. Brigham, J. C. (1980). Limiting conditions of the "physical attractiveness stereotype:" Attributions about divorce. *Journal of Research In Personality,* 14, 365-375.

14. Jones, W. H., Hannson, R. and Philips, A. L. (1978). Physical attractiveness and judgments of psychotherapy. *Journal of Social Psychology,* 105, 79-84.

15. Unger, R. K., Hilderbrand, M. and Madar, T. (1982). Physical attractiveness and assumptions about social deviance: Some sex-by-sex comparisons. *Personality and Social Psychology Bulletin,* 8, 293-301.

16. Abbott, A. R. and Sebastian, R. J. (1981). Physical attractiveness and expectations of success. *Personality and Social Psychology Bulletin,* 7, 481-486.

17. Reis, H. T., Nezlek, J. and Wheeler, L. (1980). Physical attractiveness in social interaction. *Journal of Personality and Social Psychology,* 38, 604-617.

18. O'Grady, K. E. (1982). Sex, physical attractiveness, and perceived risk for mental illness. *Journal of Personality and Social Psychology,* 43, 1064-1071.

19. Allon, N. (1975). Latent social services in group dieting. *Social Problems,* 32, 59-69.

20. Staffieri, J. R. (1967). A study of social stereotype of body image in children. *Journal of Personality and Social Psychology,* 7, 101-104.

21. Staffieri, J. R. (1972). Body build and behavior expectancies in young females. *Developmental Psychology,* 6, 125-127.

22. Wooley, O. W., Wooley, S. C. and Dyrenforth, S. R. (1979). Obesity and women. ll. A neglected feminist topic. *Women's Studies International Quarterly,* 2, 67-79.

23. Fitzgerald, F. T. (1981). The problem of obesity. *Annual Review of Medicine,* 32, 221-231.

24. Umberson, D. and Hughes, M. (1984). *The impact of physical attractiveness on achievement and psychological well-being.* Paper presented at the Meetings of the American Sociological Association, San Antonio, Texas, August.

25. *Alcock, J. E., Carment, D. W. and Sadava, S. W. (1987). *Social psychology.* Scarbourough, ON: Prentice Hall.

26. Efran, M. G. (1974). The effect of physical appearance on the judgment of guilt, interpersonal attraction, and severity of recommended punishment in a simulated jury task. *Journal of Research in Personality,* 8, 45-54.

27. Bray, G. A. (1976). The risks and disadvantages of obesity. *Major Problems in Internal Medicine,* 9, 215-251.

28. Canning, H. and Mayer, J. (1966). Obesity: Its possible effect on college acceptance. *New England Journal of Medicine,* 275, 1172-1174.

29. Karris, L. (1977). Prejudice against obese renters. *Journal of Social Psychology,* 101, 159-169.

30. Berscheid, E. and Walster, E. (1974). Physical attractiveness. In Berkowitz, L. (Ed.) *Advances in experimental social psychology* (Vol. 7). New York: Academic Press.

31. Huston, T. L. and Levinger, G. (1978). Interpersonal attraction and relationships. *Annual Review of Psychology*, 29, 115-156.

32. Biggs, T., Cukier, J. and Worthing, L. (1982). Augmentation mammaplasty: A review of 18 years. *Plastic and Reconstructive Surgery*, 69, 445-450.

33. Halmi, K. A., Falk, J. R. and Schwartz, E. (1981). Binge-eating and vomiting: A survey of a college population. *Psychological Medicine,* 11, 697-706.

34. Gray, S. H. (1977). Social aspects of body image: Perception of normalcy of weight and affect of college undergraduates. *Perceptual and Motor Skills,* 45, 1035-104 0.

35. Dwyer, J. T., Feldman, J. J. and Mayer, J. (1970). The social psychology of dieting. *Journal of Health and Social Behavior*, 11, 269-287.

36. Jakobovits, C., Halstead, P., Kelley, L., Roe, D. A. and Young, C. M. (1977). Eating habits and nutrient intakes of college women over a thirty-year period. *Journal of the American Dietetic Association*, 71, 405-411.

37. Miller, T. M., Coffman, J. G. and Linke, R. A. (1980). Survey on body image, weight and diet of college students. *Journal of the American Dietetic Association*, 77, 561-566.

38. Mrosovsky, N. (1984). Animal models: Anorexia yes, nervosa, no. In K. M. Pirke and D. Ploog (Eds.), *Psychobiology of anorexia nervosa,* (pp. 24-34). New York: Springer-Verlag.

PART III

Clinical Aspects of Activity Anorexia

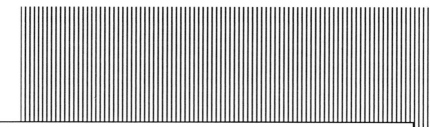

The main topics are:

- CLASSIFICATION OF ANOREXIAS
- MODEL OF ACTIVITY ANOREXIA
- ASSESSMENT CRITERIA FOR ACTIVITY ANOREXIA
- METHOD OF ASSESSMENT

Summary
- A distinction is made between the classification of anorexia based on symptoms and one based on functional causes. A functional definition of anorexia is recommended.

- Activity anorexia may be viewed as one type of functional anorexia that is lumped under the general diagnostic category of anorexia nervosa.

- A causal model of activity anorexia is outlined, showing how sociocultural factors affect dieting, exercising, and self-description through reinforcement and social modelling contingencies. These behavioral responses initiate the physiological processes that produce activity anorexia.

- The biobehavioral model has implications for assessment and treatment of activity anorexia as a clinical problem.

- Primary and secondary criteria for assessment is suggested — medical workup, behavioral history involving diet and exercise, and baseline measurement of target behavior.

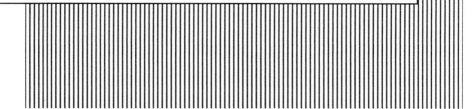

CHAPTER

Assessment of Activity
Anorexia

11

Activity anorexia is not currently recognized as a clinical problem. This form of anorexia is a natural response to sudden and severe food shortage and is not a mental illness. However, mental-health professionals diagnose almost all cases of anorexia as an expression of neurosis. To the extent that such cases of anorexia nervosa are in fact instances of activity anorexia, many people are incorrectly labelled as mentally ill. The diagnosis of anorexia nervosa is not helpful in these cases because attention is directed at personality factors rather than the objective determinants of eating. At the present time, there is no classification system for activity anorexia. In this chapter, we present assessment criteria that may be used in clinical settings. These criteria are based on our model of activity anorexia and the current research evidence. Clinical studies and practice will ultimately determine the adequacy of this classification.

1   CLASSIFICATION OF ANOREXIAS

Activity anorexia is not simply a subset of the more general category, anorexia nervosa. People in competitive athletics, dance, and recreational sports (e.g. running and jogging) appear to show a high incidence of eating disorders. Such eating problems have been described as "athletic anorexia," "athletes nervosa," and "exercise anorexia." The basic assumption of many experts is that athletes with eating problems are similar to anorectics, but athletes are not neurotic [1]. On the other hand, some researchers have claimed that runners have personality profiles similar to anorectics. The implication is that some athletes with eating problems are suffering from anorexia nervosa [2]. The more obvious link between anorectics and long distance runners is that both groups are excessively active and this may affect food intake. In our view, the personality profiles develop from the activity-anorexia process. Thus, activity anorexia is a distinct clinical problem.

Functional Classification

In order to develop assessment criteria for activity anorexia, it is important to distinguish between classification based on symptoms and one based on a functional analysis of behavior. Symptom-based diagnosis is closely tied to the medical model of disease (see, Chapter 1). From this perspective, observable behavior and physiological reactions are used to infer the underlying illness. A doctor uses fever, reports of headache, coughing, and other indicators to diagnose influenza. Once the diagnosis is made, an appropriate treatment can be implemented (i.e. drugs may be prescribed). In medical practice, the inference of physical disease from symptoms has been a successful strategy.

In our view, this strategy has not been as useful when behavior is taken as a symptom of mental illness. This is because the "disease agent" is not separated from the behavior it is said to explain. Thus, the neurotic personality is inferred from the symptoms of anorexia nervosa and failure to eat is attributed to the personality disorder. Another difficulty is that the symptoms of anorexia may change with the prevailing theory of the disorder. Thus, psychosexual symptoms may be expected from a psychoanalytical orientation while distortion of thinking may be notable within a cognitive perspective [3, 4]. A biobehavioral approach offers an alternative to the traditional method of diagnosis.

The biobehavioral model suggests that anorexic behavior results from an interplay between biology and environment. Paradoxically, such behavior is functional in the sense that it is a normal response to unique environmental conditions. An activity anorexia occurs among those animals whose ancestors have survived food shortage by increasing activity.

Physiological and behavioral processes insure that during a period of travel the animal will become anorexic until an adequate food supply is reinstated. Humans have inherited the biobehavioral processes that produce activity anorexia. These processes are triggered by cultural practices of diet and exercise and are maintained by the food restriction and activity cycle.

We prefer to define anorexia in terms of behavior rather than in terms of the desire to eat. Behaviorally, anorexia may be defined as a low probability of eating (in terms of frequency and size of meals) when body weight is below normative values (weight adjusted for height and bone structure). The decline in eating may, or may not, be accompanied by reports of loss of appetite. Such reports are not fundamental to the behavioral classification. In addition, the numerous psychological symptoms involving neurotic patterns on personality tests, bulimia, vomiting, preoccupation with food, feelings of guilt, family conflict, body-image distortion, and phobic reactions to weight are not required for the assessment. These symptoms are viewed as complex behavior that arises from starvation and social contingencies of reinforcement (see Chapter 4).

In our view, anorexia is not a uniform phenomenon. There may be several forms of anorexia that are generated by different conditions and processes Our classification of anorexia is based on an analysis of these determinants. For example, there is tentative evidence that zinc deficiency may be linked to anorexia in humans [5]. A zinc-based anorexia must be distinguished from activity anorexia in terms of the variables that initiate, maintain and change the tendency to eat. In this case, factors involving nutrition may contribute to anorexia and the distinct physiological processes that maintain it

Some forms of anorexia may arise from experiences during the lifetime of the person (i.e. ontogenetic). Thus, anorexia may occur for political or religious reasons, as when a person goes on a hunger strike or fast. Anorexic behavior may also arise from the previous consequences of eating. Cats who are punished for eating with a blast of air will starve rather than approach the food tray [6]. This suggests that the reinforcement history for eating may directly affect the probability of such behavior. Assessment of the history of reinforcement may be important in classifying and treating this kind of anorexia. For example, systematic desensitization procedures may be highly effective when eating has been punished but not when eating is reduced by zinc deficiency. Finally, a stress-induced anorexia has been reported for monkeys who were moved from their colony to a new cage [7]. This may be similar to anorexia in humans that occurs after a sudden change in living conditions.

These distinctions among the determinants of anorexia make it clear that anorexia is not a single disorder and that treatment must change depending on the causes of starvation. Based on clinical reports of hyperactivity and anorexia, we estimate that between 38 and 75 percent of the cases diagnosed as anorexia nervosa are in fact cases of activity anorexia. The remaining cases may be instances of neurotic anorexia (not functionally defined), or instances of functional anorexia as outlined above. Thus, activity anorexia is identified on the basis of functional determinants.

2 MODEL OF ACTIVITY ANOREXIA

In order to specify the functional relationships that regulate activity anorexia, we developed a model of the biobehavioral process. This model is based on the research evidence and theory presented in this book. Activity anorexia is the result of behavioral and biological processes that, in Western societies, are initiated by cultural practices. Although the model emphasizes cultural factors as the major initiating conditions, it is important to realize that the basic process may be triggered by other events. Famine, forced exercise, or any condition that combines food restriction and physical activity may increase the chances of activity anorexia.

Theories of anorexia nervosa have emphasized the importance of psychological factors. Throughout this book, we have presented analyses and evidence that these factors are not central to activity anorexia. The model shows that psychological factors such as, fear of fatness, body image distortion, eating attitudes, bulimia, preoccupation with food, depression, perfectionistic standards, hostile-dependent attitude, self-descriptions, and so on, arise from contingencies of reinforcement set by others. Family members, friends, and health professionals teach the anorexic to describe behavior, thoughts and feelings. Also, reasonable responses to situational determinants of behavior are interpreted as personality symptoms. For example, a young woman who does *not want to eat* is said to *resist* treatment. Denial of illness, evidenced by resistance to treatment, is then taken as a symptom of anorexia nervosa [8]. Psychological factors are also produced by the physiology of starvation. The Keys *et al* study found that psychologically healthy men

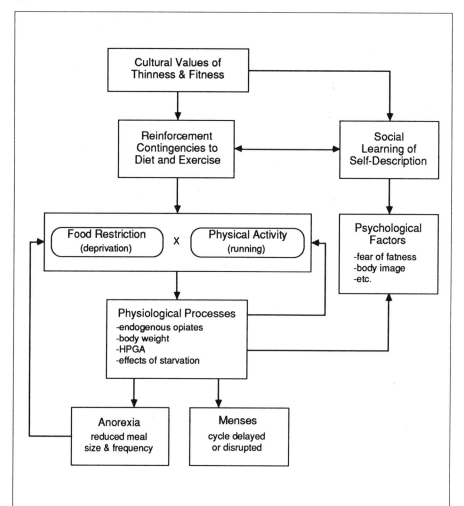

Figure 11.1   A biobehavioral model of activity anorexia. The model portrays the cultural impact on dieting and exercising. This behavior is supported by reinforcement contingencies set by family and friends. Under particular conditions, food restriction combines with physical activity to initiate the physiological processes of activity anorexia.

became neurotic, preoccupied with food, and bulimic when they were forced to starve. Although psychological factors are not the causes of activity anorexia, these effects are indicators of the major causal processes.

A major initiating condition for activity anorexia are cultural practices that emphasize appearance. In Western culture, the ideal standard of beauty for women is thin and trim (see Chapter 10). This cultural value of thinness is portrayed as an initiating factor of the model. Such ideal standards are treated as givens and are not explained by the theory of activity anorexia One measure of the value of thinness may be obtained by observing the mass media. Television, newspapers and magazines have all portrayed very thin women as beautiful.

The cultural value of thinness has been paralleled by a concern with health and fitness. This value of fitness is widely accepted in Western societies and is reflected by increased sales of sports equipment, the number of health and fitness facilities and the number of people who participate in athletic activities. In the model, this value is shown as a separate influence on individual behavior

Cultural values influence individual behavior by affecting contingencies of reinforcement. A contingency of reinforcement refers to the occasion upon which behavior is reinforced. In the model, cultural values affect the social training of self-descriptive statements that, in turn, affect reinforcement contingencies to diet and exercise. For example, social approval for women may depend on maintaining a thin appearance. Women who describe themselves as "too fat" are likely to go on diets and be reinforced by signs of weight loss. Also, the person who has gone on a diet and lost weight has probably received favorable comments from friends and relatives. This social approval increases the tendency to diet when body weight departs from the cultural ideal. It is important to recognize that each person has a unique group of friends and relatives who provide social reinforcement at different amounts and rates. Thus, the cultural impact of a value changes from person to person. In addition, social conditioning insures that one person is more (or less) affected by approval and attention than another.

Reinforcement contingencies for dieting and exercising often depend on social characteristics. People with higher status and money join clubs and sports facilities more than lower status individuals. Membership in such organizations increases the opportunity to exercise and the rate of reinforcement for such behavior. In a recreational club, people are prompted to exercise by observing others engaged in active sports and by talking about health and fitness. The members of such facilities provide companionship, privileges and social-esteem to those who excel at such activity. In terms of dieting, the reinforcement contingencies appear to differ by gender. Thus, women receive social approval and attention when dieting results in a thin appearance. The consequences of dieting are not the same for men because cultural standards of masculine appearance are not well defined (see Chapter 10). Other characteristics such as age, occupation, and education may also affect the reinforcement of dieting and exercising

The model makes it clear that cultural values affect contingencies of reinforcement for dieting and exercising. The person who chooses to participate in athletics and decides to go on a diet, is responding to the reinforcement contingencies that support such behavior. When dieting and exercising occur at the same time there is an increased chance that food restriction will combine with physical activity in a way that eventually leads to anorexia. The severity of dieting and excessiveness of exercising will determine the impact of this behavior for activity anorexia.

In order to initiate the activity-anorexia cycle, food restriction must combine with physical activity. This multiplier effect is a critical feature of the cycle. Notice that food restriction and physical activity produce an effect together that is greater than the sum of their separate influences. Laboratory research suggest that the multiplier effect is most likely when meals are reduced to one a day. Other evidence indicates that the probability of activity anorexia increases when physical activity is progressively going up. In humans, the type of exercise or fitness program may be relevant. Our best guess is that aerobic-based activities such as long distance running may interfere with eating more than other types of exercise. Thus, the person at most risk for anorexia is hyperactive with a history of increasing physical activity and is on a severe diet.

The interrelation of food restriction with physical activity affects specific physiological processes (see Chapter 9). An easily observed effect is a decline in body weight. Evidence suggests that food restriction may operate through body-weight loss to initiate physical activity. Brain opiates such as ß-endorphin are released when physical activity is intense and this release appears to reinforce such behavior. The greatest release of ß-endorphin occurs at approximately 80 percent of maximum oxygen up-take (VO2-max). As aerobic fitness increases more and more exercise is required to attain 80 percent of VO2-max and maximal release of endorphin. Thus, the reinforcing effects of brain opiates require increasing levels of exertion. This creates a feedback process between physiology and physical activity.

Endogenous opiates generated by physical activity affect the menstrual cycle. Menstrual cycle is regulated by the hypothalamic-pituitary-gonadal-axis (HPGA). Gonadotropin releasing hormone (GnRH) is secreted by the hypothalamus in a pulsatile manner. GnRH causes the pituitary gland to synthesize and release both luteinizing hormone (LH) and follicle stimulating hormone (FSH). The pituitary hormones, LH and FSH, stimulate the ovaries to secrete sex steriods and to prepare the oocytes for fertilization. In this process, endogenous opiates such as ß-endorphin may decrease pulsations of GnRH and LH [9]. A decrease in pulsatile GnRH or LH leads to problems of menstrual cycle. These relationships explain why some women athletes and anorectics experience menstrual dysfunction.

Physiological processes involving the release of endogenous opiates also affect food consumption. When body weight is low ß-endorphin appears to lower caloric intake. This reduction is observed as a decrease in meal size and frequency. Anorexia is defined at this point because body weight is low or declining and the person is eating very little. Importantly, this change in frequency and size of meals feeds back on food restriction and level of deprivation. Food restriction further augments physical activity and the person is locked into a cycle of declining food intake and increasing physical activity. This cycle explains why athletes, ballet dancers, gymnasts and anorectics have eating problems [9, 10, 11].

3   ASSESSMENT CRITERIA FOR ACTIVITY ANOREXIA

In this section, we outline criteria that may be used to identify cases of activity anorexia. These criteria are based on the biobehavioral model of activity anorexia and current research evidence. As stated earlier, clinical studies and practice may alter this preliminary system of classification.

Primary Criteria

The primary criteria for activity anorexia refer to the necessary conditions that must be present.

1. The person must show a history of low or declining food intake when body weight is below normative standards (based on weight adjusted for height and bone structure).

We have not set a weight-loss criteria. This is because the sooner anorexia is detected the better the long term outcome since the physical effects of starvation are avoided. Starvation can produce serious physiological damage that may be life threatening and irreversible.

2. The person must present a history of excessive physical activity. Aerobic exercise like long distance running, swimming, active sports are particularly significant.

3. The onset of psychological symptoms often follows, rather than precedes, anorexia and excessive exercise. For people with a history of anorexia, psychological symptoms may be present during periods of low food intake and absent when eating recovers.

It is often difficult to assess the personal history with regard to exercise and hyperactivity. People may not consider their activity level excessive or they may not wish to report it. For this reason, it may be necessary to use a structured interview that probes for type and level of physical activity. Care should be taken to reduce demand characteristics that lead the patient to report in accord with the interviewer's expectations. One way to increase accuracy is to verify patient reports with family members. An important point is that as starvation becomes extreme, activity may decline. Thus, the current level of physical activity may not be as important as the history of exercise.

Supplementary Criteria

These criteria are often present and supplement the assessment based on primary criteria. The criteria follow from our analysis of the biological, behavioral and cultural determinants of the activity-anorexia cycle. Generally, as the number of supplementary criteria increase the greater the certainty of activity anorexia.

1. Activity is particularly significant if there is evidence of a substantial increase relative to baseline levels of exertion (e.g. sedentary to active, increased sports training, increased mileage for a long distance runner, etc.).

2. History of attempts to food restrict for any reason (e.g. weight loss for aesthetic reasons, weight loss to improve athletic performance, etc.).

3. Food restriction combined with excessive and increasing levels of exercise places the person at extreme risk.

4. A decrease in the number of daily meals and snacks eaten. This may be particularly significant if the person has reduced eating to one meal or less per day.

5. Preoccupation of person and family with sports, fitness, dieting, and general acceptance of thinness as a beauty standard. High scores on the Eating Attitudes Test (EAT) may reflect such concerns.

6. Preoccupation with exercise, as when a person plans the day around exercise routines and/or engages in ritualistic behavior related to exercise (e.g. sports fanatic).

7. Persons who are required by occupation to be thin (e.g. fashion models), or physically active (e.g. athletes) are at some risk. Those individuals who are required to be thin and physically active (e.g. ballet dancers) have higher risk.

8. Persons with the time and money to belong to recreational clubs and sports facilities. High socioeconomic status is also associated with acceptance of cultural values that relate to thinness and fitness.

9. In women, menstrual problems (delayed menarche, cessation of menstruation, or irregular cycles) associated with activity and food restriction that may precede or accompany weight loss.

9. Biochemical changes including increased endorphin levels at low weight, decreased leutinizing hormone (LH) levels, and in men decreased testosterone. These changes may be accompanied by decreased sexual drive in both sexes.

Dr. Katz has reported two cases of anorexia based on several of the above criteria (see Chapter 10 for one of these cases). For example, he recognized that the onset of exercise preceded psychological symptoms [12]. In the following passage, Katz describes a man who took up long distance running after being injured in wrestling. The case is important because it shows how activity anorexia develops in athletes.

BB, a 22-year old unmarried college graduate, had been a successful varsity wrestler in high school and had never been overweight: indeed, at the age of 17 he had weighed about 150 lbs. (62.2 kg) at a height of 5' 8 1/2" (174 cm), or 98 % of ideal body weight (IBW). While concerned about his masculinity and strength (he lifted weights seriously), he had never been preoccupied with his diet or weight; he did not have difficulty making his weight class for wrestling matches. Toward the end of his senior year in high school, he injured a shoulder while wrestling. When this did not heal by the start of his freshman year at college, he began to feel 'restless' and decided to take up running, an activity he had engaged in occasionally during high school for conditioning purposes. He was able to join the cross-country team at college and began to compete with moderate success.

During his junior year, however, the patient became increasingly interested in long-distance running and gradually increased his running up to 80-90 miles per week. As his running distances increased in extent, prior moderate weight loss began to accelerate. As he worked toward improving his running times, he became increasingly preoccupied with losing additional weight. In the hope of further improving his performance, he began to consciously reduce his caloric intake and extend still further his weekly running (up to 90 to 100 miles per week). By the age of 20 1/2, his height had increased to 5' 10" (177.8 cm) but his weight had dropped to 125 lbs (56.8 kg), or 79% of IBW. He had also eliminated meat from his diet.

Over the ensuing year, the patient's marathon running performance actually worsened and he consciously recognized that he was now too weak at such a low weight for optimal running. Despite morbid fears of becoming fat, he permitted his weight to rise to within the boundaries of 130 and 135 lbs and his running times did improve. However, when he suffered a knee injury toward the end of his senior year at college (as an apparent consequence of excessive running), he became increasingly anxious and blue, felt irritable and fatigued, became socially isolated, and had difficulty falling asleep. Libido, which had diminished in association with his long-distance running over the preceding two years, dropped even further.

Concomitantly with this depressed state, the patient began to binge seriously. While previously he had engaged in only a rare binge, he now began to gorge and then vomit at least once every two weeks. This depressed him further as he now consciously began to morbidly brood about his weight. He temporarily took up bicycling. Although later in the fall his knee began to heal and he resumed running (with hopes of making the 1988 Olympics in the marathon), the patient had become so severely obsessed with his weight and calory intake that he finally decided to seek help which is when we saw him in consultation [12, pp. 75-76].

This case suggests that the assessment criteria for activity anorexia are relevant in a clinical setting. In terms of primary criteria, the client (BB) showed a history of declining food intake when he was below ideal body weight. He also had a history of physical activity that progressively became more intense. Finally, the psychological symptoms followed excessive exercise and anorexia.

In terms of secondary criteria, Mr. BB increased his running, dieted to improve athletic performance, combined food restriction with exercise, was preoccupied with running, and appeared to accept cultural values related to fitness. It is interesting that depression and binge eating appeared to follow a forced reduction in physical activity. Depression may occur as a result of the withdrawal from endogenous opiates [13] and the disruption of well established behavior patterns associated with running. Binge eating may have occurred because the man's appetite returned when physical activity was reduced (by the knee injury). Similar "feeding frenzies" occur in animals and are associated with infrequent meals and low body weight.

4 METHOD OF ASSESSMENT

The method of assessment for activity anorexia is based on the general method outlined in Dr. Stewart Agras's book, *Eating Disorders* [14]. The first phase consists of a medical work-up and a screening questionnaire that gathers basic information about activity, food intake, medical status, and so on. This phase is followed by an interview that is designed to substantiate and clarify the information obtained on the questionnaire. Finally, baseline measures of the anorectic's behavior are taken.

People with activity anorexia are locked into a cycle of food restriction and excessive activity. Physical activity increases brain opiates and the person will be motivated to continue. In simple terms, anorectics do not want to change the way they are behaving. Another reason for reluctance, is that a label of mental illness is likely to be given. In order to illustrate this point, consider what would happen if obese people were treated as though they were mentally ill. In this case, obese individuals would not seek help and would resist forced therapy. However, parents or concerned relatives typically force the anorectic into treatment. This means that clients may be uncooperative and resist efforts to modify their behavior.

At the first interview with the client, it is important to rule out physical illness. There are medical problems, such as Simmonds disease and zinc deficiency, that can produce anorexia. For this reason, it is a good idea to involve a internal medicine specialist in the assessment process. Starvation produces many dangerous physiological effects and the client should have a thorough physical examination. In terms of assessing activity anorexia, the internist may want to look for increased levels of β-endorphin, low levels of pulsatile LH in women, and reduced testosterone in men. Finally, aerobic fitness may be indicative of excessive exercising and this may be used as a check on the client's report of this behavior. Of course, if starvation is extreme, aerobic fitness will decline — in this context fitness measures may not be as useful.

The next step is to gather information on the history of the client. Such a history may be assessed by having the client complete a standard questionnaire such as the *Stanford Eating Disorders Questionnaire*. This questionnaire is reproduced in the appendix of Dr. Agras' book *Eating Disorders* [14]. This is a useful questionnaire because it is directed at objective medical, social, and behavioral events that may be functionally related to the eating problem.

It includes questions concerned with exercising, weight and food intake. Although these questions are included, there is no bias toward an assessment of activity anorexia. Other types of anorexia could be indicated on the basis of responses to this instrument.

Drs. Garner and Garfinkel have developed an *Eating Attitudes Test* (EAT) for anorexia nervosa [15]. This test is useful for identifying people who have unusual attitudes about food and body weight (see Chapter 3). In terms of activity anorexia, the test may indicate that the reinforcement value of food is low and this is especially relevant in the context of excessive physical activity. We suggest that the short version of the EAT be given at the same time as the Stanford questionnaire.

If activity anorexia is suspected based on the questionnaire, EAT scores, and medical profile, a structured interview may be conducted with the client. The interview should be directed at the activity anorexia cycle. Topics that should be discussed are based on the primary and supplementary criteria for activity anorexia. For example, any indication that client has progressively increased exercise while reducing food intake is suggestive. The therapist may also ask about the onset of psychological symptoms. Did the behavioral changes follow severe dieting and excessive exercising? If the client has experienced menstrual problems that preceded anorexia, were these problems associated with increasing exercise? Questions that probe a history of involvement in athletic activities may be important. Those sports that require intense training and thinness or reduced weight for success are particularly significant. Such activities may include long distance running, gymnastics, ballet, wrestling, figure skating, rowing, and swimming.

Because the anorectic client may not cooperate with the therapist, family members, should be made active participants during the assessment phase. In order to verify the anorectic's answers, it is advisable to interview family members when the client is not present. Subsequently, both the anorectic and family members may be brought together to discuss differences and gain consensus on the eating problem. At this interview, some attention should be paid to the family's attitudes toward beauty standards, physical fitness, dieting to lose weight, use of diet foods, and so on. Family attitudes reflect the acceptance of cultural values for thinness and fitness. If family members support these values, it is likely that they reinforce behavior that may contribute to the activity-anorexia cycle.

When it is possible, an objective assessment of the client's eating and physical activity should be attempted. This baseline phase involves one week of measurement before any treatment is implemented. In terms of food intake, it may be very difficult to accurately assess the anorectic's eating in an everyday setting. This is because anorectics may deceive the observer by hiding food or vomiting after a meal. Physical activity is also difficult to measure although devices like pedometers may be useful. More accurate baseline measures may be obtained if the person is hospitalized. Even in this more controlled setting there may be problems of measurement. Generally, the closer the monitoring by nursing staff, the more accurate the food and activity baselines.

In hospital, a known amount of food may be presented for breakfast, lunch, dinner and snacks. The amount of food eaten is determined by weight or volume after the meal period.

In order to check that food has been consumed a staff member should sit with the person during the meal and up to one hour after. The person who monitors eating should not encourage or discourage food intake. However, attempts by the anorectic to hide or otherwise dispose of food are noted and the number of trips to the bathroom should be recorded (this provides an indirect check on vomiting after the meal). Finally, a daily measure of body weight should be obtained. The weight difference from day to day may be used to validate the apparent food intake.

Physical activity should also be directly assessed. One problem with measurement of physical activity in a hospital setting is that normal exercise routines are prevented or disrupted. This means that baseline measures may not represent the activity level of the person in everyday life. Nonetheless, an attempt can be made to record overall motor activity by pedometer measurement. Also, episodes of calisthenics, running in place, going up and down staircases and so on may be recorded. It is important to recall that physical activity is displaced behavior and is not a deliberate attempt to burn off calories. This behavior occurs frequently, is intense, and may appear to be out of place and aimless. Physical activity may also be resistant to change and the person will do almost anything to exercise. These properties of physical activity should be noted and used to assess the type of anorexia. If exercising is not notable and there is no significant history, activity anorexia is unlikely.

When an assessment of activity anorexia is made, the client and family members should be brought together for an explanation of the activity-anorexia cycle. The family is told that activity anorexia is not a mental problem, although severe food restriction may produce a variety of personality and behavior changes. These changes are expected to recede when adequate normal eating and weight have been restored. The treatment goals are to interrupt the exercise and food intake feedback loop and to modify the social environment that encourages dieting and exercising. Many current approaches to the treatment of anorexia nervosa may be used in the modification of activity anorexia. Family therapy, cognitive restructuring, behavior modification, and drug therapy may be directed at the diet and exercise cycle.

REFERENCES

Although many of these references may be of interest, we have indicated (with an asterisk *) those that are written for the non-specialist reader.

1. Smith, N. J. (1980). Excessive weight loss and food aversion in athletes simulating anorexia nervosa. *Pediatrics*, 66, 139-142.
2. Yates, A., Leehey, K. and Shisslack, C. M. (1983). Running — an analogue of anorexia? *New England Journal of Medicine*, 308, 251-255.
3. *Garfinkel, P. and Garner, D. (1982). *Anorexia nervosa: A multidimensional perspective*. New York: Brunner/Mazel.
4. Rampling, D. (1978). Anorexia nervosa: Reflections on theory and practice. *Psychiatry*, 41, 296-301.

5. Bryce-Smith, D. and Simpson, R. I. D. (1984). Anorexia, depression, and zinc deficiency. *Lancet*, Nov. 17, 1162.

6. Masserman, J. M. (1943). *Behavior and neurosis*. Chicago: University of Chicago Press.

7. Bronson, R. T., O'Connell, M., Klepper-Kilgore, N., Chalifoux, L. V., and Sehgal, P. (1982). Fatal fasting syndrome of obese macaques. *Laboratory Animal Science*, 32, 187-192.

8. American Psychiatric Association. (1982). *Diagnostic and statistical manual of mental disorders (DSM-111R)*. Washington, DC: APA.

9. Mansfield, M. J. and Emans, S. J. (1989). Anorexia nervosa, athletics, and amenorrhea. *The Pediatric Clinics of North America.*, 36, 533-549.

10. Rosen, L. W., McKeag, D. B., Hough, D. O., and Curley, V. (1986). Pathogenic weight-control behavior in female athletes. *The Physician and Sports Medicine*, 13, 79-86

11. Garner, D. M. and Garfinkel, P. E. (1980). Socio-cultural factors in the development of anorexia nervosa. *Psychological Medicine*, 10, 647-656.

12. Katz, J. L. (1986). Long distance running, anorexia nervosa, and bulimia: A report of two cases. *Comprehensive Psychiatry*, 27, 74-78.

13 Angst, J., Autenrietch, V., Brem, F., Koukkou, M., Meyer, H., Stassen, H., and Storek, U. (1979). Preliminary results of treatment with ß-endorphin in depression. In E. Usdin, W. E. Jr. Bunney and N. S. Cline (Eds.), *Endorphins in mental health research,* (pp. 528-581). New York: MacMillan.

14. *Agras, W. S. (1987). *Eating disorders: Management of obesity, bulimia, and anorexia nervosa*. New York: Pergamon Press.

15. Garner, D. M. and Garfinkel, P.E. (1979). The eating attitudes test: A index of the symptoms of anorexia nervosa. *Psychological Medicine*, 9, 1-7.

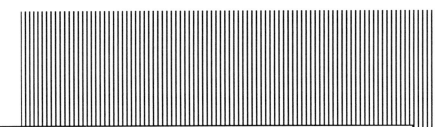

The main topics are:

- **TREATMENT OF ACTIVITY ANOREXIA**
- **PREVENTION OF ACTIVITY ANOREXIA**

Summary

- The treatment of activity anorexia is outlined based on the biobehavioral model.

- Medical, cognitive, and family therapies may be directed at the biobehavioral process of activity anorexia and the social conditions that promote it.

- Behavioral therapy is central to treatment of activity anorexia. Modification involves teaching new eating habits and safe exercise routines.

- A three-phase approach to treatment is suggested that emphasizes persuasion, contingency management by therapist and family, and behavioral contracting.

- Prevention of activity anorexia requires identifying risk factors (e.g. low baseline body weight) and sub-groups that require dieting and exercising.

- Educational campaigns by the medical profession and self-help organizations can play a major role in prevention by counteracting the cultural pressures toward thinness and fitness.

CHAPTER

Treatment and Prevention of Activity Anorexia

12

The model of activity anorexia presented in Chapter 11 suggests that many cases of human self-starvation result from biobehavioral processes activated by cultural practices. Strategies of treatment and prevention must be directed at the behavioral, physiological, and cultural factors that establish and maintain anorexia.

In contrast, current psychiatric treatments of anorexia nervosa are typically focused on mental symptoms of the disorder. Human anorexia is classified as an illness that results from a neurotic personality. From the traditional perspective, the anorectic's refusal to eat and starvation are manifestations of the mental disturbance. Treatment is designed to alter the disturbed mental state and disordered thinking that are presumed to underlie anorexia.

None of the current treatment approaches to anorexia nervosa have recognized the activity-anorexia cycle and we believe this omission is critical. Psychiatric, medical, and behavioral treatments could be more effective if therapists recognized the diet and exercise cycle. For example, behavioral treatment programs have used exercise as reinforcement for weight gain [1]. The difficulty with this approach is that the reinforcing effectiveness of exercise decreases as more weight is acquired [2]. Such a contingency may only produce modest weight gain before the reinforcer loses its effectiveness.

Current views of anorexia emphasize culture, family and personality factors and many professionals recommend a multidimensional approach to the disorder [3]. This approach includes numerous plausible conditions that may, or may not, contribute to the onset and progression of anorexia. Unfortunately, the inherent complexity of a multifactor model makes specific strategies for treatment and prevention difficult. For example, in terms of prevention, many professionals have recognized that cultural pressure to be thin has some relationship to anorexia nervosa in women [4]. In the multidimensional view, anorexic women have a personality type that makes them susceptible to the "message of thinness." This perspective is directed at the personality and thinking patterns of people and there is less concern with the cultural and familial practices that encourage dieting and exercising. In contrast, our theory of activity anorexia, focuses attention on the social practices that establish the cycle of food restriction and physical activity, the motivational interrelations between eating and exercising, and the physiological events that maintain self-starvation.

Of course, the model of activity anorexia is also multidimensional. That is, cultural, behavioral and biological conditions must be included in any approach to treatment. The difference between our multifactor model and others is that we have used a few basic principles to organize the complex interrelations among culture, behavior and biology. Thus, cultural values establish social practices that regulate the behavior of individuals. This regulation is based on social learning involving reinforcement, modeling and imitation. Based on these influences, people learn eating habits and fitness routines that may initiate the activity-anorexia cycle. This cycle is maintained by physiological processes that feed back on exercise and food intake. Finally, the physiological processes occur because of evolution and natural selection.

1 TREATMENT OF ACTIVITY ANOREXIA

Clinicians who have encountered cases of activity anorexia have usually treated their patients as though they were neurotic. This is not surprising because anorectics display a variety of unusual responses. These responses include abnormal scores on psychological tests, hostility to treatment, denial of the problem, arguments and conflict with family members, bulimia, preoccupation with food, concerns of weight and body image, and many others. Importantly, we have shown that these symptoms of anorexia are caused by either starvation or social learning. The point is that activity anorectics are not starving because they are neurotic rather they are neurotic because of the biobehavioral processes that control self-starvation. These processes include the cultural context, social reinforcement, the interrelation of food restriction and activity, and physiological responses based on evolutionary history.

Treatment of activity anorexia should be directed at the biobehavioral processes rather than neurotic symptoms. This means that current approaches to the treatment of anorexia should develop specific techniques to modify the activity-anorexia cycle. The psychological, behavioral and physiological symptoms of activity anorexia are expected to decrease when the food restriction and exercise spiral is interrupted. A word of caution is necessary since there is tentative evidence that depression may occur when exercise is prevented, blocked or interrupted [5]. This depression appears to be associated with endogenous-opiate withdrawal that occurs when excessive physical activity is reduced (see Chapter 11). Such a depressive state may be temporary and should not be used as evidence that treatment is ineffective.

In earlier chapters of this book, we have described different treatment approaches to anorexia. These approaches were shown to vary in effectiveness. That is, family therapy appears to be more successful than other indirect approaches such as psychotherapy. Also, psychiatric and psychological therapies that are based on intrapsychic forces appear to be incompatible at the theoretical level with our analysis. To illustrate, a psychoanalytic interpretation of self-starvation requires an in-depth assessment of personality. This means that the therapist spends most of the time attempting to move the patient towards an understanding of their intrapsychic motivation for starvation. Such counseling is misdirected and does not further the recovery of the person with activity anorexia. In contrast, behavior modification, cognitive therapy, family therapy, and medical treatments are more easily adapted to the treatment of activity anorexia as a biobehavioral process.

Our treatment approach uses a variety of techniques that are directed at the activity-anorexia cycle. Medical intervention is recommended when body weight is very low. When the person's life is not threatened, behavior modification may be used to alter eating and exercise habits [6]. Cognitive techniques may be used to articulate and challenge many of the beliefs that predisposed the individual to combine dieting with exercise [7]. Also, the family should be included in an overall treatment plan [8]. Although attention has focused on family conflict, this is not central in our model. A more central issue is that family members may inadvertently reinforce behavior that initiates the activity-anorexia process. This means that modification of the family's system of reinforcement is an important part of any treatment or prevention program. Medical, behavioral, cognitive and family techniques may be used in a three phase approach to the treatment of activity anorexia.

The First Phase of Treatment

From a medical perspective, the first concern will be the anorectic's health. The health status of the person is closely tied to the decline in body weight. If body-weight loss is less than 20 percent below normal, it may be possible to treat the person in an outpatient setting. However, when body weight is 25 percent or less than ideal weight, hospitalization is recommended. At this low weight, serious complications such as bradycardia, low blood pressure, seizures and imbalanced electrolytes may occur. Hospitalization is also recommended when weight loss is extreme because medical staff have more control over exercise, eating and weight gain.

We suggest that treatment be initially directed at stopping excessive exercise and dieting. Direct medical intervention is necessary when starvation has progressed to a point where it is life threatening. Confinement to bed, forced or tube feeding, and drugs may be required to save the person's life. Although we do not advocate drug control of behavior, medical doctors may prefer this kind of treatment. If drug control is used, specific agents that block endogenous opiates (e.g. naloxone and naltraxone) may be more effective and have fewer side effects than general tranquilizing or antidepressant drugs (see Chapter 9). Opiate blockers may be used to lower the motivation for physical activity and increase appetite.

A number of recent studies with animals have found that endogenous opiates affect appetite [9]. These studies have prompted researchers to speculate about brain opiates and eating disorders [10]. There is growing evidence that endogenous opiates may play an important role in the reduced eating of anorectics [11]. Additional evidence has suggested that exercise increases the release of endogenous opiates and this may explain the loss of appetite that follows vigorous activity [12]. The overall findings suggest that opiate blockers may be a useful medical therapy for activity anorexia.

Drs. Moore, Mills and Forester treated underweight anorexia patients with intravenous infusions of the opiate blocker, naloxone. They administered 3.2 to 6.4 mg. of naloxone per day for approximately 5 weeks. During this time, their patients were recovering body weight. The anorectics gained more weight when naloxone was administered than when they were not taking the drug [13].

In a recent book, Dr. Kaye reports that 5 anorexic patients were given the opiate blocker, naltrexone [14]. These patients were given oral doses of the drug several times a day (75 to 100 mg. per day). In this study, 3 of the patients gained substantial weight on the drug and continued to take it after being discharged from the hospital. Another patient gained 15 pounds but then refused to take any more naltrexone. The fifth patient did not respond to the drug.

The few studies that have investigated opiate blockers for the treatment of anorexia have been uncontrolled. Another problem is that only a small number of patients have participated in these trials. Opiate antagonists may not be effective if anorexia is a function of variables other than the exercise-dieting cycle. Although some researchers have suggested that these drugs produce few side effects, prolonged use by anorexic patients has not been tested [14]. Finally, high doses of naloxone have been associated with increased blood pressure in healthy subjects [15]. For these reasons opiate blockers should be used with caution. When drug control is used, it should be faded and replaced by persuasion and behavior modification.

The Second Phase of Treatment

Persuasion by hospital personnel involves a description of activity anorexia and its origins. The staff may explain the underlying processes and how these relate to cultural practices of our society. Cognitive techniques such as articulation of beliefs, testing beliefs against evidence, and challenging "black and white" thinking about food, figure and exercise, may be used to change self-descriptive statements [16]. Changes in self-description prompt new behavior related to diet and exercise. For example, Drs. Garner and Bemis have discussed the anorectic's unrealistic acceptance of thinness as a cultural value. They suggest the following treatment approach:

> *...We occasionally show patients examples from magazine advertisements in which unrealistic shapes are being promoted, or in which women are being subtly devalued by equating female worth with physical attractiveness in general and thinness in*

particular. Other ads recommending ridiculous or dangerous cosmetic and dietetic practices may be offered in support of the argument that women are being exploited by the fashion and diet industries. Some patients feel a healthy sense of indignation at the definition of feminine attractiveness in terms of a prepubertal shape. However, most are in continual conflict over ideals related to shape and require sustained support in challenging pernicious social norms. In all circumstances, the therapist must scrupulously avoid assault on the patient's values through true collaboration and careful dialogue. The sources of erroneous convictions may be extirpated by understanding their heritage and disputing their validity [16, p. 123].

Similar strategies may be used to combat unrealistic assumptions about fitness and exercise. Most importantly, the patient's beliefs about combining stringent dieting with excessive exercising should be challenged.

An important part of the persuasion process is medical and nutritional advice. *Nutritional counseling* has not been a prominent treatment for anorexia because the eating problem has been viewed as a mental illness. From this perspective, there is no point in telling an irrational person about proper nutritional habits. In contrast, activity anorexia is not a mental illness and nutritional counseling may be helpful in changing dietary practices that promote the cycle of food restriction and exercise.

Nutritional counseling should address the pattern and size of meals as well as composition of the diet. Based on animal research reviewed in this book, the more frequent the meals the less the tendency to exercise. For this reason, the person should be encouraged to eat frequently throughout the day. Many people with anorexia eat infrequently and this pattern may induce excessive exercising. Intense physical activity further reduces meal size and frequency. Dietary counselling can be important for interrupting this cycle.

Attitudes about thinness through diet and exercise may need to be challenged and modified. It is important to understand that the activity-anorexia cycle is resistant to change and the patient may oppose medical advice. When opposition is intense, it is useful to provide the same advise from several credible sources. Social psychological research has shown that a message that is backed up by several people has more impact than the same message given by a single person [17]. This implies that medical staff must work together to provide consistent information about dietary practices and the activity-anorexia cycle.

In addition to persuasive techniques, our review of treatment effectiveness (see Chapter 6) suggests that behavior modification is a useful approach in hospital settings. Behavior modification should be directed at the conditions that maintain the activity-anorexia cycle. Because the cycle is partially regulated by release of brain opiates, it may be difficult to interrupt. Another problem is that social reinforcement from family and others may inadvertently support the behavior of dieting and exercising. This means that interventions in hospitals may not be as effective in everyday life settings. Thus, behavior-change programs should attempt to restore normal eating, reduce the motivation for exercise, and plan for generalization of treatment. The first step in the modification of activity anorexia involves a clear statement of the treatment objectives and the consequences of meeting the objectives.

Table 12.1
Guidelines for behavioral contracting

Practical details about negotiating behavioral contracts may be found in *How to negotiate a behavioral contract* by Drs. R.V. Hall & M. C. Hall [18]. Further information may be found in *Writing Behavioral Contracts* by Drs. De Risi & Butz [19].

A Guide to Behavioral Contracting

1. Specify the target behavior.

2. Describe the behavior in a way that an observer may count or time.

3. Collect baseline data on the frequency of response or time spent responding.

4. Identify consequences that may be used to increase desired behavior (positive and negative reinforcers).

5. Find people who will monitor the behavior and provide the consequences.

6. Write the contract in clear statements of behavior and consequences (e.g. if you do "X" then you receive "Y").

7. Collect data on frequency of response or time spent responding and compare with baseline level.

8. Modify the contract if the desired behavior does not increase (e.g., try different consequences).

9. Gradually, remove arbitrary consequences and replace with natural reinforcers – rewrite the contract and monitor the behavior.

10. Plan for generalization – implement the contract in a variety of settings.

Following a baseline period of assessment (see, Chapter 11), a behavioral contract is negotiated between the client and the hospital staff. At a minimum, the contract should specify the consequences of eating. Usually, these consequences involve access to ward activities, including television, reading materials, social interaction with others on the ward, visitors, day passes, and so on. In order to make these consequences most effective, the patient's room should be sparsely furnished.

Although eating is the target behavior, it is almost impossible to accurately monitor this behavior. Often the person will hide food or vomit after a meal. For this reason, weight gain is commonly used as an indirect measure of eating. Dr. Agras has discussed behavioral contracting and weight-gain criteria for hospitalized anorexic patients.

... In almost all programs there is a 'bare bones' contract stipulating the unit contingent on gaining an increment of weight each day above the previous day's high weight. Failure to gain this amount of weight results in restriction to the patient's room. The increment of weight gain is usually set at 0.2 kg/day above the previous high weight. A smaller weight gain ... might result in room restriction for half a day. It is, of course, necessary that the patient's room not contain many reinforcing activities. In some units, television and reading material phase of weight gain is spent at bed rest, with the rationale that less energy is expended, thus making it easier to gain weight. It should be noted that this used of bed rest is an example of negative reinforcement [20, pp. 98-99].

Negative reinforcement occurs when a patient engages in some behavior that removes or avoids an unpleasant event (e.g. tube feeding). In a hospital, most people want to minimize medical treatment. When anorectics fail to gain weight, the contract should specify progressive loss of privileges and increasing medical intervention. The person may gain privileges and remove medical treatment by eating and gaining weight. Perhaps the most important long range consequence is getting out of the hospital. If the patients follow the behavioral contract their hospital stay is more pleasant and shorter.

Behavior change must involve more than the reinforcement of eating and weight gain. There should be some attempt to teach healthy eating skills that will be maintained after the patient is discharged from the hospital. We suggest that the anorectic be taught nutritional skills, appropriate eating habits (e.g. eating normal-sized bites), and eating in a social context. These skills may be made part of the behavioral contract and specific privileges should be negotiated. It is important to realize that the eating-skills training is supplementary to the overall weight-gain contingency. This is because the health status of the person is the most immediate concern.

Generalization of eating skills may be enhanced by arranging for meals that are prepared by the anorectic and attended by family and friends. The patient may be required to eat in a socially appropriate manner in the presence of significant others. Specific consequences are outlined for eating reasonable amounts of food, eating at an appropriate rate, and pleasant conversation during the meal. In order to promote generalization, breakfast, lunch and dinner should be prepared and attended by the patient. As training progresses, the meal setting should be extended to cafeterias and to the home [21].

In addition to eating skills, it is important to train sensibly and moderate exercise habits. Following sufficient weight gain, the person may be taught to discriminate between moderate and excessive exercising. This could be accomplished by allowing the anorectic to exercise for 20 minutes or less per day. If the person exceeds 20 minutes, exercise is withheld on the following day. This is a "fail-safe" contingency because the excessive exercise that generates activity anorexia is disrupted by the behavioral requirement. Discrimination of amount of exercise is part of a more general set of fitness skills. Anorectics may also be taught to choose a daily exercise routine that keeps them trim and healthy. A balanced program involving moderate walking, calisthenics and isometrics may keep the person fit without reactivating the activity-anorexia cycle

The use of exercise as a reinforcer for weight gain may not be the best long-term strategy. This is because the reinforcing effectiveness of exercise declines as the person gains weight. Based on our animal experiments, exercise is most valued at approximately 75 percent of normal weight. As body weight becomes closer to normal the person may not eat in order to exercise. At this point, the treatment program may stall and further weight gain will require a different source of reinforcement.

There is an additional problem with the use of exercise as reinforcement for weight gain. Evidence suggests that, at low body weight, physical activity increases endogenous opiates that automatically reinforce exercising and reduce appetite. If this occurs, a treatment program based on exercise may backfire and contribute to the patient's eating problem. One alternative is to decrease exercise rather than use it as a reinforcer. This procedure has been reported by Dr. Mavissakalin for two, seventeen-year-old, female anorectics [22].

These women were admitted to a hospital following excessive weight loss and other symptoms of anorexia. Mavissakalin noted that both women engaged in compulsive exercising. A behavior-modification program that required increased food consumption and a 1-hour period of rest following each meal was implemented. The rest component was added "to specifically prevent the 'compulsive' exercising which the patient(s) manifested." After leaving the hospital both patients families were told how to continue the treatment. Both patients recovered and later became overweight. Mavissakalin stated that it was very difficult to stop the compulsive exercising and that after a phenomenal number of treatment sessions the patients on their own became sedentary. Based on this study and our theory of activity anorexia, behavior modification should be most effective when procedures are designed to reduce exercise and increase weight gain.

The Third Phase of Treatment

Once the anorectic has reached and maintained "target" weight within 2 kg (5 lbs), planning for outpatient care should begin. At this point, a new behavioral contract should be negotiated. The major contingency involves longer and longer visits home if weight remains within the negotiated range. Eventually, the person is discharged from the hospital but body weight and activity are monitored by family members. As long as weight remains within the stipulated range, the person may remain at home. The contract should specify a critical weight level. If body weight declines to this level, the person is immediately re-admitted to the hospital. This contingency has two advantages: first, staying in the hospital is a powerful negative reinforcer for most people; second, re-admission occurs before the person has substantially lost weight [20].

The behavioral contract for outpatient treatment of activity anorexia is similar to the one arranged in the hospital. Consequences are planned to maintain weight, eat in an appropriate manner, and exercise moderately. The major difference is that the anorectic's behavior is monitored and reinforced by *family members*.

Effective management of eating and exercise requires the cooperation of family members. Often, however, the onset of activity anorexia will disrupt family interaction, and cooperation among family members may be difficult to obtain. In our view, these disruptions are by-products of the anorectic's refusal to eat. Family members may view the person as willfully starving for no apparent reason. The parents may plead and argue with the anorectic to no effect. Eventually, family members may blame themselves and each other for the eating problem. Conflict, hostility and marital problems may result.

When family *conflict* is encountered, it will be difficult or impossible to implement a systematic behavioral contract. This is because the family members cannot agree on the goals of the contract. Also, they may have difficulty coordinating their actions and this will make reinforcement contingencies less effective. For these reasons, family-centered therapy may be necessary [23].

Family therapy will probably start while the anorectic is in the hospital. When family and friends are used to teach appropriate eating skills, conflict can be identified. These meal sessions also provide an opportunity to resolve family conflict and train effective behavior management. In addition to meal sessions, the family should meet with a therapist on a regular basis. These sessions should be continued following discharge from the hospital. The activity-anorexia cycle may be discussed and the reasons for family conflict addressed. It may be particularly important to point out that the anorectic is not intentionally manipulating family members. This may help to diffuse arguments and gain cooperation among parents, siblings, and the patient.

A second role for family therapy involves changing family practices that may unintentionally encourage activity anorexia. A family that emphasizes the thin-fit standard of beauty may reinforce participation in sports, eating low calorie foods, and a concern with body shape. The members may be asked to critically evaluate their attitudes and behavior and how these relate to the eating problem.

Effective treatment of activity anorexia is one way to decrease the incidence of eating problems in our society. However, a more substantial decline could be accomplished by preventing the onset of the biobehavioral processes that initiate activity anorexia.

2   PREVENTION OF ACTIVITY ANOREXIA

Prevention of activity anorexia involves changing the sociocultural conditions that promote it, and identifying individuals at risk in the population. The theory of activity anorexia that we have developed in this book suggests how sociocultural practices contribute to the onset of anorexia (see Chapter 10). These practices must be modified in order to reduce the incidence of anorexia in Western society. People who strongly uphold the cultural values of thinness and fitness may be at greater risk. Other risk factors may relate to biological conditions such as age, sex, body structure, and weight set-point.

Activity anorexia in animals occurs more frequently in young females. This appears to reflect a sex difference in set point (or baseline) body weight; females animals tend to weigh less than males at a similar age. Regardless of sex or age, low-weight animals are more likely to develop activity anorexia and the onset is more rapid than in heavier subjects. Low-weight animals respond to food restriction by substantially increasing their physical activity and this occurs within one or two days. In terms of evolution, this response makes sense because these subjects have difficulty defending set-point weight when faced with food restriction. In other words, animals with less body fat should be the first to travel because they cannot afford the time to wait through a famine.

Human anorexia also occurs most frequently in young females and this may reflect a similar evolutionary adaptation to food restriction. As with the animals, low set-point weight may be a risk factor for humans who go on diets and begin to exercise. In humans, the implications of body weight for anorexia are more complicated than in animals. For example, women have a higher fat-to-lean ratio than men. On the other hand, women maintain lower set-point weight than the opposite sex. Both men and women with low set-point and fat-to-lean ratio may be at risk for activity anorexia. These biological-risk factors may influence the development of anorexia but do not seem to account for the overwhelming incidence in young women. Cultural practices of diet and exercise appear to account for the predominance of anorexia in females.

The sociocultural practices that promote anorexia involve the combination of hard training or exercise with requirements to loose weight or remain thin. Recall that anorexia is most likely to develop when intense physical activity is increasing and food restriction is imposed. Sudden increases in athletic conditioning, or a change from sedentary to an active lifestyle may also place a person at some risk. Similarly, diets that substantially change caloric intake may increase the chances of developing anorexia.

In Western culture, it is common to find people who diet, exercise, or both. Although the acceptance of such practices are widely held, there are sub-groups within our culture that emphasize these values. We have noted that there is some association between incidence of anorexia and social class. Middle and upper-middle income groups appear to have a greater number of cases than lower income groups. This association makes sense in terms of activity anorexia. People in the higher income categories have the time and money to join organizations that promote fitness (e.g. health clubs), purchase fashions that require thinness, and read magazines that encourage dieting. Finally, these individuals have the money to spend on diet foods and sports equipment.

The influence of social class and culture is mediated by the person's family. The values of some families increase the risk of activity anorexia. Such families reinforce their children's participation in active sports, emphasize fitness, and encourage eating of low calorie foods. Children accept these values and for this reason they may behave in ways that make activity anorexia more likely. We know a woman who comes from such a family:

Ms. K's father is a family physician; she has three sisters. Her father and mother show a constant concern with health, fitness and dieting. When she was a girl, the family dinner often consisted of salad, a small portion of meat, vegetable with margarine, skim milk or diet drinks, and fruit. There was always a variety of diet and low calorie foods in the refrigerator. Conversation at meal time and other occasions frequently focused on "how fat or thin" a family member appeared to be. Ms. K and her sisters were continually going on and off diets. Also, they typically went for a daily run of 3 to 4 miles. Overall, the family environment supported exercise and dieting. In later life, Ms. K met a friend who was a competitive long-distance runner. Although Ms. K had not been a running enthusiast her family history made her receptive to taking up competitive running. Her body build was ideal for running; she was tall and had long muscular legs. Over a period of 3 months she began to run and sharply increased her distance and speed.

At the end of this period, she could run for an hour and cover a distance of just under 10 miles. She was winning local races and began to train for a marathon. At this time her weight was noticeably declining - she had gone from approximately 130 to less than 110 pounds. She also gave up eating meat and her food consisted of fruit, vegetables and salads. Although it is difficult to be certain, she appeared to be entering the cycle of activity anorexia. Fortunately, she injured her leg and could not run for several months and during this time her eating improved. Several years later, she continues to be active but not at the same level [author's anecdote].

There is nothing wrong with a family promoting health and fitness. The benefits of exercise and healthy diet are well documented. However, there may be unintended consequences when these values are stressed to an extreme degree. Parents should be aware of the signs and symptoms of eating disorders (e.g. bulimia, delayed menarche, excessive exercise, and severe loss of weight) and the activity-anorexia cycle. Children should have a balanced diet and a reasonable level of physical activity. Also, parents should not be concerned about the weight gain that accompanies puberty in young women. This weight is a natural outcome of sexual development and is usually compensated by increases in growth.

Although families may inadvertently encourage behavior that leads to anorexia, there are other social groups that more directly arrange for the interaction of diet and exercise. Ballet dancers are more likely to become anorexic than other individuals [24]. In this group, young women must be thin and they must engage in hours of intense training. Any sub-group that promotes similar practices will place people at high risk.

It is of course obvious how to alleviate such conditions. Instructors, teachers, coaches and other authorities, must monitor the eating habits of their students and avoid setting requirements to lose weight when training is highly intense or increasing. One possibility is to reduce training during a period when an athlete or student is dieting. The effects of food reduction will naturally increase physical activity so there will only be a small net loss in conditioning. A better solution, in some cases, is that coaches and instructors learn to accept a body shape that is less immature.

Currently, physicians recommend dieting and exercising on a regular basis. This advice is based on sound research that indicates there are many positive health benefits for such behavior (e.g. decreased chance of heart problems and diabetes). One problem is that many fad diets are promoted on the basis of medical opinion. The companies, and authors, of such diets are more concerned with making money than with promoting people's health. Some diets ignore traditional principles of nutrition and others are extreme in caloric restriction. There are diet programs that recommend combining diet and exercise. In this case, the problem is that clinical studies have not been done to assess the possible side effects of these programs. Activity anorexia may be a serious complication that occasionally develops from such recommendations.

Prevention by Education and Self-Help

Medical doctors are in the best position to call attention to these diets and the serious consequences that may arise from them. Physicians should become more aware of the role of diet and exercise in the onset and maintenance of eating disorders. The theory and research outlined in this book, could be used to provide advice on identifying and preventing activity anorexia. The medical profession has high status and people are more likely to take advice from medical authorities than from other health professionals.

Self-help groups may also play an important role in preventing activity anorexia [25]. These groups and organizations allow people with eating disorders to meet others with similar problems. The basic idea is that people with common problems can help and support one another. At the present time, the members of such organizations do not know about the role of physical activity in the onset of anorexia. However, self-help groups who recognize the biobehavioral processes involved in self-starvation, may play an important role in preventing relapse. For example, those who have experienced this process are in an excellent position to recognize the warning signs and help the person before the cycle is initiated. Former anorectics may know, from personal experience, techniques and strategies that interrupt the activity-anorexia cycle.

A second major function of self-help groups is education and social change. The groups may send speakers to schools, public meetings and professional conferences. In addition, self-help groups organize their own conferences and solicit media attention. These groups may also lobby government agencies, private organizations and public companies. Because of this active and organized involvement, self-help groups may be the most important source for prevention of activity anorexia.

The Bulimia Anorexia Self-Help (BASH) is a prominent example of an effective self-help organization for eating disorders (see Chapter 6). This group rapidly expanded into a national-level organization under the direction of Dr. Felix Larocca [26]. Today, BASH publishes a monthly magazine that is widely circulated and informs readers about research, personal experiences, and treatment of eating disorders. BASH hosts an international conference on eating disorders where prominent researchers present their recent findings. The group promotes public awareness (e.g. National Eating Disorders Week), and maintains a toll-free telephone crisis line. In the future, BASH could help reduce the incidence of activity anorexia by educational programs and direct attempts to influence those sectors of society that promote the thin and fit beauty standard.

In the last analysis, activity anorexia is the outcome of cultural practices and biobehavioral processes. Major changes in the incidence of activity anorexia will occur when cultural standards of beauty and fitness are modified by large scale socioeconomic factors. Our review of beauty standards (see Chapter 10) shows that cultural trends in beauty and health may naturally change over years. The determinants of such changes are not well understood and may be exceedingly difficult to alter. Since this is the case, immediate prevention must rely on educating doctors, parents and people who are at risk for activity anorexia.

REFERENCES

Although many of these references may be of interest, we have indicated (with an asterisk *) those that are written for the non-specialist reader.

1. Blinder, B. J., Freeman, D. M. A. and Stunkard, A. J. (1970). Behavior therapy of anorexia nervosa: Activity as a reinforcer of weight gain. *American Journal of Psychiatry*, 126, 1093-1098.
2. Pierce, W. D., Epling, W. F. and Boer, D. P. (1986). Deprivation and satiation: The interrelations between food and wheel running. *Journal of the Experimental Analysis of Behavior*, 46, 199-210.
3. Garfinkel, P. E. and Garner, D. M. (1983). The multidetermined nature of anorexia nervosa. In P. L. Darby, P. E. Garfinkel, D. M. Garner and D. V. Coscina (Eds.), *Anorexia nervosa: Recent developments in research,* (pp. 3-14). New York: Alan R. Liss.
4. *Bruch, H. (1978). *The golden cage*. Cambridge, MA: Harvard University Press.
5. Angst, J., Autenrieth, V., Brem, F., Koukkou, M., Meyer, H., Stassen, H. and Storek, U. (1979). Preliminary results of treatment with ß-endorphin in depression. In E. Usdin, W. E. Jr. Bunney and N. S. Kline (Eds.), *Endorphins in mental health research,* (pp. 521-581). New York: McMillan.
6. Bachrach, A. J., Erwin, W. J. and Mohr, J. P. (1965). The control of eating behavior in an anorexic by operant conditioning techniques. In L. P. Ullman and L. Krasner (Eds.), *Case studies in behavior modification,* (pp. 153-163). New York: Holt, Rinehart & Winston.
7. *Beck, A. T. (1976). *Cognitive therapy and the emotional disorders*. New York: International Universities Press.

8. Yager, J. (1982). Family issues in the pathogenesis of anorexia nervosa. *Psychosomatic Medicine, 44*, 43-60.

9. Morley, J. E. and Levine, A. S. (1980). Stress induced eating is mediated through endogenous opiates. *Science, 209*, 1250-1261.

10. Givens, J. R., Wiedmann, E., Anderson, R. N. and Kitabchi, A. E. (1980). Beta-endorphin and beta-lipotropin plasma levels in hirsute women: Correlation with body weight. *Journal of Clinical Endocrinology and Metabolism, 50*, 975-976.

11. Marrazzi, M. A. and Luby, E. D. (1986). An auto-addiction opioid model of chronic anorexia nervosa. *International Journal of Eating Disorders, 5*, 191-208.

12. Epling, W. F and Pierce, W. D. (1988). Activity-based anorexia: A biobehavioral perspective. *International Journal of Eating Disorders, 7*, 475-485.

13. Moore, R., Mills, I. H. and Forester, A. (1981). Naloxone in the treatment of anorexia nervosa: Effect of weight gain and lipolysis. *Journal of the Royal Society of Medicine, 74*, 129-131.

14. Kaye, W. H. (1987). Opioid antagonist drugs in the treatment of anorexia nervosa. In P. E. Garfinkel and D. M. Garner (Eds), *The role of drug treatments for eating disorders,* (pp. 150-160). New York: Bruner/Mazel.

15. Cohen, M. R., Cohen, R. M., Pickar, D., Weingartner, H. and Murphy, D. L. (1983). High dose naloxone infusions in normals. *Archives of General Psychiatry, 40*, 613-619.

16. Garner, D. M. and Bemis, K. M. (1985). Cognitive therapy for anorexia nervosa. In D. M. Garner and P. E. Garfinkel (Eds.), *Handbook of psychotherapy for anorexia nervosa and bulimia,* (pp. 107-146). New York: The Guilford Press.

17. Tanford, S. and Penrod, S. (1984). Social influence model: A formal integration of research on majority and minority influence processes. *Psychological Bulletin, 95*, 189-225.

18. Hall, R. V. and Hall, M. C. (1982). *How to negotiate a behavioral contract.* Lawrence, Kansas: H. & H. Enterprises, Inc.

19. DeRisi, W. J. and Butz, G. (1977). *Writing behavioral contracts: A case simulation practice manual.* Champaign, Illinois: Research Press.

20. *Agras, W. S. (1987). *Eating disorders: Management of obesity, bulimia, and anorexia nervosa.* New York: Pergamon Press.

21 Halmi, K. A. (1985). Behavioral management for anorexia nervosa. In D. M. Garner and P. E. Garfinkel (Eds.), *Handbook of psychotherapy for anorexia nervosa and bulimia,* (pp. 147-159). New York: The Guilford Press.

22. Mavissakalian, M. (1982). Anorexia nervosa treated with response prevention and prolonged exposure. *Behavior Research and Therapy, 20*, 27-31.

23. Sargent, J., Liebman, R. and Silver, M. (1985). Family therapy for anorexia nervosa. In D. M. Garner and P. E. Garfinkel (Eds.), *Handbook of psychotherapy for anorexia nervosa and bulimia,* (pp. 257-279). New York: The Guilford Press.

24. Garner, D. M. and Garfinkel, P. E. (1980). Sociocultural factors in the development of anorexia nervosa. *Psychological Medicine, 10*, 647-656.

25. Enright, A. B., Butterfield, P. and Berkowitz, B. (1985). Self-help and support groups in the management of eating disorders. In D. M. Garner and P. E. Garfinkel (Eds.), *Handbook of psychotherapy for anorexia nervosa and bulimia,* (pp. 491-512). New York: The Guilford Press.

26. Larocca, F. E. (1986). An intermediate care model for the treatment of eating disorders: The BASH Approach. In F. E. F. Larocca (Ed.), *Eating disorders: Effective care and treatment,* (pp.129-139). St. Louis: Ishiyaku EuroAmerica Inc.

INDEX

215